MW00576483

They Made Us Happy

They Made Us Happy

Betty Comden and Adolph Green's Musicals and Movies

Andy Propst

OXFORD

UNIVERSITY PRESS

Oxford University Press is a department of the University of Oxford.
It furthers the University's objective of excellence in research, scholarship,
and education by publishing worldwide. Oxford is a registered trade mark of
Oxford University Press in the UK and certain other countries.

Published in the United States of America by Oxford University Press
198 Madison Avenue, New York, NY 10016, United States of America.

Library of Congress Cataloging-in-Publication Data

Names: Propst, Andy, author.
Title: They made us happy : Betty Comden & Adolph Green's musicals & movies /
Andy Propst.
Description: New York : Oxford University Press, [2019] | Includes
bibliographical references and index.
Identifiers: LCCN 2018004387 (print) | LCCN 2018004819 (ebook)
| ISBN 9780190630942 (updf) | ISBN 9780190630959 (epub)
| ISBN 9780190630935 (alk. paper)
Subjects: LCSH: Comden, Betty. | Green, Adolph. | Lyricists—United States. |
Librettists—United States. | Musicals—United States—History and
criticism. | Musical films—United States—History and criticism.
Classification: LCC ML423.C78 (ebook) | LCC ML423.C78 P76 2019 (print) | DDC
782.1/40922—dc23
LC record available at https://lccn.loc.gov/2018004387

3 5 7 9 8 6 4

Printed by LSC Communications
United States of America

For Erik and Joe

CONTENTS

In the course of their careers Betty Comden and Adolph Green wrote the books and/or lyrics for 18 musicals. They also penned screenplays for nine movies, two of which are considered landmarks in cinematic history. Beyond this they enjoyed healthy careers as performers and, oh yes, had rich lives offstage as they raised children and mingled with the glitterati of New York and Hollywood.

As I surveyed their artistic legacy and considered their personal lives, I suddenly came to understand how daunted they must have been when Arthur Freed assigned them the task of writing *Singin' in the Rain*. There they had hundreds of songs, written for a wide variety of projects, at their disposal. Their task was to take both hits and lesser-known tunes and somehow fit them together within the context of a cohesive story for a movie musical that wouldn't run more than a couple of hours.

The same task lay in front of me for *They Made Us Happy*. How was I to include something about each of their works, including projects that never made it past planning stages, as well as their lives, on stage and off, and not walk away with a manuscript for a book running 700 or 800 pages?

In the end I decided that I needed to borrow from my subjects, who realized that the period in which so many of Freed's songs were written provided them with the key to *Rain*: They made it a movie about the dawn of talking pictures. In my case, in order to offer you, the reader, a satisfying but not unwieldy portrait of Comden and Green, I have adopted the sort of loose storytelling style that so often informs their work, be it for stage or screen. The result, I hope, is a book that will allow you to experience their highs (and lows) professionally while providing some insight into their offstage lives.

In addition—and this is the genuine toast to Comden and Green—I've tried to give a sense of offbeat fun to *They Made Us Happy*. So, as you read, you'll find that inserted boxes are used on the page as the equivalent of "in ones." These are the scenes in musicals played in front of the curtain that were so often used to help cover the moments when the sets were being changed. Generally, an "in one" related tangentially to the show's action and more often than not got a laugh.

It's something of a nontraditional approach to biography or criticism, but as Comden quipped in the early 1980s, "It's good to do something new."

—Andy Propst, June 2018

They Made Us Happy

CHAPTER 1

Childhood Dreams

Hailing from Brooklyn and the Bronx, respectively, Comden and Green grew up in two distinctly different homes. He was the older of the two, born on December 2, 1914. His parents, Hungarian immigrants Daniel and Helen Green, came to the United States before they were teenagers and married before they turned 20. Daniel, according to the 1930 census, was a tradesman, but according to Green's son, Adam, Daniel was "a stock specu-lator and bootlegger." In the same census, notations indicate that Daniel and his wife were proficient in English. Nevertheless, they used Magyar, a difficult Hungarian language, at home, and as he was growing up, Green, according to his son, made "an instant goulash"[1] of both it and English.

Comden was born Basya Cohen two years, five months, and one day after Green, on May 3, 1917. Her parents, Leo and Rebecca Cohen, were also im-migrants, but, unlike the Greens, the couple came from Poland and at mark-edly different ages. Rebecca arrived in the United States in 1888 when she was just barely five, while Leo arrived in 1902 at the age of 19. In addition, the Cohens married relatively late in their lives, when they were both 29. They had waited to establish themselves professionally and financially. Until her marriage, Rebecca worked as a teacher, while Leo practiced law in Manhattan.

But while Comden and Green might have been growing up in different boroughs and with dissimilar parents, both discovered an affinity for the arts and demonstrated a penchant for inventiveness while they were still just grade-school age.

For Green, who was speaking what could jokingly be termed "Magyarlish" at home, love of theater and the elegant use of English started out thanks to school plays. One of his earliest stage experiences came when, in third grade at P.S. 39 in the Bronx, he played an evil dwarf in a production of *Snow White and the Red Rose*. Other age-appropriate productions followed, and then Green played the more adult role of Lord High Executioner in Gilbert and Sullivan's *The Mikado*. It was a seminal moment for the boy; Green was so taken with the wordplay in the operetta that he memorized the entirety of the team's canon.

Comden was showing her own inventiveness at just about the moment when Green was developing a demented laugh and violent demeanor for his performance in *Snow White*. She, however, was re-creating herself. It started at the age of five, when she grew tired of her peers' inability to pronounce "Basya." She told her father about the problem and of her desire to have a new name. His response, she recalled, was, "You can take any name you like as long as it begins with B."[2] She settled on "Betty." As for her surname, the family took an equally liberal approach, and she adopted "Comden"—a name used by other branches of the family—before she turned 20.

In Brooklyn Comden, too, was discovering the allure of make-believe. At home she fashioned costumes for herself from what she would later describe as her "dress-up bag … a large pillowcase filled with old clothes of my mother's."[3] Further, at the Brooklyn Ethical Culture School, Comden got a taste of both writing and performing when she and her class adapted and presented a stage version of Sir Walter Scott's *Ivanhoe*. Looking back on the experience, Comden would quip in her memoir, *Off Stage*, that it was "[her] first experience with the dramatic form and with collaboration, twelve writing partners," wryly adding, "Later on in my career I did cut down the number somewhat."

And even as the two were getting their first tastes of theater as performers in school, they were also experiencing professional productions as theatergoers. Green's first trip to Broadway came when he was 13 and his uncle took him to a production of George Bernard Shaw's *The Doctor's Dilemma*. Not long after this, Green remembered seeing the original production of Jerome Kern and Oscar Hammerstein II's *Show Boat*. Comden's theatergoing included productions in Manhattan (her first Broadway show was the operetta *Rose Marie*) and in her native Brooklyn, where she was a frequent attendee for performances of theater and opera at the Brooklyn Academy of Music.

It wasn't just live performances that captured their young imaginations. The two had an equal fondness for movies. Green would attend anything. "I didn't care what it was—a masterpiece or the crudest melodrama or most witless comedy."[4] As with the Gilbert and Sullivan librettos he memorized, Green committed each detail of the movies he saw to memory, including the bit players' names.

One of his idols on screen was Charlie Chaplin, and the two men would later become fast friends. In her book *Just in Time*, Green's wife, Phyllis Newman, described the first time that she saw Green and Chaplin together and witnessed just how encyclopedic her future husband's knowledge of movie history was: "Adolph hummed every note of Chaplin's movie scores, if called on, and filled in any word of a film title or bit of business."[5]

A FIRST MEETING

Green self-deprecatingly described his first meeting with Chaplin in the April 9, 1989, edition of the *New York Times*, writing that he had made "an absolute fool" of himself. "I followed him around the room relentlessly all evening, singing his musical scores to him, my face pressed close to his face." This continued until Chaplin and his wife, Oona, left, and Green felt sure that Chaplin would "look the other way if we ever met up again." He discovered, however, that his antics had not put the star off: Oona called Green a few days later to invite him to dinner at their home.

The specifics of the movies Comden saw while still a girl, whether it be at Loew's Kameo Theater in Brooklyn or the Whalley in New Haven (which her uncle owned), remained with her all her life. In the 1980s she wrote: "Vividly before my eyes, after many a decade I can still see scenes from what must have been one of the first movies I ever saw, *The Magic Skin*, based on a Balzac story."[6] Another seminal film for her as a young person was Noël Coward's *The Scoundrel*, and she would discover in adulthood that her fondness for the picture was shared by both Green and another collaborator, Leonard Bernstein. The effect the movie had on her was so profound that it even informed her wedding-day plans.

The pair's stories diverge following their high school graduations. Green, having attended DeWitt Clinton High School in the Bronx, enrolled at City College but only lasted a short time. Some, such as columnist Rex Reed, would report that Green remained there only one semester. Other accounts put his time at the school as only one day. Many years later Green would regret his decision to leave school, thinking that if he had stayed, "It would have been good for my discipline."[7]

As for Comden, after matriculating from Brooklyn's Erasmus Hall she enrolled at New York University (NYU) and eventually received a bachelor's degree.

It was during Comden's time in college that the two entered one another's spheres. Green, working a variety of jobs while also pursuing his goal of becoming a performer, had a penchant for hanging out in Greenwich Village and at New York University in particular. His goal was to meet interesting people. During one of his sojourns downtown he encountered Comden. He would later wryly describe this introduction, saying, "She was studying drama at New York University and I was a full-time bum."[8]

Actually, Green was anything but a bum. He worked tirelessly, and years later columnist Whitney Bolton would colorfully describe the writer's life at this time, asking his readers to imagine "a 17-year-old boy slugging things out for his uncle in the garment district [trudging] along the gutters of Seventh Avenue, hating his job and dreaming of the theater."[9]

But their shared aspirations to a life on stage did not mean that lightning struck when Comden and Green first met at NYU. Nor did it happen whenever they would run into one another as they made the rounds of producers' offices, looking for work as so many aspiring performers did at the time.

In fact, their paths diverged significantly. Comden managed to get some work and further training as an actress following her graduation from NYU. In early 1938 she was cast in a post-Broadway tour of Arthur Kober's *Having Wonderful Time*, a play about life among the denizens of the Catskills' adult summer camps at which Green was actually working during this time. The show, which had enjoyed a healthy year's run on Broadway and would later inspire the musical *Wish You Were Here*, toured within the tri-state area, and although Comden's role was not substantial enough to warrant reviews, her presence in a company that included many of the original Broadway performers was her first foot in the door of the theater.

After the tour she received a scholarship to Leighton Rollins' School of Acting in East Hampton, New York, for the summer of 1938. The school's founder had established himself in Boston and was just starting his second year operating on Long Island. His capacity for recognizing talent had been witnessed both in Massachusetts and the Hamptons, where, in his first summer, student performers included Van Heflin and Henry Fonda. Rollins received support from Mary Woodhouse, a patron of the arts in the Hamptons. Through her generosity he had access to the Guild Hall's John Drew Theatre and the elegant manor house Greycroft, both of which were on the grounds of Woodhouse's country estate.

During Comden's time at the Rollins school she performed in both new experimental works and other then-modern classics, such as Oscar Wilde's *The Importance of Being Earnest* and Ferenc Molnar's *Liliom*, which would ultimately be transformed by Richard Rodgers and Oscar Hammerstein II into *Carousel*. Her reviews that summer—courtesy of an unnamed critic for the *East Hampton Star*—were uniformly excellent. In writing about her performance in *Earnest*, the critic noted, "Miss Comden has an amazing technical range. We are already accustomed to expect a splendid performance from her and we were again satisfied."[10]

Similarly, in a review of *First Lady*, one of the new works that was part of the season, Comden's performance as the wife of a Supreme Court justice garnered this effusive, and curiously hyperbolic, praise: "She brought to her characterization an exciting power and a command of her role that must far exceed her years of experience. We can now imagine Miss Comden playing with distinction any role which is given to her. . . . If the floods which we have been having these last days should wash us all away we prophesy that

Miss Comden would survie [sic] on a raft which for her would be success in the theatre."[11]

Green, too, was performing in the summers, but far away from the genteel climes of the Hamptons and critical eyes. In 1937 he accepted a job as an actor at a summer camp in the Berkshires in Massachusetts. Specifically, Green was invited by a friend to play the Pirate King in a production of Gilbert and Sullivan's *The Pirates of Penzance* at Camp Onota in Pittsfield. The musical counselor for the camp that summer was a young pianist named Leonard Bernstein, who had just completed his sophomore year at Harvard.

Green and Bernstein became good pals immediately thanks to Green's self-education in music. Green's son, Adam, described the moment that solidified what would become a lifelong friendship: "Bernstein had heard about my father's uncanny knowledge of classical music, dragged him into the dining hall and challenged him to identify a Shostakovich melody, which he played on an upright piano. After a few bars, my father said, 'I don't know what that is, but it's not Shostakovich.'"[12] Bernstein was overjoyed by the response, and Green had passed his new friend's test. It turned out that Bernstein had played one of his own compositions.

Years later Green would recall this moment, saying, "I felt a sudden, complete exuberance, the fresh air of 1,000,000 windows opening simultaneously and a sense that my life had been building towards a turning point and that it had happened—now."[13]

The following summer Green was once again plying his craft as a performer outside of the city, not as an actor for hire but rather as a member of a group called Six and Company, which was touring its productions of short plays to several adult summer camps that were scattered in the mountains of Pennsylvania, New York, and Massachusetts. These places were spots where women and children could escape the city's summer heat. On the weekends, men would join their families at these establishments, which were generally built near some body of water to allow for swimming and boating. In addition to accommodations of both private cabins and shared bungalows, the camps also boasted a communal dining hall and generally a recreation facility with a stage for dances and other entertainment.

It was at one of these in the Poconos in Pennsylvania (by most reports the International Ladies' Garment Workers' Union's [ILGWU's] "Unity House") that Green struck up a friendship with one of the camp guests, a recent high school graduate named Judith Tuvim, who would later use the English translation of her surname, "holiday," to transform into the award-winning actress Judy Holliday.

In 1938, Tuvim, like Green, was hoping to establish a career in the theater and had found a job working as a switchboard operator for Orson Welles and John Houseman's adventuresome Mercury Theatre. It was a position that she felt would serve as a good "foot in the door" of the industry.

Tuvim came to the camp after a severe bout of ill health that started just as the Mercury was going on hiatus for the summer. She had mostly planned on resting and reading while she was out of New York and had not anticipated taking part in activities. Green's innate charm and gregariousness soon changed this. He convinced her to join in his group's work as a stagehand. He would later describe the summer by saying, "The shows we put on at camp were dreadful, and the work she did on them was drudgery, but she performed it as though the world depended on it. Even then, she was a perfectionist."[14]

When Tuvim and Green's time together at the camp ended, they exchanged phone numbers and promised to stay in touch. Tuvim did, in fact, call Green not long after they left the Poconos, and in doing so she set the trajectory that his and Comden's professional lives would take for the next sixty years.

CHAPTER 2

The Revuers Emerge,
Soar... and Coast

S tories about the next phase in Comden's and Green's lives are, to put it
mildly, different. Memory seems to have started playing tricks on everyone involved beginning in the mid-1940s, when their career together—as
well as Judy Holliday's—began kicking into high gear. As years passed, all
three, along with their chroniclers, embellished or revised.

Many incarnations of the tale about how they all began working together
start with the fact that it was a late summer or early fall day in New York City
featuring an afternoon storm that brewed up quickly and dramatically.
Another general constant in the story is that Judy Tuvim, who had still not
adopted the surname Holliday, got caught in the downpour without an umbrella on Seventh Avenue South, just around 10th or 11th Street.

From these basic starting points narratives diverge. One of Holliday's biographers, Gary Carey, has her following a group of stray cats into a seemingly deserted stairwell, believing that they were leading her to a place to
stay dry. Another version of this artistic-creation myth mentions her hud-
dling in a doorframe of a club, the Village Vanguard, on the west side of the
street, and being invited in by the place's proprietor. In still another she takes
the initiative of descending the Vanguard stairs and ends up in the small
triangular basement space that would become the world-renowned jazz club.

Regardless of how she came to be in the cellar at 178 Seventh Avenue
South, Tuvim did end up in the club and found herself in conversation with
its owner, Max Gordon.

At that time the Vanguard was—and had been for nearly four years—an
artistic refuge for the bohemians of lower Manhattan. Gordon, a Lithuanian
immigrant who earned a degree in English literature from Oregon's Reed
College and then went to New York in the mid-1920s, opened it in 1935.
In his memoir, *Live at the Village Vanguard*, Gordon writes that he imagined

running a place where "when the conversation soared and bristled with wit and good feeling, perhaps a resident poet would rise and declaim some verses."

Gordon had achieved that goal, so much so that poet Eli Siegel, who would ultimately receive a nomination for the Pulitzer Prize for poetry, served as master of ceremonies for the space. Other writers who frequented the Vanguard and sometimes declaimed there included Maxwell Bodenheim, John Rose Gildea, and Harry Kemp.

Gordon doesn't mention rain when he describes his early encounters with Tuvim in his memoir. Instead, he describes her as being a regular denizen of his establishment. "There were nights when I'd sit in the back and talk to a pretty, shy, blonde girl, sixteen, maybe seventeen years old, who used to hang out in the place," Gordon writes, adding, "She hung out in the Village, like a lot of kids, because she could breathe more freely, so to speak, than uptown."

With or without rain and whether or not it was Tuvim's first time in the club, there is a consensus about one conversation that she and Gordon had. She started talking about her interest in performing, as well as her friends with similar ambitions. As she spoke, Gordon realized that she might be presenting him with a solution to a conundrum with which he was struggling: how to diversify what he was presenting at the Vanguard. He suggested that maybe the venue would be a spot for Tuvim and her friends to perform.

Tuvim left the club and in short order called Green to tell him about Gordon's offer. A series of other phone calls ensued. Green got in touch with Comden and another performer he knew, Alvin Hammer, who had been involved in a two-man troupe that, like Green's Six and Company, had played at adult summer camps and around the city. After hearing from Green, Comden also reached out to an acquaintance, John Frank, whom she knew from NYU and who was both an actor and a musician. Hammer and Frank were intrigued by the opportunity, and so the quintet got together to figure out what they might be able to perform at the Vanguard.

PERHAPS GREEN WAS THERE

In the April 2, 1951, issue of *Life* magazine, Winthrop Sargeant described yet another scenario that led to the formation of the Revuers: "One day in 1938, with a young actor named Adolph Green, [Holliday] dropped into a Greenwich Village basement hangout for a sandwich and a cup of coffee." During the course of a conversation with Gordon, Sargeant reported, "Miss Holliday suggested that she and her fellow borscht-circuit actors could put on a performance a week in exchange for the privilege of using the place for rehearsals. Gordon agreed, and 'The Revuers' were launched."

As with Tuvim's descent into the space, there are varying reports about what the group's first performance at the Vanguard consisted of. When Gordon writes about the evening in his memoir, he describes their debut by saying that after they'd taken to the cramped stage, "they explained how happy they were to be at the Village Vanguard to sing about New York. The opening number sounded as if it had been written the night before. It had, Judy told me later. They loved New York, but they had some beefs about New York that they were now going to sing about."

In Will Holtzman's biography, *Judy Holliday*, he describes the group's debut quite differently: "The five of them gathered at the Vanguard one Sunday night and performed individually. There was no act." Holtzman goes on to describe how denizens of the place walked out during the performance but says that Gordon remained supportive: "He told the kids to keep at it."

Holtzman's recounting of the group's inaugural effort seems the more apt, given that in later years both Comden and Green would quip about how they came to be primarily writers rather than performers after they learned that if they intended to perform others' work, they would have to pay royalties. "We couldn't afford that," Comden would later recall, adding, "so we all chipped in and bought a pencil and started to write material for ourselves—lyrics, sketches, music, everything."[1]

Once the group had written their sketches and numbers, which appears to be what Gordon describes, they invited family and friends, including Green's father and brother and Comden's future husband, Steven Kyle, to attend a performance. Unsurprisingly, they all enjoyed what they saw, as did Gordon, who writes in his book, "I found myself liking it too," and it was at this moment he hired them to appear on a regular basis.

He even agreed to pay them. Their fee would be a split from the receipts for the food and setups that were charged for people who brought their own liquor. As a result, each member of the group ended up earning about $5, and it marked the first moment of Comden and Green's reinvention of themselves from would-be actors to professional writer-performers.

Gordon's decision to have them appear on an ongoing basis meant that they needed to come up with some sort of name for the group. He suggested Judy and the Kids (which would ultimately become his way of referring to them for the rest of his life), but as this was a collaborative effort, they felt that no one deserved "top billing." For a while they performed as the Village Vanguarders and later just as The Vanguarders, but ultimately they opted for The Revuers, believing that it simultaneously described the sort of work they were doing and encompassed the cooperative nature of the material they were developing.

THE REVUERS ON THEIR NAME

Roughly one year after their debut at the Vanguard, the group penned a column for vacationing radio commentator Jo Ranson in the *Brooklyn Eagle*. The September 4 piece related how they became The Revuers. They quipped that they considered using the initials of their first names, but that "'Jajab' and 'Bajaj' sounded like dishes on an Armenian menu." They further joked that their decision to go by The Dionne Quintuplets was nixed after they discovered "another act had been using that name for some years." In the end they explained that they derived their name from "the initials of the words Rhododendron, Earthquake, Varnish, Uncle, Egg, Ragweed, Salami."

By the end of 1938 columnists covering the nightclub scene began to take notice of the change in programming at the Vanguard. It wasn't until March 1939, however, that the Revuers themselves started receiving official reviews. One of the earliest came from Richard Manson in the *New York Post*, who wrote, "This troupe puts on a bright, fast show that is a credit to the 'little theatre' movement.... The material has a liberal slant but doesn't make a barbecue out of the propagandist urge; and the production has a lightning pace that makes you forget their working with two dollars' worth of props."[2]

Manson hastened to remind readers that they would need to bring their own liquor, as Gordon had yet to earn enough to secure a liquor license. What the critic neglected to mention was that until spring had fully arrived, patrons might want to dress warmly. The space was so frigid that one of the Revuers' earliest pieces of material was set on a subway, so that they could stay in their coats while they performed.

A second review from Manson helped solidify the Revuers' reputation, and just after it ran Comden and Green arrived to find that they were not able to enter the Vanguard. The staircase leading down into it was crammed with people attempting to secure seats for their show.

Once warmer weather arrived, so too did new notices and opportunities. Among the most effusive write-ups they received came from Theodore Strauss in the *New York Times*, who said that they had written "the cleverest, sauciest and altogether most entertaining topical skits we have seen in a year of midnight travels."[3] As for performing elsewhere, the first stint they had outside of the Vanguard took Comden and Green closer to their goal of working in the theater itself. It also took them out of the city and back to the realm of summer theater; they were invited by the Westport Country Playhouse to be part of a new revue called *Magazine Page*.

The show was an amalgam of acts that the theater culled together, and it also included performances by two Rainbow Room alums, satirists Sheila Barrett and John Hoysradt (who, as John Hoyt, would go on to enjoy a lengthy television career); magician Francis Carlyle; and comedienne Hildegarde Halliday. Another performer on the bill—and also the show's choreographer—was a man who would become a lifelong friend of Comden and Green: Gene Kelly. In a *Billboard* review of the show on September 9, 1939, Samuel A. Lefkowitz described the future screen legend as "a personable juvenile [who] taps his way into the hearts of the audience."

Magazine Page had been billed as a pre-Broadway engagement, but a transfer, despite favorable notices, never materialized. However, that didn't mean that Comden and Green and their compatriots were either out of work or relegated to returning to their tiny cellar stage. Instead, they had a swank gig lined up to immediately follow their Westport appearance.

John Roy, manager of the Rainbow Room, had been one of the many who had flocked to see the Revuers at the Vanguard, and he hired them to play a brief engagement at the opulent nightspot at Rockefeller Center. Roy placed them on a bill with Jack Cole (another choreographic talent who would later go on to work with Comden and Green), whose work had previously been seen and acclaimed at the supper club.

The combination of old and new at the venue was hailed by most of the critics, and Roy himself was applauded for being so "experimental" in his programming of the swanky nightspot. Paul Dennis in his September 23 *Billboard* review wrote that bringing the Revuers to the Rainbow Room was "a bold departure from the conventional entertainment policies of most class spots."

Unfortunately, the group's work did not click in this space the way it had downtown. Part of the problem was simply one of scale. Their routines were geared toward a smaller, more intimate room, such as the Vanguard, not a large one with a chasm of a dance floor in its middle. At the Rainbow Room their relative lack of experience was also more apparent. Words such as "amateurish" and "undeveloped" surfaced in review after review.

Nevertheless, critics did their utmost to be supportive because of the talent they saw in the quintet. In his September 15 *New York Sun* review, Malcolm Johnson wrote: "Their material is literate, witty and clever. We wish, therefore, that we could be unqualified in our praise of their work as exhibited uptown." Johnson went on to seesaw between the pieces in their act that he liked and those he didn't. In the former category he hailed one in which they satirized the work of Clifford Odets and Noël Coward; in the latter was a satire on the movie industry that Johnson reported "fell flat."

In later years, when recounting this moment in their show *A Party With*, Green would quip, "We began in this cellar, the Village Vanguard, and in less than six months we were up 65 floors atop the glamorous RCA building in the magnificent Rainbow Room, and less than a year after that, we were back at the Village Vanguard." Indeed, that was their arc, but in the self-deprecating joke Green utterly minimized the exceptional strides the group continued to make as 1939 turned into 1940 and the opportunities that came their way, even after they had returned to the Vanguard.

ALONGSIDE THE REVUERS

During their time at the Vanguard, the Revuers worked with other artists. One of them was Julian Claman, who served as their sometime stage manager. He would go on to write the play *A Quiet Place*, which starred Tyrone Power and featured incidental music by Leonard Bernstein, and also produced the TV series *Have Gun—Will Travel*. Also, at some performances jazz pianist Eddie Heywood, who was just starting what would become an acclaimed career, accompanied the group.

What's most striking about what was happening for Comden and Green and their compatriots in the last part of 1939 (less than a year after they began performing) was that they started to garner a national profile. Magazines such as *Collier's* and *Life* offered extensive features on them, their meteoric rise, and their work. *Vogue* editors even went so far as to include them in an "Under 20" feature in the October 15 issue of the magazine, dedicating a full page to these "five gay satirists." Cleverly, the group had been included not because of their ages but because they spent less than $20 on an entire production.

Most impressively, and as a sort of precursor to the work that Comden and Green would go on to do on both the big and small screen, the Revuers made several television appearances during this period. One program actually had them paired with Kelly, and, fascinatingly, the show was described in a *Billboard* review on October 21 as potentially solving "the variety-tele problem."

The Revuers also began making guest appearances in the far more pervasive medium of radio as 1939 drew to a close, and by spring of 1940 they had both recorded an album for the Musicraft label and begun appearing on their own weekly program for the NBC network.

Their work at the Vanguard prepared them well for creating a new show for listeners each week. They had been writing new material on an ongoing basis while appearing downtown, meeting on Mondays to discuss new sketches that they might integrate into their sets. During these sessions they would also start writing, and then during rehearsals they would revise the new material so that it would be polished by the time they added it to their Vanguard sets each weekend. They continued this process once they made the leap to the airwaves, even as they found ways in which they could use some of their best sketches on air.

Listening to recordings of the Revuers' routines (such as those heard on their *Night Life in New York, No. 2* album from the period) or reading through their archived scripts can often be bewildering, as time has dulled some of their topical jabs. A prime example is a piece they wrote in the first part of 1939, "The Joan Crawford Fan Club," which was included in the Westport show and later recorded. In it they imagine the heresy of a fan club member arriving for a meeting and proclaiming that she had switched loyalties and now idolized Norwegian figure skater Sonja Henie, who had just begun to make movies. It's a curious conceit, and one that might inspire a bemused smirk today. In 1939, however, it carried a deeper comic punch, given that in March MGM's *Ice Follies of 1939*, headlined by Crawford, had opened and, indeed, this woman so famed today for her portrayals of strong women does don a pair of skates during the course of the movie.

The irony is that Crawford's appearance in *Ice Follies* was dictated by her fan clubs, which proliferated nationally. They were given scenarios for the various projects she was considering and then asked to vote on which they would most like to see the glamorous star appear in. Because these details would have been fresh in the minds of many of the Revuers' audiences, the "Fan Club" musical sketch would have had a far deeper resonance than it does for listeners today.

Other material fares better, such as "Psychoanalysis Blues," a number in which they take aim at some of the screen's most villainous film stars and their movies. Charles Laughton, Robert Montgomery, Boris Karloff, Peter Lorre, and such classic movies as *Mutiny on the Bounty*, *Night Must Fall*, and *Frankenstein* are all skewered. The number even becomes political when Lorre sings about the movie *M*, made in Germany before Hitler's rise to power. In it he laments, "But since Adolf became Germany's favorite child/ They banned my picture . . . it was much too mild."

Equally amusing when taken out of its period is the group's lyric for the song "Variety Says." In it they mock the paper's idiosyncratic argot, which extended to giving reviewers bylines by only using four letters from their names, "Abel." or " Helm.," for example. In the song the Revuers took aim specifically at the newly coined words and invented abbreviations used in the paper's headlines. In the lyric, which the editors at *Variety* re-ran in full in their October 30, 1940, edition, the group described an article about a series of six films that had met with disastrous reviews when playing in regional movie houses. It would carry the headline of, they quipped-sang, "Hicks nix six pix."

The Revuers' sketches also point toward topics and targets that would become staples of Comden and Green's stage and screen writing careers. Beyond Hollywood, their penchant for scenarios involving the New York City subway surfaces repeatedly, as does their gift for lovingly satirizing popular culture. One episode parodies Thornton Wilder's *Our Town*, casting Green as a stage manager and having "Radio City" stand in for the playwright's Grover's Corners.

Beyond giving the Revuers national exposure, the radio shows were also providing Comden and Green with some important lessons in structure that would come to serve them well. Most notable is how they learned to handle the introduction of outside singers and songs within the programs. In the earliest shows, singers are introduced beyond of the scope of the material that the Revuers are performing, but in later ones, performers and their songs, even far outside the realm of their theme for the week, are integrated into the program's overall scenario.

The group wasn't relying simply on these broadcasts for work during 1940. In June they took up residence for several weeks at the World's Fair, where they offered two shows a day. Their performances took place in a prime spot at the event: the World of Fashion building, which was located directly across from the iconic Trylon and Perisphere, the gigantic spire and globe that were connected by what was then the world's longest escalator.

By the end of the year the Revuers got a gig that generated live audiences larger than any they had yet experienced. They were hired to be the first speaking act to appear in Radio City Music Hall's stage show accompanying its screening of the movie *Escape*, an early drama about the concentration camps in Germany that starred Norma Shearer and Robert Taylor.

The group returned to Radio City for two additional appearances. The first, in the summer of 1941, was in the stage show that played alongside the film musical *Sunny*. The second, in October of that year, came as the Charles Laughton–Deanna Durbin movie *It Started with Eve* premiered. Unfortunately, they lasted only a single performance for this engagement because their material did not mesh with the other pieces of the stage show, which had been conceived as being four different dreamscapes.

It was the beginning of a rocky 18-month stretch for the group, a time when the meteoric arc of fame that they had enjoyed for two years hit a plateau. It wasn't that they couldn't find work. During this period the group continued to appear at clubs in New York City, and they took to the road with engagements in cities such as Pittsburgh and Chicago. They were also frequently asked to take part in special events around Manhattan, including a Russian War Relief fundraiser at Carnegie Hall. It's just that they seemed to have stopped building on their previous successes.

It was during mid-1941 and early 1942 that both Comden and Green married. He was the first to wed, and his nuptials to Elizabeth Reitell took place on June 20, 1941, just before the Revuers had their second engagement at Radio City. In the *Variety* announcement about their marriage a few weeks later, Reitell was identified as a costume designer. Her credits at this juncture, however, were slim. Perhaps most notable was her work on a production of an experimental poetic drama, *The Bridge*, seen at Vermont's Bennington College in December 1939.

The Green-Reitell relationship began after she, some school friends, and future choreographic great Merce Cunningham visited the Vanguard to see the Revuers. When writing years later about his father's first marriage, Adam Green described it merely as an "unhappy union."[4] It ended in divorce after only 14 months.

Comden's wedding to Steven Kyle, born Siegfried Schutzman, came six months after Green's, and the marriage endured until Kyle's death in 1979. The couple met while she was studying at NYU and he was a student at the Art Students' League while simultaneously working for his father. In her memoir Comden describes him as "a young god...beautiful in every way" and recalled wondering "how this paragon could possibly want me."

Their romance had flourished (despite Comden's insecurities) since their meeting, and he had watched and supported the Revuers' work from their first Vanguard performance. Finally, in January 1942, Comden and Kyle married in a private ceremony attended by a few family members. Afterward they enjoyed a wedding luncheon at Hapsburg House in Manhattan's East 50s. It had figured prominently in Noël Coward's movie *The Scoundrel*, and to Comden it seemed "the most romantic setting in the world."[5] The couple's honeymoon period was short-lived, because in May 1942 Kyle enlisted in the army and was soon deployed to a camouflage unit.

Just before Kyle was sent overseas, Comden, Green, and their Revuers colleagues saw a glimmer that the group might finally break through to a new level in their craft when they were cast in the Broadway-bound show *My Dear Public*. It was the brainchild of Irving Caesar, who had a diverse array of credits. He had collaborated with George Gershwin, writing the lyric for "Swanee." Caesar also put lyrics to Vincent Youmans's melodies in *No, No Nanette*, which boasts the standard "Tea for Two," and was coauthor of the book for Richard Rodgers and Lorenz Hart's *Betsy*. With *My Dear Public*, Caesar was not only providing book, music, and lyrics (working with Charles Gottesfield, Sam Lerner, and Gerald Marks); he was also making his debut as a producer.

The play centers on a producer who believes that his newest show will be critic-proof if its author has died before it opens, and the wan comedy seesaws between scenes about the producer's machinations, the making of the show-within-the-show, and portions of the fictional piece itself. For Comden and Green the opportunity must have seemed to be a realization of childhood dreams of becoming performers on the Great White Way.

Unfortunately, *My Dear Public* received disastrous notices when it played its tryout engagement in Boston in March 1942, and Caesar closed the show, sending the Revuers back to their lives as nightclub entertainers. Over a year later, *My Dear Public* did reach Broadway, but without the presence of the group.

BENEFICIAL FOR BERNSTEIN

My Dear Public provided a somewhat happier end result for Green's old friend Leonard Bernstein. When the show opened in Boston, Bernstein was among the guests at the opening night party and provided impromptu entertainment. Caesar, impressed with the young musician's skill and believing him to be a genuine successor to Gershwin, promised him work if he should ever move to New York. One year later Bernstein took him up on his offer. Caesar got Bernstein a job working for the music publisher Harms Inc., and this provided him with some of the financial resources necessary to sustain himself before his career as a composer-conductor hit its stride.

As 1942 turned into 1943, the Revuers transformed from a quintet to a quartet after John Frank left for health reasons. The change in the group's composition did nothing to undermine their ability to get work, nor did it dim the remaining members' desire to move to a new level in their careers. And when July 1943 came around it looked as if they had finally succeeded in moving out of the world of nightclub entertainment, as reports came that they were scheduled to appear in their first motion picture, *Duffy's Tavern*.

The group pooled their money, borrowed some more, and set off for Hollywood. Unfortunately, they had not signed contracts for the film; they only had a verbal promise from the producers. When they arrived in California they discovered to their dismay that the movie had been called off. Thankfully, they had managed to secure other work in anticipation of their arrival on the West Coast, and in August 1943 they began performing at the famed Trocadero, which had recently been renovated and was reopening to both critical and popular acclaim. *Variety* critic "Helm." heralded the renovations of the spot in an August 11, 1943, review and commended the Revuers for being "smart, fresh and nicely adaptable to this intimate room."

In the absence of film work, the quartet stayed in Hollywood, looking for other engagements and finding sporadic gigs. There were radio guest shots and special events. Further, studio execs were eager to sign Comden and Tuvim to contracts, but the women refused, asserting their loyalty to the group.

Eventually, the Revuers did secure a film deal for themselves. They were contracted to appear in the Don Ameche and Vivian Blaine movie *Greenwich*

Village, which centers on a young composer who's swept up in the colorful bohemian life of New York's downtown artistic scene. The Revuers were contracted to do several of their sketches for the project, but most of their work ended up on the cutting-room floor. Still, the group can be seen in the final version of the film during one large party sequence, all attired in color-ful, vaguely Elizabethan costumes. Additionally, Comden can be glimpsed uttering one line as a hatcheck girl at a club that Ameche's character visits. After filming was completed on the project in early 1944, Tuvim and Hammer opted to stay on the West Coast to pursue careers in films while Comden and Green made their way, disconsolate, back to New York, uncer-tain of what the future would hold for them.

COMDEN'S FIRST SCREENWRITING CREDIT

Comden came up with her one bit of dialogue—"Check your hat, sir?"—that remains in *Greenwich Village*. In July 1975 a joke that Green made about the line was carried in newspapers around the country in a syndicated "Behind the Scenes" column. He said, "They were sitting around on the set one day wondering what kind of dialog a hatcheck should have when Betty came up with her line. They all cried, 'That's IT!'"

CHAPTER 3

Taking the Town

C omden and Green made individual exoduses from Hollywood after
the debasing experiences they had there in late 1943. She journeyed
back to New York first in order to be with her husband, who had a scheduled leave from the army. Green followed a few weeks later, and when he
arrived at Grand Central Station, Comden was there to cheer him up with a
sign that read "Adolph Green Fan Club."

Almost concurrent with Comden's and Green's returns to Manhattan
was a terpsichorean tsunami of sorts that washed over the city: the premiere
of *Fancy Free* as part of the Ballet Theatre's season at the old Metropolitan
Opera House on Broadway just above 39th Street. With music by Leonard
Bernstein and choreography by Jerome Robbins, the piece premiered on
April 18 and was heralded in the *New York Times* the following day by John
Martin, who labeled it "a smash hit."

For Robbins, who had been dancing with the company for years, *Fancy
Free*, which centers on the friendly competition between three sailors on
leave in New York, marked his breakthrough debut as a choreographer. In
his *Times* review Martin made particular note of how the dance fit with
Robbins's previous work as a performer, writing that it boasted "the same
quality of humor which has always characterized his personal dancing."

As for Bernstein, it was the second in a pair of life-altering events. The first
had come just six months before. He became something of an overnight sensation when, as assistant conductor for the New York Philharmonic, he sub-
stituted at the last minute—and without the benefit of rehearsal—for an
ailing Bruno Walter. The November 1943 concert was heard both in New
York and nationwide on radio, and Comden and Green, out in Hollywood
and feeling down about the Revuers' fortunes there, heard it. "We were sitting
on the sticky tar paper roof in back of our weird apartment," they recalled,
adding that after they heard the ovation Bernstein received "Our depression
about our own state faded as we yelled and leapt with joy and excitement."[1]

The following morning papers around the country carried news of the historic debut of this 25-year-old wunderkind, who before these successes had been cobbling together an existence and career, sometimes even serving as accompanist for the Revuers and penning one number with them, "The Girl with Two Left Feet."

And even as Bernstein was occasionally working with the group and also enjoying a close friendship with them (Green and he shared an apartment together at one point), Comden and Green are said to have assisted him in his endeavors. According to one report the two played a part in bringing his first major symphonic work to the concert hall in early 1944. In the July 25, 1960, issue of *Life* magazine, Tom Prideaux wrote, "When Bernstein was rushing to copy out parts for the premiere of his *Jeremiah Symphony*, Betty and Adolph got out their fountain pens and helped him all night."

More significantly, they had a hand in ensuring that the premiere of *Fancy Free* went smoothly. The dance opens in a small bar where a pop tune is meant to be playing on a Victrola. Specifically, audiences were supposed to hear a recording of Bernstein's "Big Stuff" delivered by his sister, Shirley. On opening night, however, the record player refused to function.

Bernstein—knowing his old friends Comden and Green had a working Victrola and also aware that they were in the house for the performance—got word to them about the technical issue facing the company. He asked if they could bring their machine to the theater in time for the beginning of the dance. Comden and Green hurried out of the theater and into a cab. Just as Bernstein was taking the podium to conduct *Fancy Free*, the working record player was being installed on stage. No one in the house—critics included—had any sense of the problem that could have undermined the opening moments of the dance.

Fancy Free remained a new centerpiece for the company as it continued—and then extended—its season at the Opera House, and by June 1944 reports were circulating that the ballet, described as "indispensable" by dance critic Martin in the *Times* less than a month after its premiere, would become a Broadway musical under the auspices of a first-time producing team, Oliver Smith and Paul Feigay.

Wisconsin-born Smith had designed *Fancy Free* as well as two other pieces in the company's repertoire, including Agnes de Mille's *Rodeo*, and was the first to see the potential in creating some sort of musical from the dance. He approached both Robbins and Bernstein about his idea and learned that they were already contemplating working on a musical together, although not one inspired by the ballet. After some discussion, Robbins and Bernstein both agreed to scrap the piece they had begun and develop a new work stemming from *Fancy Free*.

Like Smith, Feigay was also a first-time producer, but he was not untested in the entertainment industry. His first job after graduation from Yale had been staging a presentation in the Hall of Pharmacy at the 1939 World's Fair. After that he worked for the Ringling Circus and then moved on to the New Opera Company, where he served as assistant director. It was in this latter capacity that Feigay came to know Smith, who provided the scenic design for the company's production of *Rosalinda*, an adaptation of *Die Fledermaus* that ultimately moved to Broadway and enjoyed a 15-month run.

As Smith and Feigay contemplated who might join them, Robbins, and Bernstein in expanding or reinventing *Fancy Free* as a full-scale musical, the choreographer suggested two friends. He thought Arthur Laurents, an aspiring playwright at this juncture who had written scripts for army shows, could provide the aborning musical's book. In addition, Robbins suggested as lyricist John Latouche, whose résumé included both *Cabin in the Sky*, which contained the standard "Taking a Chance on Love," and the highly acclaimed cantata *Ballad for Americans*, for which Latouche had provided the conception and text.

Bernstein, who at the time and until his death could perform many of the Revuers' routines from memory, believed that Comden and Green would be better suited to the project. Realizing that the best way to introduce the pair to his artistic partners was in performance, Bernstein took Smith and Robbins to a spot where Comden and Green had just begun an engagement, a supper club on the Upper East Side called the Blue Angel.

Of course, they were now just a two-person act, but they still performed as the Revuers, and when Bernstein and his artistic partners dropped in to see them, they were offering up a combination of new pieces and older ones they had adapted for themselves. During their show they performed one number that would be a staple for them for the balance of their careers: "Reader's Digest," in which they imagine classics distilled to just three rhyming lines, including such hefty tomes as *Les Misérables* and *Gone with the Wind*. Also new, and another number that they would continue to perform for years to come, was a routine inspired by their experiences in Hollywood, imagining a story conference among a group of screenwriters.

Their song-sketches and their spirit convinced Smith and Robbins that Bernstein's instincts were correct, and in short order Comden and Green joined the team for the musical that would evolve from *Fancy Free*. Smith would later recall his reaction to them and their work in a conversation for the Bernstein Archive Oral History project: "I was enchanted with them."

Official reports about the creative team for the piece began appearing on June 7, 1944, the same day that papers were emblazoned with headlines about the Normandy landing 24 hours before. Even the front page of entertainment bible *Variety* was primarily devoted to the impact that the D-Day invasion had had on radio programs and movies, but on page two a small story carried a headline that blared: "Young Talents Map Broadway Musical."

This item, as well as ones that ran concurrently in the *New York Times* and the *Christian Science Monitor*, all stated that the book would be a collaborative effort among Comden, Green, Bernstein, and Robbins. But no mention was made of who would be providing lyrics for the piece that was being "written, produced and staged by 23- to 25-year-olds."[2]

FOREVER YOUNGER

Neither Comden's nor Green's age was accurately reported in the *Variety* announcement of the show that would become *On the Town*. At the time they were, respectively, 27 and 29. The subtraction of a couple of years from both of their ages presumably was the invention of a press agent who hoped to set the show apart in a season that was shaping up to feature primarily new musicals by older, experienced pros. The revisions to their birthdays had a lasting impact on Comden and Green, who for the remainder of their careers would obfuscate their ages. During a Dramatists Guild symposium in 1981, Bernstein even joked about this, saying: "We were all twenty-five years old—at least I was, and they all said they were."

Given that the new musical had no announced director, it's surprising—and telling—that the initial reports about it in June also noted that the show would be going into rehearsal the first week of August. Clearly, neophyte producers Smith and Feigay believed both that they would be able to raise the money needed to present the show in short order and that Comden and Green, along with Bernstein and Robbins, would be able to produce a completed script and score in just seven weeks' time.

When Robbins's friend Latouche was announced as the lyricist for the project just a month later, the show had been given an official title, *On the Town*. Also, in a signal that the producers' original timeline for the show had been too aggressive, the starting date for rehearsals, for a production that still lacked a director, had been shifted into September.

Thus began an intensive summer of writing for Comden, Green, and Bernstein. Latouche, who would disappear quietly and without explanation from the show within two months of his announcement, appears to have never begun work on the piece, although according to Comden's remarks in the notes for Ben Bagley's *Leonard Bernstein Revisited* LP, Latouche may have done some rewriting of the preexisting song "It's Got to Be Bad to Be Good," which already had a lyric by Hughie Prince, lyricist of "Boogie Woogie Bugle Boy," and was sitting in Bernstein's trunk.

The creative process of developing the show was a collaborative one among all the members of the creative team from the outset, although there was one specific task that fell to one member of the group. Comden, just as she had with the Revuers, served as the official note taker, and some of the earliest scenarios for the piece exist to this day in her handwriting. She would later joke about her duties when chatting with Richard Morrison for a March 4, 2005, London *Times* feature: "As I had foolishly learnt to type, I was the one who had to write it all down."

The closeness of the way in which *On the Town* was written can be best understood by the lengths to which Bernstein, Comden, and Green went to be together during the summer of 1944. When Bernstein traveled to California to conduct *Fancy Free* at the Hollywood Bowl, Comden and Green went with him, and they worked together on the cross-country train ride. Later, when Bernstein learned that he needed an operation to relieve a chronic sinus infection, Green scheduled an operation for himself (a tonsillectomy) so that they could recover simultaneously, meaning that work on the new piece would not be interrupted. Shirley Bernstein would later recall how, several days after the operations, she found "Betty perched on their beds," and that in the hospital "they all worked on the show. The floor nurses and patients in nearby rooms were alternately amused and irritated by the singing and laughter that erupted from Room 669."[3]

As they didn't want the new musical to replicate *Fancy Free* and its story-line about three soldiers competing for the same girl during their leave, they started to develop other New York–centric scenarios that might allow for the same sort of creative freedom that the ballet had afforded Bernstein and Robbins.

In one they imagined a septuagenarian actor who takes a young aspiring actress under his wing just after she's arrived in New York from Small Toe, Iowa. While she looks for work, buoyed by the reviews she received for her performances for the Big Toe Dramatic Society in the Midwest, she also volunteers at a Times Square nightspot for servicemen, and it's there that she meets the man of her dreams. Unfortunately, before they speak she overhears him talking about wanting nothing to do with the actress types whom he has encountered at the Stage Door Canteen, so she has to pretend to be someone else.

Another scenario that the team dreamed up centered on a down-on-his-luck sculptor whose fortunes change after he receives a hefty commission to create a huge statue meant to stand in front of the headquarters of the Face-O-Firm cosmetics company. Comden and Green imagined that the artist would have to contend with the ambitions of the women who were to be immortalized in his work and their desire to be at its fore. Romantic complications would ensue for the aspiring models, the artist, and his female assistant, who unsurprisingly carries a torch for her boss.

Both of these tales contain the sort of comic verve that had been the hallmark of Comden and Green's writing with the Revuers, with the names of the small town in Iowa and the beauty company saying it all. Further, strong women's roles are central to the stories, and each contains the basic tropes of musical theater comedy of the period.

Ultimately, the team opted to stick with the idea of three Navy men on leave in the city. The guys, however, would not be in competition for the same girl. Instead, they would each go off in search of adventure and a romance that would sustain them after they had shipped out. Envisioned as a whirlwind tour of the city, the musical would chart the guys' travels throughout the city and leave the writers ample room to create a theatrical valentine to New York. Comden, who had seen her own husband deployed, recalled a personal credo that informed the writing: "New York's streets were full of servicemen, all searching for joy before being sent into the war.... We wanted to capture the poignancy of those times."[4]

As they wrote, Comden and Green made one additional mandate for themselves: "We decided what would give our show life would be a book so involved in, and involving[,] the other elements that it would be hard to tell where one department left off and another began."[5]

From the earliest handwritten drafts of what would become On the Town, the show's starting point—the Brooklyn Navy Yard—remains a constant. After this, though, Comden and Green's work goes through both dramatic and subtle changes, many of which were influenced by the show's director, George Abbott.

Unlike the as-yet-untested (at least on Broadway) artists behind On the Town, the 57-year-old Abbott was a playwright-director with a long history of hits on the Main Stem. Among the shows he had staged were Rodgers and Hart's The Boys from Syracuse, Pal Joey, and On Your Toes. The team only approached Abbott after disappointing encounters with others, including Elia Kazan, who had staged such groundbreaking plays as Waiting for Lefty and Golden Boy and who had recently made his debut as a musical theater director with One Touch of Venus.

Eventually, Smith recalled, "Suddenly we asked ourselves, 'Well, if we could have anybody in the world, who would be our first choice?'"[6] The answer was Abbott, and so they sent a script to him. He had already heard about the project through the industry grapevine and his response was: "I know about this—it has a very good smell to me."[7] On the Town had its director.

The addition of Abbott to the project meant not only that the piece would benefit from the eye and judgment of a seasoned Broadway professional; it also assisted Smith and Feigay in their efforts to secure the necessary financial backing. Smith would later recall that although they had not had difficulty raising a small amount for the show initially, finding additional money was hard because "the typical Broadway crowd didn't fancy it, didn't think it was commercial."[8]

After Abbott was announced as director, Smith and Feigay had no problem raising money. Indeed, MGM made what is reportedly the first pre-production deal for film rights to a stage musical because of Abbott's involvement, providing a quarter of the show's $250,000 capitalization and advancing $100,000 to the creators for the screen rights. Ironically, Smith and Feigay eventually found that they had too many investors and tried to return some of the money. And just as the show was opening they found themselves in the position of having to cope with an injunction from one of these people, who was refusing to take back his investment.

The version of the script that the producers gave to Abbott was one that had already been heavily revised by Comden and Green during the summer. Their ability to self-edit can be seen in some of Comden's earliest notes as she and Green rethink what their central male characters are to be called. They start off as Gabey (short for Gable), Donny, and Mitch. It's not long, however, before Comden begins to substitute "Chip" for Donny and Ozzie for Mitch.

Their lyrics, too, went through careful rewriting before Abbott's arrival. Perhaps one of the most noticeable changes comes in the iconic opening song for the men, "New York, New York." Before the city was a "helluva town" it was a "feverish spot" where instead of the Bronx being up and the Battery being down it was "either freezing or horribly hot."

Not all of the lyrics in the first drafts belonged to Comden and Green. Some came from Bernstein because of inserted trunk songs, pieces he had written previously that had gone unused and unrecorded. All of these tunes would eventually be removed from the script as Comden and Green crusaded for new numbers that were organically tied to the story and its characters.

Among the Bernstein songs was "Ain't Got No Tears Left," which, at one point, was slotted in as a number to be performed by an African American bartender at a Times Square dive into which Gabey stumbles. The song appears to have made it as far as the show's first rehearsals because in one casting announcement that ran in the November 13 edition of the *New York Times*, a listing of the show's principals included African American actress Ann Robinson. By the time the show reached Boston, however, neither she nor the song was still in the show, and it would seem that after excising "Tears" from the score, Robinson's role was eliminated. Bernstein would later go on to use some of the music from it in the masque movement of his Second Symphony, "Age of Anxiety."

The script, when it was presented to Abbott, also included a framing device of a hearing in night court in which the three sailors are accused of various minor crimes they have committed during their time in the city. In this version audiences would come to learn exactly what the sailors had done to land themselves on the wrong side of the law.

In later years Abbott would remember that in addition to his excitement about the script, he also felt that "some things were wrong, and it seemed best to say so early in the game. For instance, there were many long and involved interruptions of the main plot by a judge and an old lady, two characters I thought unnecessary." Abbott also recalled how Comden and Green fought him about cutting these sequences until he issued an ultimatum: "You'll have to take your choice between me and the old lady." Abbott then added, "They chose me, and we used the old lady simply as a crossover."[9]

Much of what Abbott bristled at in Comden and Green's draft script resembles the sort of writing that they done for the Revuers' radio shows, where scenes were connected by the thinnest of plot threads. The night court sequences, for example, allowed the writers to shift the action of the script as needed, with each character telling stories that were essentially unrelated to each other.

After Comden and Green agreed to remove the framing device, they made another significant change to the script: They gave all of the sailors a common goal. In the original version, as in the final one, Gabey falls in love at first sight with a picture of Ivy Smith that touts her as the Miss Turnstiles for the month. He vows to find her during his 24-hour leave. Ozzie and Chip understand what their bud needs to do and wish him luck before heading off to find girls of their own. All three agree to bring the women they meet to Times Square and Nedick's, which Chip believes to be a famed nightclub. (In actuality it was just one in a chain of eateries that were known for hot dogs and a signature orange drink, sort of like an early 20th-century version of Gray's Papaya, which proliferated throughout the city starting in the 1970s.)

WARTIME TIMES SQUARE

For generations who have only come to know New York's theater district as either dilapidated, dirty, and dangerous (as it was in the 1970s) or Disneyfied (as it became in the late 1990s), it's difficult to imagine what the guys of *On the Town* would see once they arrived. One terrific description of the area at the time appeared in a July 1946 syndicated column from theater reporter Jack O'Brian. In it he describes the "war-born adjuncts of the Main stem" that were feeling a pinch because servicemen were no longer thronging into the city: "shooting galleries, penny arcades, [and] flea circuses."

In the final version of the *On the Town* script Comden and Green still have the guys deciding to part company and meet at Nedick's (minus Chip's mis-assumption about its being a swank nitery), but instead of striking off with individual quests for a girl, they all go off to various spots where they think they might be able to find Ivy. This change—perhaps at the request of Abbott, whose sense of structure and plot was renowned as impeccable—adds one important element to the script. It gives it a solid dramatic through-line that simultaneously allows Comden and Green to giddily portray the city they love.

Feigay paid tribute to Abbott's contributions to the show and the benefit that his age and experience brought to shaping it when he said, "He showed us how we must space the musical numbers…and entered wonderfully into the effort we were all making to do something fresh in a musical and was a good check-up because of his experience in the theater, in reminding us at times that some things we thought were new had been done before, and well done."[10]

As they wrote *On the Town*, Comden and Green, who had always dreamed of lives as Broadway performers, crafted two central roles for themselves: the man-hungry anthropologist Claire DeLoone and the wildly extravagant sailor Ozzie. And even though they wrote these two parts for themselves, "tailored to what we hopefully thought were our histrionic talents,"[11] they still needed to audition for Abbott. They were in good company. Other people who auditioned for the veteran director were Bernstein's sister, Shirley, who had recorded "Big Stuff" for *Fancy Free*. She was cast in the ensemble and performed as Shirley Ann Burton, adopting another brother's name as her surname.

A future Hollywood luminary, Kirk Douglas, was also one of the actors who auditioned for Abbott, who had cast him as a replacement in the Broadway production of the play *Kiss and Tell*. Douglas, in his book *The Ragman's Son*, describes how after his audition "They all applauded, and George Abbott told me I had the role of Gabey." Douglas goes on to discuss working with the creators and then, developing a psychosomatic case of laryngitis that forced him to depart the production. Bernstein remembered it differently years later, saying "We turned down Kirk Douglas because he couldn't sing."[12]

When Abbott finished the casting process for the show, it turned out that all three sailors would be played by men making their Broadway debuts, with John Battles playing Gabey, Cris Alexander as Chip, and Green in the role he had crafted for himself, Ozzie. The principal female roles went to Sono Osato (Ivy), a colleague of Robbins's from Ballet Theatre, who had just appeared in *One Touch of Venus*; Nancy Walker (Hildy), who had enjoyed a breakout debut in the Abbott-directed musical *Best Foot Forward*, had gone to Hollywood and was released from a film contract to do the show; and Comden in the role of Claire.

WHAT'S IN A NAME?

In the Revuers' routines Comden and Green created zany names that also had double meanings. They continued this practice in *On the Town*, co-opting two classical music references in their character's names. The anthropologist's name is a homonym for "Clair de lune," one of Claude Debussy's most famous piano works. Similarly, the writers' joviality extends to the surname they assigned to the female cabbie who shanghais Chip. On its surface Brunhilde ("Hildy") Esterhazy is just a silly sounding Teutonic name, worthy of the strong-willed character. For anyone, such as Green, with an encyclopedic knowledge of classical music, the last name has a deeper resonance; it belonged to a Hungarian prince who was one of Joseph Haydn's principal benefactors.

First rehearsals were set for November 13, and an abbreviated tryout, only ten days, was scheduled for Boston's Colonial Theatre just one month later. In finding a New York venue, *On the Town* fell prey to a logjam of shows. It was initially booked into the International Theatre on Columbus Circle (which later became the site for the New York Coliseum and currently contains the Time-Warner building) at the northernmost edge of the theater district. Eventually, it found a home in the only slightly more advantageous Adelphi (later the George Abbott) Theatre, which lay just a bit closer to the theater district on 54th Street between Sixth and Seventh Avenues. This house, however, had a history of being a home for flops.

During the casting and rehearsal process, Comden and Green continued to refine the book and lyrics. In writing the character of Madame Maude P. Dilly, Ivy's zanily unconventional vocal teacher, they allowed reality to shape their work. Osato remembered telling Comden and Green about how she had begun seeing a voice teacher, Susan Steell, to ensure that her voice was up to the demands of a lead role. According to Osato, they "were amused by my struggles with Susan [and] they wrote a scene into the show caricaturing my lessons." Eventually, Steell auditioned for the role of Madame Dilly. Osato said that her "hilarious audition . . . had just the screwy quality they wanted and won her the part hands down."[13]

On the Town was scheduled to open for critics on December 13 in Boston, but because of "a shortage of stagehands"[14] Smith and Feigay asked that the reviewers refrain from attending for two days. Theatergoers, many of them Bernstein's friends and family, were still able to attend on the original opening date, which chagrined the composer, but it wasn't until December 15 that reviewers had the opportunity to take in the wholly original new work.

The delay in inviting critics may also have been calculated to allow the creators to fully integrate one last addition to the show, the new song "Some

Other Time." Comden later recalled, "This one we had to write in Boston, writing most of the night." She added that Bernstein composed it "in the window of a music store because that was the only place we could find a piano we could use."[15]

Comden's memory makes it sound as if the tune was a traditional out-of-town addition to the show, a song added after critics had reviewed it. "Some Other Time," however, appears in the opening-night program for the musical and is mentioned in first-night reviews, indicating that the number might have been on the creators' minds even before the company arrived for the tryout on December 10, and that they and Abbott had simply needed time to complete it and stage it between their arrival on December 11 and the opening on the 15th.

The reviews on December 16 showed that Boston critics thought they had encountered an important new musical, though they also believed that the show was still in need of reworking. In the *Boston Post* Elliot Norton wrote, "It is now too long, too loose, too leisurely, and sometimes a little too coarse," before comparing it to *Oklahoma!* and adding that it could be considered "a new American institution."

The *Variety* review that ran on December 20 was less charitable, but even in critic "Elie."'s derision there was a hint of respect for the brashness and freshness of the show, found in his quip that the musical had inspired "the feeling that Art Has Come to the Musical Stage and It Took Us Kids to Do It."

Bearing in mind critics' specific complaints and also gauging audience reaction, the team began retooling the show. Abbott instituted two major cuts, which substantially streamlined a first act brimming with 12 songs and dances. One was "Intermission Number," a sequence that took Gabey to the theater in search of Ivy. Much as they had done in their Revuers' sketches, Comden and Green used the scene and song to lampoon wildly diverging opinions of theatergoers as they filtered into the lobby at an act break. It merely proved extraneous.

The other cut number was listed in the Boston program as "Pick Up Song," and it came just before the show's sensational first-act closer, Robbins's "Times Square Ballet." The excision of this sequence, also known as "Gabey's Comin'," pained Bernstein, because he had woven its melody into other parts of the score; he used it both as the basis for the verse in Gabey's song "Lonely Town" and as thematic underpinnings for the climax of the "Imaginary Coney Island" ballet in the second act.

Along with the cuts, one new song was added, the wry "Carnegie Hall Pavane (Do-Do-Re-Do)," which was performed by Steell, Osato, and young women in the rehearsal rooms at Carnegie Hall. Osato recalled how Robbins created the number one night after the curtain fell on a Boston performance. "He took me back on the stage before I could even remove my makeup and kept me there until the wee hours of the morning." The dance for the number, which has a deliciously silly lyric from Comden and Green, was, as Osato describes it, "a burlesque of all of the steps that had always caused me trouble."[16] Finally, the writers significantly restructured the song order in the second act.

With these major changes and a handful of minor ones, *On the Town* had its official New York opening at the Adelphi on December 28. Comden and Green would write jokingly about their first opening night many years later, noting that they didn't feel at all like writers but instead "much more akin to Dick Powell and Ruby Keeler and, as the final curtain fell to legitimately tumultuous ovation…we expected to see a title 'The End—W.B.' come zooming toward us, growing larger and larger, till it filled the screen and enveloped us."[17]

The next morning Comden, Green, and their partners discovered that their work had received the kind of accolades of which most artists can only dream. Lewis Nichols's review in the *New York Times* began, "There can be no doubt about it: 'On the Town' is the freshest and most engaging musical show to come this way since the golden day of 'Oklahoma!'" Jack O'Brian announced at the top of his AP wire service review that the show's premiere was a rare moment for both the theater and himself as critic: "Almost once or twice in a decade a reviewer gets an opportunity to heave his hat into the stratosphere, send up rockets and in general start the sort of journalistic drooling over a musical comedy that puts an end to all adequate usage of superlatives."

Given how frequently the show was compared to *Oklahoma!*, it's curious that *On the Town* did not receive a full cast album. Just two years before, Decca had broken with a long-standing tradition of recording singles, featuring either cast members or popular singers, to allow songs from musicals to reach home listeners. For *Oklahoma!* a set of 78s that featured the stage company with its theater orchestra was released. The recording was a phenomenal success artistically and financially and began the tradition of original cast recordings as they are now known.

Perhaps it was the elaborate and shrewd blend of jazz, pop, and classical sounds in Bernstein's score that kept record companies away. Another factor might have been one of length. Many numbers would not fit easily onto one side of a 78, which could contain just about three minutes of music. Or perhaps it was the fact that Comden, Green, and Bernstein had done so well at integrating the songs into the book that executives felt it would be impossible to enjoy a majority of the numbers outside of the show.

Still, for musical fans outside of New York who wanted a taste of Broadway's new critical and popular hit, Decca reverted to old practices when the label released a trio of 78s in March 1945 that featured Walker,

Comden and Green, and Mary Martin delivering some of the show's tunes. For anyone who had not been able to see the musical and who wanted a fuller sense of its score, they would need to wait until 1960, when the original principals, along with John Reardon (a vocal replacement for John Battles), went into the studio to record what would become the closest thing to a cast album for the production.

Profiles of Comden and Green in New York and around the country proliferated both before these records and alongside them, and the two, who less than a year before were wondering how they would support themselves, settled in for a long run in the show they had co-created. They wouldn't be with the musical as performers for its entire year-long run (which included a move to the more centrally located 44th Street Theatre and then the Martin Beck—now Al Hirschfeld—Theatre on West 45th Street), but that's only because their lives as Broadway wordsmiths had begun.

ANOTHER KIND OF LEGITIMACY

Beyond giving Comden and Green their first Broadway credit, *On the Town* provided them with another kind of legitimacy. In a December 13, 1999, *Billboard* feature about the 70th anniversary of the American Society of Composers, Authors, and Publishers (ASCAP), Comden recalled: "Back in 1944, we were nightclub performers writing material one day—and the next we were suddenly musical dramatists, with a publisher and membership in ASCAP, getting four checks a year!"

CHAPTER 4

Turning to the 1920s

The morning after *On the Town* opened, Comden and Green had a surprising revelation about life on Broadway. It wasn't at all like what they had learned from movies that centered on the backstage drama of making a musical. Most of these, *42nd Street* for example, end with their fictional show's successful premiere and do not portray what happens after. In their case they realized that it was time to go on, and as they headed to the theater on December 29, 1944, they were also "nursing massive hangovers."[1]

Their morning-after malaise passed, and in short order they were enjoying the benefits of having written—and starring in—a hit Broadway show. First and foremost was the assurance of a steady income, something they had not had since they began working together six years earlier. Neither, however, became spendthrifts with their newfound good fortune. As James Thrasher reported for an NEA wire report in March 1945, "Miss Comden still retains her modest fourth floor walk-up apartment in the West Sixties." Similarly, he noted, "Mr. Green has bought some new suits and a pair of galoshes, and is having his teeth fixed."[2]

Even as they were enjoying their good fortune with *On the Town*, they were also aware that their future as writers meant that they needed to start working on something new. They were concerned that they might not be able to write a second show. "The suspicion that we couldn't scared us," Comden told the *New York Herald Tribune*'s Helen Ormsbee for a May 19, 1946, feature. She added, "We had to find out."

Thus, whenever they were not on stage during their smash hit, they started contemplating a new show and developing scenarios for it. Green told Ormsbee: "We could see the first scene and the last—the little gold digger in Staten Island starting out to get what she wants in the boom of the 1920s and winding up with her wedding just as Wall Street crashes."

The public got the first news about their second musical on May 15, 1945, when Bert McCord told readers in his *New York Herald Tribune* theater column that "the same quintet that was responsible for 'On the Town,' the hit musical now at the Adelphi Theater, will be reunited in the fall for the production of another musical."

At this juncture, no one—including *On the Town* producers Oliver Smith and Paul Feigay, who were reuniting with Comden and Green for the show—would disclose what the show was about. The piece, in fact, didn't even have a title. Nevertheless, whatever Comden and Green had conceived was enough for *On the Town* director George Abbott. McCord reported in the same story that the director liked "the idea so much that he has again committed to stage the show for them."

Fans of the writers' first musical did not have to wait long for more news about their next to start circulating. Before May had ended, Morton Gould was announced as the new musical's composer. He had not been, however, the writers' first choice. They had hoped that Leonard Bernstein would once again write the music, but as reported in the May 30 issue of *Variety*, Bernstein wanted "to continue with his serious music...having proved himself with a 'popular score.'" The same story indicated that the producers and writers had approached Arthur Schwartz, who, with lyricist Howard Dietz, had written songs such as "Dancing in the Dark" and "I Guess I'll Have to Change My Plan" (for the revues *The Band Wagon* and *The Little Show*, respectively), but he had "refused" the offer.

The show, now provisionally titled *There She Goes!*, would mark Gould's Broadway debut as a songwriter, but the fact that the producers and Comden and Green turned to him is not surprising. He, like Bernstein, was at the forefront of making classical music accessible and popular and also had a strong jazz sensibility. His versatility as a composer could be seen in the multiplicity of works he'd written, everything from the songs for the movie *Delightfully Dangerous* to orchestral works such as *Cowboy Rhapsody* and *Harvest*, along with *American Concertette*, which Jerome Robbins used for a dance piece later that year.

Beyond his work as a composer, Gould had enjoyed several high-profile radio engagements, and yet he still did not see himself as a celebrity. Comden, in fact, would later remember with amusement their first encounter. "The phone rang, and someone said, 'Hello, this is Morton. You know, Morton Gould'—and he whistled the 'Pavanne,' as if I didn't know who he was. It was a very funny, self-satirical thing to do."[3] Given their own sensibilities, Gould's amusing introduction of himself appeared to signal that Comden and Green had found a good match for their new project.

The writers, still appearing in *On the Town* at this juncture, needed to concentrate on finishing the book and lyrics for their new show, so in July they took a two-week hiatus from their roles. A sense of how much progress they made during this break can be gleaned from an August 2 column in the

New York Herald Tribune announcing that Abbott had said that the title *There She Goes!* "will definitely not be used."

Even as Comden, Green, and Gould continued to write, speculation about who would choreograph the show arose. There were some reports that Jack Cole, who had been on the same bill with the Revuers at the Rainbow Room and who was just starting his lengthy career as a creator of dances for Broadway and Hollywood, would serve as the musical's choreographer, but the task eventually went to Comden and Green's *On the Town* collaborator Jerome Robbins.

As for the casting, one of the earliest names floated in the press was Mitzi Green, who began her career as an entertainer as a child, working in her parents' vaudeville act and appearing in films like *Tom Sawyer* and *Little Orphan Annie*. She made her Broadway debut at 17 in Rodgers and Hart's *Babes in Arms*, in which she introduced the songs "My Funny Valentine" and "The Lady Is a Tramp." Interestingly, she, like Cole, also had appeared with Comden and Green during their Revuers' days: in the ill-fated *My Dear Public*.

Mitzi Green's name was first mentioned by Leonard Lyons as a mere rumor, but it was a solid one. She and Joan McCracken, who was hired to play the leading character, were the first two casting choices, confirmed in early September, a little more than a month before the still-untitled tuner was to begin rehearsals.

It was Comden and Green who first suggested McCracken. Abbott, however, balked at the idea. He knew her work and the acclaim that she had received for her dancing in *Oklahoma!* and *Bloomer Girl*. His problem was not her talent as a dancer but rather her appearance. The show's central character was to be a beauty-pageant contestant, and given that he thought McCracken "fat, squat, [and] unsensitive,"[4] she was not at all what he was looking for in a leading lady for the show.

Comden and Green knew of Abbott's resistance and devised a way to get the performer in front of him so that he might be willing to let go of his preconceptions. They scheduled her audition for the end of the day at the end of the week, when he would naturally be somewhat tired and ready to move on. Additionally, they advised her on what to wear, so that she might appear both taller and more slender. The ruse worked, paving the way to McCracken's first starring role on Broadway.

The show's cast ultimately grew to include David Burns, whose career started in vaudeville and had expanded to encompass Broadway with shows such as Irving Berlin's *Face the Music* and Moss Hart and George S. Kaufman's *The Man Who Came to Dinner*; James Mitchell, another of the performers in *Bloomer Girl* and one who would go on to leading roles in *Brigadoon, Carousel,* and *Carnival!*; William Tabbert, whose future roles would include Lt. Cable in *South Pacific* and Marius in *Fanny*; and Robert Chisholm, whose string of Broadway credits stretched back to the 1920s and who left *On the Town* to appear in this new Comden and Green show.

Most of these performers were announced before the show had officially received its title, which was revealed only five days before rehearsals were to start. The musical would be known as *Billion Dollar Baby*.

Like *On the Town*, Comden and Green set *Baby* mostly in New York, and in it they tell the story of Staten Islander Maribelle Jones (McCracken), who wants to get in on the boom times the entire country was enjoying in the 1920s by snagging a rich husband. Maribelle's pursuit of a wealthy man takes her through gangster-run nightspots, into a Ziegfeld-like extravaganza, and, in the end, to the rarified Upper East Side.

Comden and Green never sugarcoated Maribelle's cunning and ruthlessness in pursuing a fortune, and they depicted the other characters as equally self-involved: from Dapper Welch, the kingpin who helps launch her, to Georgia Motley, Dapper's songstress girlfriend who's less than thrilled about Maribelle's arrival in their lives. Even Champ Watson, Maribelle's sweet boyfriend, a guy who earns his living working on the Staten Island Ferry, wants to get in on the good times and some fast money. After Maribelle dumps him for wealthier men, Champ heads off to earn a big prize and fame in dance marathons. The violence associated with gangsters also figures prominently in *Billion Dollar Baby*. Before the curtain falls there has been a trio of murders.

Comden and Green leavened their darkness with joviality and giddily goofy details. Champ finds himself taking part in a dance marathon that lasts 143 days, and Maribelle's conniving mom munches on a 10-pound box of candy. Furthermore, as the show draws to a close their work takes on the tone of high farce as a pair of Maribelle's jilted beaus and her rival Georgia dart in and out of hiding places in a swank hotel suite.

What intrigues most about their book for the show is its pitch-black ending, which finds Maribelle, having bagged the fabulously wealthy M. M. Montague, tossing jewels at the guests at her wedding as he, having lost everything in the stock market crash, scrambles to retrieve them. As Green commented during the run of the show: "We had no nostalgia for the '20s. It was a dreadful decade."[5]

COMDEN'S "FLAPPER" AUNT

Neither Comden nor Green was an adult during the decade they were chronicling, but a new member of Comden's family, a career woman her uncle David married, made an indelible impression on the not-yet-teenager. This "flapper," as Comden calls her in her memoir, was "a tall, willowy creature with blue-black hair parted in the middle and coiled into a graceful chignon at the back of her neck." More important, as Comden later recognized, this woman was someone who also "married, had children, and worked at a career in what had been known as a 'man's world,'" forging a trail of sorts for Comden herself to follow.

For this musical trip back in time, Gould matched Comden and Green's dual tones of lighthearted musical comedy and weightier musical satire. In some instances he wrote melodies that aptly evoke the sounds of the 1920s, such as in "Lovely Girl," where he echoes the simplicity of early 20th-century tunes from composers like Irving Berlin. In fact, the Comden and Green lyric for this song, a production number in a *Ziegfeld Follies*–like show Maribelle joins, seems to pay tribute to Berlin's "A Pretty Girl Is Like a Melody." Even the line "A lovely girl is like a lovely bird" matches the rhythm of Berlin's title as it simultaneously ribs its central simile.

Elsewhere, though, Gould's music has a decidedly '40s jazz sound and appears to be attempting to echo Bernstein's work in *On the Town*. In "Bad Timing," during which Maribelle and one of her suitors lament the futility of their love for one another, the shifts to minor of Gould's melody provide the sort of musical melancholy present in Bernstein's "Lonely Town."

Perhaps the creators, director Abbott, and choreographer Robbins might have had the opportunity to make the dichotomous tones of the book and score for *Baby* more cohesive during its tryouts in New Haven and Boston, but events conspired against them. Abbott was sidelined by illness while the show was out of town, as was his star. In fact, the opening was delayed in Boston so that McCracken could recuperate from laryngitis.

There were also difficulties between the lyricists and their composer. Late in life Comden succinctly summed up the collaboration by saying, "It wasn't the happiest experience.... Morton Gould wasn't Lenny Bernstein."[6] And Gould himself admitted to making the process difficult, starting with billing and extending to orchestrations. "I was stupid. I always wanted to control it. I did all the big things, the overture, the ballet music," he later admitted.[7]

When the show ultimately went in front of critics in New Haven on November 15, reviews were dire. The worst came nearly a week later after the show moved on to its tryout in Boston. In the November 21 issue of *Variety*, critic "Laza." wrote: "On the basis of its preem, first reaction is to state that a more pertinent admonition than the usual 'Do not open until Christmas' would be 'Do not open, period.'"

Given that illnesses would make wholesale revisions difficult, the creators opted to make only one major change to *Baby* as it moved from New Haven to Boston and then New York. It was a shrewd addition to the show's first act: a ballet called "Dreams Come True." The dance injected a note of sympathetic humanity into McCracken's character as she imagined what life would be like if she were to be wooed by three screen idols from the period. Beyond helping to make Maribelle look more like a young kid who had just gotten swept up in the hype of the era, the dance also addressed a concern that surfaced in many of the reviews from the New Haven engagement: Most felt it was unfortunate that McCracken did not have a showpiece in the first half of the evening.

With Robbins's addition (effected in just a week's time), and after the delay due to McCracken's laryngitis, *Billion Dollar Baby* officially opened at Boston's Shubert Theater on November 22. The next morning the *Boston Herald*'s Cyrus Durgin announced that it "has the makings of a good show and conceivably a hit." His concern was that while the first act "is a grand summation, in satire and burlesque, of those fabulous days when money was easy and the stock market was high," the second act "will have to show more gayety than it did last night."

Elliot Norton in the *Boston Post* that day noted that theatergoers' enjoyment of the show would depend largely on their age. For those who were old enough to remember the era, he noted: "It comes close to being a classic, despite its first night faults."

When the show finally arrived at Broadway's Alvin Theatre, where it opened on December 21, Abbott and Robbins had made no major changes, and reviews of the show ran from guardedly positive to ecstatic.

Howard Barnes's review in the *New York Herald Tribune* on December 22 praised the writing: "The book and lyrics by Betty Comden and Adolph Green are slyly refreshing and curiously nostalgic." The odd oxymoron in his description led to his final summation of the show: "'Billion Dollar Baby' is as bouncing and sometimes as random as the crazy few years to which it puts a mirror, but it is great good fun."

The *Billboard* review from Bob Francis on December 26 compared the new musical with Comden and Green's first: "*Billion Dollar Baby* looks set for a longer run than its predecessor. *Baby* rates a niche among the top hits." The reviewer added: "Comden and Green have concocted a bang-up book to rib the era....Also by way of originality they have written a heroine who is a complete heel thruout [*sic*], a sort of female *Pal Joey*."

The *New York Times*'s Lewis Nichols certainly didn't have as good a time as some of his journalistic brethren, and yet he did try to be supportive. In his December 22 review he wrote that the creators should "be credited this morning with a good idea and with some good material off the beaten track, but they must also be blamed for allowing their product to waver, to let its course run far from even." Nichols continued, "Often the book sounds as though neither Miss Comden nor Mr. Green had his heart in it."

The critics' assessment of Gould's music frequently bordered on the dismissive or condescending. There were, however, champions of his freshman Broadway effort, perhaps most notably *Billboard* critic Francis, who opined about the future that some of the songs could have: "*Bad Timing* listens well enough for solid pop play, and several of the laugh-pitch chants, such as *Broadway Blossom, Speaking of Pals, A Lovely Girl* and *Faithless*, pack plenty of merit."

Interestingly, given Francis's assessment of these numbers and Gould's work as an orchestra leader, no covers of the songs from the show emerged during its run, nor was any sort of cast recording made. It wasn't until nearly 20 years later, when Comden and Green released a recording of their theater songs for the Heritage record label, that two of the numbers ("Bad Timing" and "Broadway Blossom") were preserved. Gould even distanced himself from the score for the remainder of his career. On the many albums he released after the show closed, he recorded just one number from *Baby*, "I'm Sure of Your Love," including it on his orchestra's 1962 album *Love Walked In*.

Regardless of the mixed critical reaction, *Billion Dollar Baby* took on the aura of a decided smash. The producers were able to run quote ads promoting their "Billion Dollar Hit." Demand for tickets held steady, and through the middle of May it appeared that the show would enjoy a run through the summer. At the end of that month, however, the production fell prey to an economic slump that was hitting the theatrical community. One of the chief reasons was that New Yorkers, who previously had not been able to head out of town because of gasoline rationing during the war, resumed their summertime habits; they were taking to the roads, driving for vacations in the mountains or at the shore. As a result, box-office receipts for *Baby* tumbled by more than 30 percent, and Smith and Feigay posted a hasty closing notice. The musical ended its run at the Alvin on June 29, having played 220 performances.

SETTING TRENDS IN NEW YORK AND BEYOND

Billion Dollar Baby never reached a year's anniversary on Broadway or had a national tour, and yet it had a surprising impact on fashion trends. Just as the show was opening, the December 24 edition of *Life* magazine chronicled in photos how "brave girls in a new show sacrifice long locks for old-time short bobs, ear puffs and bangs," and in early 1946 columnists throughout the country were touting how stylists were creating "Billion Dollar Baby" hairdos for their clients. Following suit, fashion designers began crafting retro hats to suit the hairstyles.

In the first months of 1946, Comden and Green took time to tend to both personal and professional matters. In the latter regard they both went out on tour with *On the Town* after it closed at the beginning of February, and they reprised their original performances as Claire and Ozzie in the show's first tour stop in Philadelphia. However, by the time the show had reached Chicago, less than two months later, only Green remained with it.

Neither at the time nor in the years that followed did either of them comment on the reasons they had not both stayed with the tour, but it seems most likely that they separated because of their primary relationships outside of their partnership.

Comden's husband, Steven Kyle, was just back from the war, living in New York and tending to an opening of his own. On February 26, 1946, he launched Americraft, a designer accessories store, in Manhattan. The boutique at the corner of First Avenue and 51st Street featured wares ranging from decorated tiles to table lamps and portable radio cabinets, all of which were made by hand by Kyle and some two dozen of his fellow veterans. In addition to being a retail shop, Americraft boasted a full-scale workshop for its former–military personnel artists. Kyle would continue to run the store and contribute his own designs to its inventory until his retirement from the business in 1970.

QUIPPING ABOUT KYLE'S DESIGNS

Throughout her marriage Comden, along with Green, would readily acknowledge Kyle's support of their work and careers. Similarly, Comden was a champion of her husband's design work; some pieces were showcased in their home while others might be found in her purse. One such item, a cigarette case, made it into one of Leonard Lyons's columns at the end of August 1949: "[Comden] showed Zero Mostel an unusual cigaret [*sic*] case she carries in her bag. It was made by her husband....Mostel lifted the large, heavy cigaret case and said, 'With this, you should carry an end table around with you.'"

As for Green, the compelling reason for him to stay with the *On the Town* tour was its new leading lady, Allyn McLerie, with whom he was romantically linked and who would eventually become his second wife. McLerie was a dancer in the ensemble of the show's original company and subsequently stepped into the leading role of Ivy Smith on Broadway before going out on tour. Rumors of Green's relationship with the dancer, who would go on to lead roles in musicals such as Frank Loesser's *Where's Charley?* and Irving Berlin's *Miss Liberty*, became fodder for columnists even before *Town* had concluded its Broadway run. By the time he and she were back in New York in May after the *Town* tour had shuttered, popular speculation was that they would marry before the summer was over. However, the two wouldn't tie the knot until March of the following year.

One reason for the delay (provided the columnists had gotten their original information from reliable sources) was due, most likely, to Comden and Green's joint efforts to capitalize on their Broadway successes as writers to leverage a film deal. And while members of New York's theatrical press speculated about what their next Broadway project might be, they were diligently working with their agents, A. & S. Lyons, toward getting a studio contract.

It might have appeared to the writers that shifting their careers to California should have been effortless. After all, MGM had purchased the film rights to *On the Town*, and in August 1946 Samuel Goldwyn finalized a deal for the rights to make a movie version of *Billion Dollar Baby*. Unfortunately, they found, as Green later commented, "there weren't many takers"[8] for their talents.

Comden and Green did, however, ultimately get an offer from Hollywood. MGM hired them to write the screenplay for a new film version of the stage musical *Good News*.

The show had a book by Laurence Schwab and B. G. ("Buddy") DeSylva and a score by Ray Henderson, Lew Brown, and DeSylva. It played a 557-performance Broadway run from 1927 to 1929 and was turned into a movie by MGM in 1930. Some of the tuner's success stemmed from its buoyant songs, which include "The Varsity Drag," "The Best Things in Life Are Free," "Just Imagine," and "Lucky in Love." The early talkie version of the musical only retained the first two of those numbers. The balance of the film's score consisted of interpolated songs by a bevy of different writers.

Among the songwriters who contributed new material were the team of Nacio Herb Brown and Arthur Freed, and by 1946 they had penned such hits as "Singin' in the Rain" and "You Are My Lucky Star," which had been used in MGM's movie musicals. Freed had since become the unofficial head of the studio's musicals department and had already produced an impressive array of hits, including the Judy Garland classics *Meet Me in St. Louis* and *The Harvey Girls*.

Public announcements about Comden and Green's film deal came in October 1946 as they were headed to the West Coast. Comden remembered feeling "being taken aback" by the project, but she also recalled realizing that "they probably thought we were authorities on the twenties, because *Billion Dollar Baby* was laid in the twenties just like *Good News*." [9]

Unlike their sophisticated satiric musical, though, *Good News* is a lighter-than-air collegiate romp set on the fictional Tait College campus, where star football player Tommy Marlowe might not be able to play in the big game because he is failing astronomy. There's nary a gangster or a nightclub anywhere to be found in the lark.

Comden and Green asked to watch the original movie and was told that all copies of the film had been destroyed. It was only later that they discovered the studio deemed the original screen *Good News* "a mistake" and that "they were not to be contaminated"[10] by seeing it. Unable to view the project's cinematic precursor, the team got hold of the stage script to use as a reference point.

As they read, they were disheartened to discover that they were adapting what Comden would later describe as a "hokey campus football story from 1925"[11] that did not suit their artistic temperaments or their writing style. In response, Green recalled that they tried "to come up with new and clever ways to rewrite it." He also remembered Freed's response: "No, kids, just write *Good News*."[12]

Thus, they found themselves turning out a script that still featured the crisis of whether or not football hero Tommy Marlowe would be able to play in the big game at Tait. At the same time, however, they enhanced the dramatic thrust of the piece and injected it with substantial wit.

How they get to Tommy's academic crisis involves a very clever revision to the romantic triangle of the original stage musical. They decided not to begin their version with the academic crisis, which is the starting point of both the show and first movie. Instead, they opt to have Tommy fall for Patricia, a bombshell who's recently transferred to Tait. She wants nothing to do with him, though, because his biggest asset is his athleticism. He decides he'll learn French to get her attention. His first lessons come from Connie, something of a wallflower at Pat's sorority and a girl who's working her way through school.

Chemistry sparks between Tommy and Connie, but he's too smitten with Patricia to pay real attention to it. Instead, he opts to enroll in a French class to solidify his use of the language. Academically it works, but he finds that even with his ability to *parlez-vous français* he still gets the cold shoulder from Patricia. It's only after she's misled by another member of the sorority into thinking he's the heir to a pickle fortune (a detail that's pure Comden and Green) that she begins to accept his amorous advances.

Their romance has its downside, however, and once they're an item, Tommy's grades slide. He passes (barely) in most subjects, but, ironically, he fails French. It's at that moment he has to return to Connie, whom he has basically ditched, for help. She does it, begrudgingly, because she doesn't want the team to lose, and in the process of their tutoring sessions Tommy comes to realize whom he genuinely loves.

Comden and Green wind the plot tighter for the two, throwing in a few more reversals, including a couple that happen on the playing field at Tait in the middle of the big game, but eventually they do get Tommy and Connie to a happy ending. They also send Patricia off to an uncertain future with a lunkhead from the team, one who may or may not be the heir to a dairy fortune.

This story still may not have the sort of urban sophistication that had been the hallmark of Comden and Green's work since they began penning Revuers material, but nevertheless it had more logic and genuine dramatic momentum for the characters than the original. Even more impressive in their reworking is how they inserted clever satiric digs. Particularly choice is one at the end of the movie, when the money-hungry Pat drops Tommy after Connie misleads her about him having lost his fortune because of a "cucumber blight in Iowa."

Beyond crafting a screenplay that would meet some of their own artistic sensibilities, Comden and Green had to write one that would fulfill the expectations of film audiences in the late 1940s, which meant propelling action toward production numbers. They also had to cope with the studio's desire to interpolate a song into the movie called "Pass That Peace Pipe."

It's a tune with an impressive pedigree. Its melody is by Roger Edens, who had established himself in Hollywood as a vocal arranger, vocal coach, and composer. He worked extensively with Judy Garland in the 1930s and since then had become one of the most valued members of the Freed unit. In fact, he was serving as *Good News'* associate producer. The lyric for "Peace Pipe," originally intended for the studio's *Ziegfeld Follies*, is by Ralph Blane and Hugh Martin (who provided the tunes for *Meet Me in St. Louis*, notably "The Trolley Song" and "The Boy Next Door").

Comden and Green inserted the song into a scene at a campus malt shop and used it as a way of commenting on the ongoing friction between Tommy and Patricia. It's delivered by another co-ed as she tells him to relax about the situation.

A PRE-OPENING CONTROVERSY

More than a year before *Good News* began preproduction, one of the songs in the film was already causing a stir. In late 1945, MGM was holding on to its rights to "Pass That Peace Pipe" for use in a future but still undetermined film. Dinah Shore recorded the number after the writers gave her a copy, but MGM halted the release of her RCA Victor single after restricting its usage because the song had never been published.

Beyond this interpolation Comden and Green discovered that there were moments when the characters would naturally sing, and so they wrote a pair of new, integrated numbers with Edens. One of the new numbers is "The French Lesson." With Edens's lilting and ever-accelerating melody and Comden and Green's fun bilingual pairings of words, the song allows for both glee and a sense of romance to spark between Tommy and Connie.

The other number the trio penned was "An Easier Way," written for Connie and the other girls at the sorority. It's perhaps the most progressive of the team's embellishments for *Good News*, and in it she sings about her disdain for the ruses women employ to entrance men. "Easier Way" ultimately makes Connie a young woman reminiscent of the three leads in *On the Town* and less of a doe-eyed coed. The tune was filmed but ultimately excised from the final cut of the movie, a decision that was not about its content but rather one of pacing; it came too early in the film and slowed the forward momentum of the picture.

Good News commenced filming in March 1947, and just before it started Green joked in a letter to Bernstein about the rapidity with which the screenplay had moved into production. "[It's] causing a minor revolution at M.G.M. No picture has ever before been done there without 4 years of preparation, 15 scripts, etc., etc."[13] And later that year Comden and Green would enthuse publicly, "Arthur Freed, the producer, went wild over the story and ordered it before the cameras immediately."[14]

At the center of the movie were a trio of stage vets in the leading female roles: June Allyson, who, like Nancy Walker, had appeared in *Best Foot Forward* on Broadway, played Connie; Pat Marshall, who had appeared in Alan Jay Lerner and Frederick Loewe's first two Broadway shows, *What's Up?* and *The Day before Spring*, was cast as Patricia; and *Billion Dollar Baby*'s Joan McCracken took on the central comic female role of Babe. At their side were Peter Lawford, who had been steadily establishing himself in movies in his native England and Hollywood and would now be appearing in his first musical role, playing Tommy, and Mel Tormé, at the start of his career, who was cast as a campus crooner.

Under the direction of Charles Walters, who had been dance director on a number of the studio's major releases, including *Ziegfeld Follies* and *Meet Me in St. Louis*, but who had never helmed a full movie musical, *Good News* filmed from March until the middle of May. However, as the project was getting under way Comden and Green returned to New York. As they left California, what they didn't know was that their work on a "hokey" collegiate puff piece would provide them with a valuable artistic and professional safety net before the end of the year.

CHAPTER 5

Theatrical Disaster...
Cinematic Success

Almost immediately upon Green's return to New York, he and Allyn McLerie finally tied the knot in a ceremony held on March 21, 1947, in the chambers of Judge Ferdinand Pecora. The wedding party for the small ceremony included Leonard Bernstein, who served as Green's best man. Just a month earlier Green had confided in a letter to Bernstein that he had had some doubts about the union and then added, "I feel completely sure now that I want to marry her, and I'm very anxious to get back and do it."[1] For her part the Canadian-born McLerie had two bridal attendants: Comden and Felicia Montealegre, who four years later would become Mrs. Leonard Bernstein.

Green had no time for a honeymoon because he and Comden were already at work on developing their next theatrical project. Even before the filming of *Good News* had started, the New York press was heralding their Hollywood success while reporting that they would be penning a new revue for Broadway that would be produced—as had the team's two previous Broadway works—by Paul Feigay and Oliver Smith.

The strength of Comden and Green's desire to return to New York and begin work on a stage show can be best indicated and judged by an offer from Arthur Freed that they declined. Just after they turned in their *Good News* screenplay, Freed "offered a second picture, at mightily increased salaries."[2] Tentatively titled *Easter Holiday*, it was to use songs by Irving Berlin and star Judy Garland, Gene Kelly, Frank Sinatra, and Kathryn Grayson. Freed even offered to allow them to work in New York. As Green shared this news with Bernstein, he wrote, "We are therefore tempted...maybe we'll write this thing."[3]

About a week after Green's nuptials, Lewis Funke told his *New York Times* readers that "[they] say they have given up on their idea for a revue and instead are trying to think up a book for another musical comedy. As for the straight play [which had been mentioned over the years], it's still in the rough draft status."[4]

By May their new tuner had a name and a composer. It would be called *Gold Diggers of 1898*, and Saul Chaplin would write the music for it.

Hollywood-based Chaplin, no relation to Green's screen hero Charlie, had known Comden and Green since their first unfortunate foray in Hollywood five years before. He and his wife had attended one of their Revuers performances at the Trocadero. "We were bowled over. They were superb," Chaplin recalls in his memoir *The Golden Age of Movie Musicals and Me*, and he, his wife, and Comden and Green quickly became, as he put it, "virtually inseparable."

The new Comden-Green show was marking Chaplin's Broadway debut, but he was anything but a newcomer to the entertainment industry. He had been working on movie musicals since the mid-1930s in a variety of capacities and was a sometimes songwriter, equally adept at providing music or lyrics. Among his most notable works at the time were two collaborations with composer Sammy Cahn: both an original song, "Please Be Kind," and an adaptation, "Bei Mir Bist Du Schön," which they had based on a song with Yiddish words by Jacob Jacobs and music by Sholom Secunda, who sold their rights to Cahn and Chaplin. The composer had also collaborated with the film star Al Jolson on another revisionist piece of songwriting, "The Anniversary Song," which was a reworking of a 19th-century Romanian waltz by Ion Ivanovici. Eventually, Chaplin would go on to win three Academy Awards, sharing honors for film scoring for *Seven Brides for Seven Brothers*, *An American in Paris*, and *West Side Story*.

As the writing team was just diving into work on the show, they learned that they would have to come up with a different title for it, because Warner Brothers asserted its ownership of the phrase "gold diggers." The studio had bought it from David Belasco, who produced Avery Hopwood's play of that name, a work that is believed to have popularized the term as it relates to women searching for wealthy husbands.

The new musical quickly became known as *Free for All*, a title that was abandoned two months later when it was redubbed *Bonanza Bound*. Soon after this the producers added a third partner, Herman Levin (a relative newcomer to Broadway at the time and later the producer of hits such as *Gentlemen Prefer Blondes* and *My Fair Lady*) to their ranks. As his participation was confirmed, he announced he was headed to Hollywood to search for a director for the show. Not long after, rumors surfaced that Groucho Marx was considering making a return to Broadway to appear in it.

Marx, who would become a lifelong intimate of Comden and Green, seems as if he would have been an ideal choice for the screwball comedy they had written. Set in Alaska during the Gold Rush, *Bonanza Bound* focuses on a con man, one Waldo Cruikshank, who sets out to build a fortune and small empire for himself. First, he floats a false rumor about a vast lode in the vicinity and then he fleeces the people who, hoping to strike it rich, have flocked to the town he has established.

One of Cruikshank's chief patsies is Peter Fleet, a milquetoast Easterner with financial and literary aspirations, with both his sense of adventure and his poetry inspired by the likes of Rudyard Kipling. Also duped by the self-serving Cruikshank is the elderly Cornelia Van Rensaleer, a dowager who has trudged to Cruikshank's eponymous outpost in the hopes of unearthing a rich vein that will allow her to once again live in the manner to which she was born.

The other primary characters in *Bonanza Bound* are a trio of vaudevillians, the Versatile Da Vincis. These three siblings—Leonard, Belinda, and Toodles—arrive under the impression that they will be appearing at the Alaskan equivalent of Manhattan's ritzy Delmonico's and are stunned to discover Cruikshank's pedestrian saloon.

As it begins, the book for *Bonanza Bound* boasts an ungainly mix of melodrama involving Cruickshank's nefariousness and Comden and Green's signature satire, notably about greedy monopolistic tycoons. Ultimately, the musical gives way to complicated romantic plotting in which all of the characters are at odds with one another. Peter falls for Belinda just as Cruikshank decides that she's the woman for him. His daughter, Eustasia, dotes on Leonard from the outset, a relationship that Cruickshank vehemently opposes. He does everything in his power to keep them separate while also ensuring that Peter stays far away from Belinda. And while he's trying to woo her himself, he also needs to fend off Mrs. Van R, who falls head over heels for Cruikshank from the moment she arrives, much to the chagrin of her faithful servant, her butler Digby, who's hopelessly in love with her.

Once *Bonanza Bound* was in rehearsal, Comden told a reporter that they had chosen to set their show in the milieu "because we thought we could put ANYTHING into it."[5] And when one considers other elements of the show, such as the poor Eskimo, Chokkilok, whom Cruikshank essentially enslaves, it seems as if they almost succeeded in their goal of stuffing it with myriad plots and themes.

The show's score became as far-flung as its story. In "Inspiration," a number that Comden and Green would later often perform, Chaplin riffs on Beethoven and Rimsky-Korsakov. Elsewhere he provides overblown melodies that sound as if they might have been penned for operettas. In these instances, it would appear that the goal had been to make *Bonanza Bound* sound as if it had come from a musical era as bygone as the one in which it was set. The one notable exception is a raucous ensemble number, "Fill 'Er Up," which eschews the frigid climate in which the musical takes place and is charged with the buoyancy of New Orleans jazz.

Given the zany nature of the project, the producers made a somewhat surprising choice when selecting a director: Charles Friedman, who had an impressive array of such serious-minded Broadway credits as Oscar Hammerstein II's Americanization of Bizet, *Carmen Jones*, and the Kurt Weill–Langston Hughes–Elmer Rice musical drama *Street Scene*. Concurrent with their announcement of Friedman, the producers named Jack Cole, who had devised dances for the Ethel Merman stage vehicle *Something for the Boys* and the Ann Miller movie *Eadie Was a Lady*, as the choreographer for *Bonanza Bound*.

These announcements came in mid-September, even as Feigay, Smith, and Levin were working to secure the last pieces of funding necessary to capitalize the show. Concurrently, they and director Friedman were hastily at work on assembling a cast in time to begin tryout performances at the end of the year. As the capitalization came together, so did the company.

George Coulouris, who had distinguished himself on stage in Orson Welles's Mercury Theatre productions and in films such as *Citizen Kane*, came on board to play the nefarious Cruikshank, and McLerie was cast as his daughter, Eustasia. Conveniently enough, Green was to play Leonard Da Vinci, meaning the real-life newlyweds would be able to play love scenes on stage. Leonard's sisters were to be played by Carol Raye, a British actress-singer who was making her American stage debut, and Betty Lou Barto, who just happened to be Nancy Walker's younger sister. For the other principals the producers turned to Hal Hackett, who had recently appeared in several minor film parts, for the role of Peter, and Zamah Cunningham, a Broadway vet with credits that included playing Madame Dilly as a replacement in *On the Town* who was cast as the imperious and needy Mrs. Van R.

The company, which also happened to have future Broadway star Gwen Verdon in its chorus, started rehearsals during the last week of November, and just one month later it was in Philadelphia's Shubert Theatre offering the first public performance.

The show had been scheduled to premiere on December 25, but technical problems necessitated a day's delay. The morning after *Bonanza Bound* faced the public for the first time, the response from the city's chief critic, Edwin H. Schloss in the *Philadelphia Inquirer*, was as chilly as the weather that had accompanied the opening (a storm had blanketed the city in seven inches of snow that day). Schloss praised the sets and costumes (by Smith and Irene Sharaff, respectively) and Cole's dances. Additionally, he found kind things to say about the performers, but their successes came in a musical that suffered from, as he bluntly put it, "a dull book and ailing lyrics."

Just four days after opening, the producers announced that they were temporarily shutting the show down for "repairs and cast revisions,"[6] and that after this it would return to the stage in the spring. As if validating the producers' decision were the reviews that appeared as *Bonanza Bound* played its last week in Philadelphia. In the December 31 issue of *Variety*, for instance, critic "Waters." wrote: "The show's book is so bad now that it would seem better to throw it out, virtually in toto, and start from scratch."

For the next year news stories would occasionally mention the show and the revisions that Comden and Green were making to it under the guidance of George Abbott, who had helped bring their first two musicals to the stage. But before 1948 drew to a close any such plans of reviving *Bonanza Bound* were scrapped, and the costumes, "which once cost $48,000, were picked up at the bargain price of $2,500 by Eaves,"[7] a costume supplier that would have rented out the garments for other productions in New York and beyond.

Years after the failure of *Bonanza Bound*, director-lyricist Barry Kleinbort asked Green about when he knew he had become a theater professional. He said it was just after he returned to New York following the show's closure and walked into Sardi's. Someone asked him what had gone wrong, and his response was, "We had an idea for the show and it wasn't very good."[8] Taking the responsibility for this was the moment he knew he was a "real" theater professional.

A COMDEN AND GREEN FIRST (ALMOST)

Given that the team's first two Broadway successes had gone unrecorded, it seems ironic that *Bonanza Bound* did receive a cast album. As 1947 was drawing to a close, the industry was bracing for a strike brought on by the American Federation of Musicians, and producers of shows scheduled to open in early 1948 made hasty plans for studio sessions during the final weeks of the year. Such was the case for *Bonanza Bound*, which was recorded in sessions during the company's final days of rehearsal in New York and first days of performance in Philadelphia. After the show shuttered, however, RCA canceled plans to release what would have been the first official cast recording of a score featuring Comden and Green lyrics.

After the drubbing that *Bonanza Bound* got in Philadelphia, Comden and Green could take solace in knowing that they were at least being lauded for their film work. *Good News* had opened in early December in New York at Radio City Music Hall in the prime Christmas season slot at a time when movies were still accompanied by a live show that would morph into

The Radio City Music Hall Christmas Spectacular. As was the norm at the time, engagements around the country began only after this New York premiere.

Some reviewers in Manhattan and elsewhere may have bristled at the nostalgia in which *Good News* traded, but they also generally had to admit to having had fun, on some level, with the collegiate tuner. Other writers were more enthusiastic about the movie overall. In the December 3 *Variety* review, for instance, "Brog." said that *Good News* had "an infectious appeal that should click with all type audiences." For Lew Sheaffer, the critic in Comden's native Brooklyn, the movie was simply "an hour-and-a-half of unadulterated pleasure." One review that might have been most heartening to Comden and Green (if they ever received it via a clipping service) appeared in the *Pittsburgh Post-Gazette* on the morning that *Bonanza Bound* was closing. In it, the critic, acknowledged with the initials E. F. J., recognized that the buoyant, feel-good movie had "some bite, too, in the satire of sorority life, of the importance of money to falling in love, and of the football coach in his half-time diatribe."

In addition to enjoying the warm reception *Good News* was getting from critics and audiences alike, Comden and Green could also be heartened by having more work waiting for them at MGM, and they left for the coast in January 1948. For Green it was the first time that he would be separated from his wife of less than a year, but she, like her husband, was rebounding quickly from the failure of *Bonanza Bound*, segueing almost seamlessly into the Broadway production of *Finian's Rainbow*, serving as a replacement in the role of Susan Mahoney. The more than 3,000-mile divide between the couple didn't last for long, however. Three months after assuming the role, McLerie departed the production, preferring to be with Green in California.

Once she arrived she found him at work with Comden on their first assignment. They were developing a treatment for a new picture, tentatively titled *You Made Me Love You*, which would be a vehicle for Fred Astaire and Judy Garland, one that would capitalize on the popularity of their pairing in the studio's phenomenally successful *Easter Parade*. The new picture was even being directed by Charles Walters, the man who had choreographed its predecessor and cut his teeth directing movie musicals with *Good News*.

The scenario that Comden and Green devised for the picture involves Josh and Dinah Barkley, a successful husband-and-wife musical comedy team who have a prickly, but still loving, offstage relationship. After opening in their latest hit (for which he provided lyrics and also directed), she meets a more serious-minded writer who believes that she should be the star of his next play, which centers on the early years of Sarah Bernhardt's career. After much turmoil at home, Dinah accepts the offer and before long discovers that she is in over her head. When Josh learns that his wife is flailing in her new venture, rather than taking self-satisfied glee in what could be an abysmal failure that would send her straight back to him, he begins to coach her over the phone, disguising his voice to sound like the auteur.

Of course, there's a happy end for the Barkleys after her successful opening in the play and her discovery that the reason for her success has been, all along, Josh.

Unlike their previous screen outing, which was an adaptation, Comden and Green had the opportunity to spin an original story for the film that ultimately became *The Barkleys of Broadway*. But even as they were able to allow their fertile imaginations to play in their beloved milieu of backstage storytelling, they had constraints to contend with. Astaire had devised several pieces of specialty dancing that needed to be integrated into the story. One, which became the number "Shoes with Wings On," took place in a shoe store where he would play a clerk surprised to find that the footwear comes to life around him.

Another—and this required some special work from composer Harry Warren and lyricist Ira Gershwin, who were providing the movie's songs—was based on a new dance step Astaire had created, "The Swing Trot." Begrudgingly, Warren and Gershwin provided a number with that title, knowing full well that it was a dance that would also serve as a new piece for use in Astaire's successful string of dance instruction studios.

Comden and Green's backstage scenario made it easy enough for these and other far-flung numbers that Astaire devised to be integrated into the film. Song-and-dance routines could just become part of the show-within-the-movie in which the Barkleys are starring. Similarly, Comden and Green created opportunities to showcase the keyboard virtuosity of the film's third star, Oscar Levant, who plays Josh's composer partner, Ezra. Scenes at an opening night party where he's conscripted into performing and a hospital benefit easily allowed for the insertion of classical pieces, such as Aram Khachaturian's "Sabre Dance."

Once the script was finished Comden and Green sat down with Astaire, Garland, and Freed and read through it. Astaire would later recall the moment in his autobiography, *Steps in Time*: "We flipped with delight and said we'd have a hard time following them in the parts. They are noted for their brilliant readings of their own material."

In May 1946 Astaire started rehearsing the intricate "Shoes with Wings On" number with choreographer Hermes Pan and special-effects man Irving G. Ross. In June, Garland reported for work and rehearsed for two weeks, but there were issues with her health. In short order it became apparent that she was in no condition to be working, and Freed took her off the film.

As for her replacement, Freed sensed that *Barkleys* might serve as a terrific vehicle for reuniting Astaire with Ginger Rogers. The two had not appeared opposite one another on screen for nearly 10 years. Freed sent a request to her, and she agreed, although she "didn't relish the idea" of reteaming with Astaire because of someone's illness. Still, as she said, "The role was waiting and I knew somebody would have to fill it...."[9]

Comden and Green, much as they would on the road, had to go into revision mode once the new leading lady been signed, and their changes to the script continued for several months as the film was rethought for the Astaire and Rogers pairing. Numbers written for the Astaire-Garland combination were dropped during this time, and one song, "They Can't Take That Away from Me," written by Ira and George Gershwin for the previous Astaire-Rogers film *Shall We Dance*, was inserted.

Other changes that occurred with the picture's revised casting were not as dramatic. For instance, the nationality of the playwright-director who lures Dinah away was changed. After Rogers's arrival he became French rather than British. Also, as Astaire recalled, "Our rehearsals brought forth a new set of gags and jokes."[10]

Beyond making the project notable for bringing the renowned dancers back together, Rogers's presence also helped to solidify the credibility of certain aspects of the script. Certainly the notion that she and Astaire were husband and wife became more plausible. There was, after all, an eighteen-year difference in Astaire's and Garland's ages. Furthermore, Rogers's forays into dramatic roles on the screen, notably her Oscar-winning performance in *Kitty Foyle*, added resonance to Dinah Barkley's resounding success impersonating Sarah Bernhardt on stage.

The Barkleys of Broadway script doesn't shout with satire, but as they had done with the gentle digs in *Good News*, Comden and Green manage to insert barbed humor in the movie from first to last. The most cutting of the details they include centers on a conceptual artist who has created a portrait of the Barkleys. When they arrive at the gallery for the piece's unveiling, they discover that the work is a frying pan mounted on the wall; in it there is a likeness of Dinah, seemingly made out of pancake batter. The Russian artist's explanation for his work is that he believes Josh to be the pan and Dinah to be the batter. In his vision it is only after coming into contact with the heated skillet that Dinah (and her performance) can take shape. "It's like Pygmalion breathing life into Galatea," he says. This parody of high-concept surrealism amuses and, impressively, propels the story as it magnifies Dinah's insecurity about her ability to create without the assistance of her husband, helping to push her toward accepting the role in the Sarah Bernhardt play.

Elsewhere in the picture a running joke about the string of interchangeable blond girlfriends found on Ezra's arm gives the sometimes scattershot story a thin comic sense of unity, while the brief appearances of Billie Burke (forever to be thought of as Glinda the Good in *The Wizard of Oz*) as a flighty society woman who's always imposing on Josh, Dinah, and Ezra provide wry commentary about the cloying nature of certain hangers-on in the theatrical community.

Comden and Green even manage to insert an old Revuers-era joke into the screenplay: a jab at photographic magazines such as *Life*. It comes after a shoot with the Barkleys has gone awry. Josh suggests that the newsmen just run a spread on an appendectomy in lieu of pictures of the "happy" couple at home.

COMDEN AND GREEN AND HOLLYWOOD'S
SOCIAL WHIRL

Parties, particularly weekly Saturday night fetes at the home of Gene Kelly and his wife, Betsy Blair, were often on Comden and Green's agenda when they were in Hollywood. Blair recalls in her memoir, *The Memory of All That*, one night in particular when Comden and Green got to entertain for one of their heroes from when they were younger: Noël Coward. "He charmed us all, and everyone was eager to entertain him. Betty Comden and Adolph Green performed some of their old Revuers' routines brilliantly. Gene and the fantastic dancer Carol Haney improvised a dance. Judy sang. And then Coward was persuaded to the piano."

Concurrent with the beginning of preproduction for and shooting of *The Barkleys of Broadway*, another film with Comden-Green material was also just starting. This one was *Take Me Out to the Ball Game*, a movie that was reteaming their old pal Gene Kelly with Frank Sinatra, the two having scored big together in *Anchors Aweigh*.

Ball Game, with a screenplay by Harry Turgend and George Wells, was based on a scenario that Kelly devised with an old friend, Stanley Donen, a dancer who had been in the ensemble of *Pal Joey* on Broadway, in which Kelly had starred. And because of his New York roots, Donen, like Kelly, also had a long-standing relationship with Comden and Green. Comden warmly recalled, "Gene and Stanley are old friends of ours. With them we have a lot of the same frame of reference. They knew our nightclub act very well. They knew our kind of humor, our craziness."[11]

The treatment the two men developed was inspired by a story Kelly had read about a pair of baseball players in the early 20th century who during the off-season toured vaudeville with their song-and-dance act.

The movie imagines two such players, Eddie O'Brien (Kelly) and Denny Ryan (Sinatra), who, along with their teammates, are appalled when they discover their team's new owner is a woman (played by screen swimming sensation Esther Williams). Before long, the sweetly awkward Ryan's pining for her, while the wolfish O'Brien's feuding with her. Ryan also has to fend off the advances of an aggressive fan (played by Betty Garrett).

Romance gets sorted out, and O'Brien and Ryan, along with their best pal, Nat Goldberg (Jules Munshin), take their team, the Wolves, to first place and the pennant race. At the same time an unscrupulous gambler works to undermine their success. He lures O'Brien into rehearsing nights (in the age before the electric light there were no evening games) for a show that will open just after the season ends. For a while it looks as if the team might go down the tubes because O'Brien's so exhausted, but of course it all works out in the end for the team (and the two couples).

Comden, Green, and Edens wrote four numbers for *Ball Game*, which would be the last film directed by a man who had at one time been the master of the movie musical, Busby Berkeley. Almost as if to signal a change in tastes and trends in movie musicals between the 1930s and the 1950s, *Ball Game* also served as the first screen collaboration for Kelly and Donen, who jointly created its dances.

The Comden-Green-Edens songs all amount to specialty material for the leading men and their hoofing, but when compared with the rosy-cheeked story and the cornball humor found in the rest of the movie, the team's lyrics have particular bite. A reference to Herzegovina, for example, crops up in "It's Fate, Baby, It's Fate," a song for Garrett's character as she pursues Denny with a drive similar to Hildy's in *On the Town*. In fact, Edens's jazzy melody makes this number a distant musical cousin to that stage musical's "Come Up to My Place."

A STRONG WOMAN BEHIND THE FILMS

Almost as if to echo the sort of strong, independent women who were a hall-mark of Comden and Green's stage and screen musicals throughout their careers, *Take Me Out to the Ball Game* had a female editor, Blanche Sewell, who proved herself time and again in a profession dominated by men. She died before the film's opening, and in obituaries and tributes in both general and trade publications she was deemed a pioneer. Among the credits she amassed during her 25-year career were such classics as *The Wizard of Oz*, *The Big House*, and *Born to Dance*.

In a more period number, "Yes Indeed-y," O'Brien and Ryan jokingly sing about their romantic adventures while on the vaudeville circuit, and while the tone of the number overall is lighthearted, Comden and Green inject it with some dark humor. One of Ryan's supposed lady loves commits suicide, and as he describes the mock-woeful events they rhyme "her teachers wouldn't pass her," "she just turned on the gasser," and "the sweetest gal at Vassar." It's simultaneously grim, clever, and definitely funny as this section of the lyric ends with "she's in the cold, cold ground."

Among the other songs that Comden, Green, and Edens completed for *Ball Game* was "O'Brien to Ryan to Goldberg," a humorous paean to the guys' ability to complete double plays. The lyric was also a take-off on "Baseball's Sad Lexicon," a poem by Franklin Pierce Adams that celebrated the Chicago Cubs' infield ("Tinker to Evers to Chance") in 1910.

The fourth piece of Comden and Green material in *Ball Game* was the lyric for a love song for Sinatra, "The Right Girl for Me." The latter became the first song they wrote to receive multiple covers in early 1949 as the film was gearing up for release. Naturally, a single from Sinatra was on the market. There were others by the likes of Tony Alamo, singing with the Sammy Kaye orchestra, and Gordon McRae, the smooth-voiced baritone who would ultimately become immortalized as Curly in the film version of *Oklahoma!* A review of this single in the March 19 issue of *Billboard* praised both his vocals and the song itself, labeling it a "beautiful new ballad."

Both *Barkleys* and *Ball Game* completed shooting in the early fall of 1948. Their releases came the following spring, opening within weeks of one another. *Take Me Out to the Ball Game* was the first to reach audiences, debuting at Loew's State in Manhattan on March 9. Both in New York and throughout the country the film got tepid notices, and there was scant recognition for the tunes that Comden, Green, and Edens had written.

The Barkleys of Broadway opened on May 4 in New York, also at Loew's State. The screen reunion of Astaire and Rogers was, understandably, the critics' chief consideration, and, whether in New York or elsewhere around the country, their chemistry and the nostalgia factor of seeing them back together on the big screen was warmly and sometimes enthusiastically received.

Beyond this, Comden and Green's work on creating a showcase for Astaire and Rogers also caught the attention of reviewers nationwide. In the May 5 edition of the *New York Times*, Bosley Crowther groused about what he felt was an imbalance of their comic script to the central couple's dancing, but then said that "this might be a matter for umbrage if it weren't that the comedy is good." That same day, in the *New York Herald Tribune*, Otis L. Guernsey Jr. labeled the screenplay as being "a perfect vehicle" for the Astaire-Rogers reappearance.

And a week later in his *Washington Post* review, Richard L. Coe described the writing as "fresh and crisp" and went on to say that their work was "a model of excellence. The pace is sparkling." Of course, the review that mattered most to Comden and Green had come months earlier (in December 1948) just after an early preview of the film. The head of MGM, Louis B. Mayer, reportedly loved the film from start to finish, so much so that he invited them for a lunch in his private dining room. During it he marveled that "this tiny little girl"[12] could have penned such a grand picture.

By the time the critics' notices were appearing, the team had already completed a third project for MGM and were in New York, at work on other projects and enjoying home life with their spouses. Thanks to their still-unfilmed screenplay, they were about to wind down 1949 on a note higher than they might ever have imagined possible when they were barely a year into their working relationship as the decade began. Little did they know that even greater things were waiting for them in the new decade of the 1950s.

COMDEN AND GREEN LOOK BACK

In later years, Comden and Green discovered that reporters wanted to know their thoughts on their early films. For a while they would admit to not caring for their first one, but by April 1986 they felt differently. They told the *New York Times*'s Alvin Klein that they were developing a "growing fondness" for *Good News*. As for *Barkleys*, when the film got a late-night TV airing in the 1950s, Comden, according to Burt Boyar in the February 11, 1958, edition of the *Philadelphia Inquirer*, "shuddered" at the listing, quipping, "We all make mistakes when we're young."

CHAPTER 6

Broadway to Hollywood
and Back Again

I n late 1948, MGM opted to move forward with making the movie version of *On the Town*, which had been languishing as a studio property since before the musical's Broadway premiere in 1944. Louis B. Mayer himself had authorized the purchase of the rights to the Comden-Green-Bernstein-Robbins show after a call from one of his favorites in the studio's story department, Lillie Messinger.

At the time of the call she was in New York to secure a deal for the movie rights to the musical *Bloomer Girl* and had visited Bernstein. He had yet to complete his work on the new project, but he, Comden, and Green had accomplished enough on the story that he was able to describe it to her and play small fragments of music he had begun to compose for it. Messinger was entranced and began lobbying for the studio to purchase the rights to the show, even though it was unfinished and by a group of artists who all were making their first forays into musical theater.

Mayer implicitly trusted Messinger's tastes, saying, "Something happens to your voice, Lillie, when you feel that strongly,"[1] and MGM made its substantial preproduction investment in the aborning show.

After *On the Town* opened, Mayer traveled to New York to see it. His response was not favorable. In fact, he was offended; he found it, according to Gene Kelly's biographer Clive Hirschhorn, "'smutty' and 'Communistic.'"[2] In particular, Mayer reportedly blanched at the white and black performers dancing together. By this point, however, the die was cast, and MGM had the rights to film *On the Town*.

Mayer's thoughts on the project, of course, were enough to damn it to obscurity, and yet *On the Town* faced another opponent at the studio: Arthur Freed himself. For Freed, who had begun his career as a song plugger for Tin Pan Alley, the problem wasn't the content of the show but rather its sound. Bernstein's music was simply too symphonic and avant-garde. As Stanley Donen—who, along with Gene Kelly, would make his directorial debut on the movie—later commented, "He thought Bernstein was off on cloud nine."[3]

Thus, without the support of either man, the thought of transferring *On the Town* to the screen evaporated, and, in fact, Hugh Fordin, in the book *The Movies' Greatest Musicals*, writes: "At the time Comden and Green set out for Hollywood with their newly signed M-G-M contract, they had been admonished by their agents and their lawyers never to bring up the subject of *On the Town*."[4]

Varying reasons exist for why *On the Town* resurfaced in late 1948. Some recollections say that it was the show's original director, George Abbott, who, on a trip to Hollywood, was informed that he could direct any project he wished and unhesitatingly said that he wanted to transfer *On the Town* to the screen. Other reports suggest that it was Dore Schary who brought the project back to the fore.

Schary, recently named MGM's head of production, was working to shore up the studio's profitability and productivity. To that end he had, as a *Variety* report described it, "been combing the Metro story department shelves with the result that a half-dozen properties long owned by the studio are now in preparation for the cameras."[5] One of the properties he stumbled on was *On the Town*, and in October 1948 the studio announced it would be moving forward with a film version of the stage hit.

Within a month of this news, MGM announced that Comden and Green would be adapting their work for the screen. But their involvement came about only after some soul-searching on their part and extensive negotiations among the studio, their agent, and Bernstein. To begin with, they were reticent about Freed's demand that the film use only a handful of Bernstein's songs. He was, after all, an old friend, and what's more it had been at his insistence that Comden and Green had become involved with the musical in the first place. Beyond this, neither writer wanted to relocate to California to pen the screenplay.

With regard to the Bernstein issue, nothing in the contract that accompanied the studio's original investment stated that MGM had to use all of the music from the show. At the same time, however, he did have the right of first refusal with regard to any new songs that might be needed for a film version. As Bernstein had no interest in writing new numbers for the movie, the basic issue had been dealt with, and yet the studio made an additional concession: The rights to all of the songs that were included in the original contract that were not used in the movie reverted to Bernstein. This satisfied the composer, who also agreed to travel to California to write the music for the movie's climactic ballet.

Comden would eventually describe Bernstein's actions and his contribution to the movie as "very generous," adding, "He came out and worked on the film and put the ballet music together for Sollie Chaplin."[6]

Over the years Bernstein sent mixed signals about his feelings with regard to the studio's decision. As the film was being rolled out he was supportive of what had been done when questioned by reporters. He was, however, less generous years later during a symposium about the show, saying, "I asked them to take my name off the full-frame credit, and credit me only for the songs I wrote."[7]

To secure Comden and Green's services for the movie, MGM agreed both to allow them to do a preponderance of their writing in New York and to be paid additional compensation beyond what they had received from their portion of the studio's original investment. There was an $85,000 fee for the new screenplay and an additional $25,000 for the new lyrics. In 2017 terms they were splitting the equivalent of $1.1 million.

COMDEN AND GREEN ON WORKING CONDITIONS IN HOLLYWOOD

"We had an office in a big administrative building that they used to call 'The Iron Lung,'" Comden told Pat McGilligan for her book *Backstory 2*. Comden went on to say, "It was a bleak office and we went to work every day about nine o'clock. People always think you go to Hollywood, whee! Playing tennis! Wow! But we worked very hard....Almost around the clock." Green added, "No one was at us with the whips, but it was a good idea to get the job done and do it right."

For Comden, Freed's concession that they be able to write the screenplay in New York was particularly important. She and her husband, Steven Kyle, wanted to start a family, and just as negotiations for the *On the Town* movie began she discovered that she was pregnant with their first child.

Green also had a reason to stay close to home. His wife, Allyn McLerie, had just opened in a new Broadway hit. She was starring opposite Ray Bolger in *Where's Charley?*, the musical that brought composer-lyricist Frank Loesser to Broadway. While she had been able to be with Green while he was working in California during his time on *Good News*, this time she was obligated to stay in Manhattan.

Comden and Green had professional reasons for staying on the East Coast as well. Since returning from California, they had begun to reintegrate themselves into the fabric of the New York entertainment community. What's more, producers Oliver Smith and Herman Levin, who had first teamed up with *Bonanza Bound,* approached them about writing another 1920s-set musical, the adaptation of Anita Loos's *Gentlemen Prefer Blondes.* However, on this they demurred, later saying, "We were asked to write the book for [*Blondes*] and we said no, we'd already done our 20s show."[8]

In Manhattan they were also getting the opportunity to occasionally indulge their desire to perform, often for good causes. For instance, on November 29 they, along with performers such as Perry Como, Patrice Munsel, and Guy Lombardo, took to the stage of Madison Square Garden for an event that raised money for the Hospitalized Veterans Program of the Musicians Emergency Fund. It was also during this period that Comden began her work with the Dramatists Guild, becoming a member of its executive council. Comden would remain deeply committed to and involved with this organization for the rest of her life.

As they set out to write the screenplay for *Town,* Comden and Green faced numerous issues in recalibrating their original, starting with the characterizations of two of the three sailors. Kelly was set to play Gabey, and the lovelorn, starry-eyed character from the stage incarnation of the movie was not exactly suited to Kelly's more outgoing screen persona. Similarly, while they had tailored the highly flamboyant Ozzie to suit Green's own performance style, the role was being played on screen by Jules Munshin, who brought less of an oversize comedic sensibility and more of a goofball one to the role. As for the third sailor, Chip, Frank Sinatra lent qualities of awkwardness and sweetness to the role that matched the part as originally envisioned.

The same can be said of Betty Garrett, who was cast as female cabbie Brunhilde Esterhazy, and in pairing her with Sinatra *On the Town* harkened back to *Take Me Out to the Ball Game.* The other two female leads, however, were also adjusted. Vera-Ellen's girl-next-door quality made her Ivy Smith a stark departure from Sono Osato's sensuous, exotic beauty, while Ann Miller, in the role of Claire, radiated a boisterous sunniness that was far afield from the urbane giddiness of Comden, for whom the role had been crafted.

The screenplay not only reframes the roles to fit the stars; it also shifts the story in gentle directions to fit studio (and moviegoer) sensibilities. For instance, in the movie it takes longer for the guys to split up for their search for Ivy, affording them the opportunity to share a number beyond the opening "New York, New York." For this Comden, Green, and Edens devised "Prehistoric Man," a replacement for Claire and Ozzie's "I Get Carried Away," and in it the characters cavort in the natural history museum donning masks and tribal regalia. In addition, the number, featuring a jagged, jazzy melody that attempts to approximate the Bernstein score, provides Miller with a tap specialty.

Other changes included recasting the backstories for Gabey and Ivy, making them two babes from the midwestern woods in New York, both coincidentally from the same Indiana town, and altering Claire's reason for her anthropological research. She's still a woman who has spent a great deal of time pursuing romance, but she's not doing it at the expense of her fiancé.

In both of these instances and elsewhere in the film—such as in "Main Street," a saccharine duet for Gabey and Ivy in which they extol life in a small town—one can sense how Comden and Green were diligently working to take the bite out of the tale and substitute a wholesomeness appropriate for the post–World War II, pre-Eisenhower era.

Comden and Green did find ways to insert their signature wit and gentle sardonic touches into the screenplay, most notably in the film's early moments, when the sailors reach the subway. They walk onto the platform and ask a man for directions. A train roaring by obliterates his answer. The guys try a second New Yorker only to find the same thing happens. It's familiar to anyone who has ever tried to have any sort of conversation in the tunnels of the subway system.

Other signature quips surface, such as the choice one that comes after two cops hear on their radio about the dinosaur skeleton that Ozzie inadvertently toppled at the museum. One of the two officers mis-hears the dispatch and believes that they have been informed that Dinah Shore has collapsed. He comments, "That's a shame. She was always my favorite singer." Similarly, as Kelly's Gabey scours Symphonic Hall in search of Ivy, he overhears one ballet instructor tell her pupil that she has "taught them all, from Nijinsky to Mickey Rooney."

SUITING A MOTHER'S SENSIBILITIES

One noticeable change Comden and Green made for the screen version of *On the Town* is in the rephrased lyric for "New York, New York." The city is no longer a "helluva town" but rather a "wonderful town." Though undoubtedly mandated by the Hollywood Production Code, it's a change that would have most likely pleased Comden's mother. In her memoir *Off Stage*, Comden remembers how she worried about her mother's reaction to the original line, so much so that for years "some deep inhibition from my past made me avoid singing the song to my mother." It wasn't until Comden was in her mid-forties that she found the courage to sing it—complete with "helluva"—to her mother.

On the upside of events surrounding the *On the Town* movie was one significant fact: Neophyte co-directors Kelly and Donen brought a vision to the film that perfectly suited the material and even echoed the creation of the original. They felt that New York had to be a central character in the movie, and to this end they vigorously campaigned for portions to be shot on location on the East Coast rather than just on the soundstage at MGM. Eventually, Kelly and Donen prevailed, and they were allowed several days of filming in the Big Apple, including the footage for the now-iconic opening sequence in which the sailors take a whirlwind tour of the city, from the Brooklyn Navy Yard to the upper reaches of Manhattan and Grant's Tomb.

Similarly, the picture's intimate scale, largely eschewing singing choruses and lavish dance ensembles, may not seem remarkable today, but it was unusual at the time. Kelly and Donen were attempting to break ground in their co-directorial debut, which intentionally or not echoes the freshness of the stage original. As Ezra Goodman noted in a May 22, 1949, *New York Herald Tribune* feature written as the film was shooting: "Kelly is attempting some innovations for Hollywood, in this film. There will be no regular chorus line. The principals will be backed in song-and-dance specialties by other members of the cast."

The filming of *On the Town* took place between the end of March and the beginning of July, and the picture opened at Radio City Music Hall in December, giving Comden and Green their second cinematic debut at the art-deco showcase in midtown Manhattan. Reviews were generally ecstatic. Bosley Crowther enthused in his December 9 *New York Times* review that "gaiety, rhythm, humor, and a good, wholesome dash of light romance have been artfully blended together in this bright Technicolored comedy." Otis L. Guernsey Jr. in the *New York Herald Tribune* that same day echoed with "This 'On the Town' is as exuberant as a kid at Christmas, or as a sailor on shore leave, which is what it is all about."

The public flocked to see the movie in New York, so much so that records were set at Radio City. One report in the *Christian Science Monitor* on December 30, 1949, noted that so many people had wanted to see *On the Town* the day before that "a waiting line of four abreast wound around Rockefeller Center skyscrapers for seven blocks." A week later the venue's manager, Gus Eyssel, presented Comden and Green with a photo that captured a portion of the roughly 10,000-strong crowd.

"LONELY TOWN" AND SINATRA

According to Sinatra biographer Will Friedwald, Sinatra had been lured to appear in *On the Town* because he wanted to sing "Lonely Town." Nevertheless, the ballad was cut, because the studio considered the romance between his and Garrett's characters to be secondary, and the powerful love song wouldn't suit that positioning in the film. On the last day of filming "That's a wrap" was shouted, and Friedwald quotes Comden as recalling, "Sinatra said, 'Well, where's my song? When do I do "Lonely Town?"' And they just said to him, 'It's out. You're not going to do it.' And he was very, very angry."

As 1949 wound down and 1950 dawned, new reviews of *On the Town* began appearing as engagements elsewhere in the country opened. In Mae Tinee's January 2 write-up in the *Chicago Tribune*, she noted that the comedy was "hilarious" and warned readers, "You may miss some of the lines because the audience is still hooting at previous ones." And Marjory Adams, echoing reviewers both in New York and nationwide, complimented the songs as being "outstanding" and added "each one good for laughs" in her January 2 *Boston Globe* review.

On one level the success of the film—and at Radio City in particular, where less than 10 years before the Revuers had lasted a mere performance during the third of their three stints there—had to be gratifying. At the same time the movie wasn't entirely a representation of what they, Bernstein, and Robbins had created. It was a cinematic approximation. In later years Green would comment that the decision not to use Bernstein's full score was "very sad."[9] And Comden would lament the studio's decision not to use the full score, saying that she wished that they had "had more faith in the score and in the undercurrent, which was meant to be bittersweet."[10]

Comden and her husband, Steven Kyle, had another reason to celebrate during the 1949 holiday season. They were enjoying it for the first time with their daughter, Susanna, who had been born July 29. But life as a new mother had done nothing to diminish Comden's workload with Green. They were already at work on a new Broadway show, writing the book for a new Cole Porter musical, *Out of This World*.

They came to the project in November at the request of Porter himself. "They are bright as buttons and write very fast and I believe they will deliver the goods in time so we can start rehearsals during the second week in January," Porter wrote to his friend Samuel Stark.[11] Comden and Green were taking over as writers from Dwight Taylor, who had turned in a draft only weeks before they were invited to work on the show. Taylor agreed to their being called in, ostensibly because of his preexisting film commitments.

Out of This World, which was much anticipated thanks to the smash-hit status of Porter's recent *Kiss Me, Kate*, was based on Jean Giraudoux's *Amphitryon 38*, a variation on the myth of Zeus's seduction of the mortal Alcmene. The French playwright's decision to put the number 38 at the end of the titled stemmed from his wry belief that his was the 38th time the tale had been reconstituted.

Comden and Green wrote two draft versions of the script in just as many months, confirming Porter's faith in their speed. In these the story has been made contemporary, and Jupiter has fixed his eye on an American woman, Helen, who is on a Mediterranean cruise with her husband, Arthur. For Helen the atmosphere, even before Jupiter comes on the scene, is charged with romance, but for Arthur the onboard movies and reports about how his beloved Yankees are doing back home are enough.

Jupiter enlists one of his sons, Mercury, to help him secure a night with Helen, and while Mercury disguises himself as a member of the ship's crew to help his father, he has to both distract Arthur and fend off the attempts his mother, Juno, makes to catch Jupiter in his act of infidelity.

As Comden and Green were writing, reports circulated that the show was to star David Wayne (who originated the role of the impish leprechaun Og in *Finian's Rainbow*) as well as their former Revuers partner Judy Holliday, who catapulted to fame in *Born Yesterday* on Broadway shortly after Comden and Green scored their breakthrough success there with *On the Town.*

Comden and Green's *Out of This World* caters to the comedic talents of both these performers. They make Mercury simultaneously frantic about the many directions in which he's being pulled and cleverly wily as he works to maneuver Arthur away from Helen. He does this by promising the Yankees fan the ability to catch a couple of games on a 1956 prototype television that will get reception from the United States in Greece.

As for the Juno they crafted with Holliday in mind, they devised a way to allow the actress to display her multitude of gifts. When the goddess arrives on the scene to thwart Jupiter, she disguises herself as what she believes to be a typical American, basing it on the one gangster film she has managed to watch on Mount Olympus, a little opus called *Kick Me, My Sweet.* On Earth she adopts the persona of Laverne Ballou, a sultry siren who is a ludicrous combination of femme fatale and Jimmy Cagney and Humphrey Bogart.

Beyond writing plum parts for these two performers, Comden and Green penned a script that integrated the songs that Porter, who had been at work on the project since the beginning of 1949, had already written. Their draft indicates placement of 15 numbers, including "Nobody's Chasing Me" and "Cherry Pies Ought to Be You," although this latter number is indicated just by "Ought to Be You." Further, they used the project as an opportunity for musical theater innovation. As if inspired by the intimate scale of Kelly's work on the movie *On the Town*, their *Out of This World* has no indications of dance numbers or ballets.

After turning in their second version, Comden and Green withdrew from the project because of further revisions that producers Saint Subber and Lemuel Ayers, the team who had brought *Kiss Me, Kate* to Broadway, were requesting. Eventually, Dwight Taylor, returned, and, working with Reginald Lewis, delivered a script that suited the producers.

Unlike Comden and Green's vest-pocket version, Taylor and Lewis's draft and their final Broadway script more closely resemble the sort of musical that audiences would have expected at the time. In the Taylor-Lewis book a standard comedic love plot gets added for two newly devised roles of Greek locals, Juno becomes a less flamboyant role, and spots for large-scale dances are inserted. Additionally, most of Comden and Green's witty jabs at contemporary life are excised.

Out of This World reached Broadway at the end of 1950 after a rocky tryout period in which Agnes de Mille, who had broken ground as the first woman to direct a Broadway musical in 1947 with Rodgers and Hammerstein's *Allegro* and was repeating that role here, was unofficially replaced as director by George Abbott. The production's dances were by Hanya Holm, who created a trio of major numbers, including a ballet that concluded Act One. As for the cast, neither Holliday nor Wayne appeared. Instead, the show's star names were theater veterans Charlotte Greenwood, as Juno, and William Redfield, as Mercury, while a relative newcomer to Broadway, George Jongeyans (who later changed his surname to Gaynes), played Jupiter.

Comden and Green's exit from the project in February 1950 wasn't the end of their relationship with the piece, however. After the show opened they contested how the producers had paid them for their work, nearly going to arbitration over it. Eventually, the producers agreed to provide them with a portion of royalties for their contributions to the musical.

The collapse of *Out of This World* was accompanied by a welcome professional honor for Comden and Green. Just days before it was announced that they were withdrawing from the project, they got word that they were nominated for a Screen Writers Guild Award for their screenplay for *On the Town*, a prize they went on to win just a month later.

Comden and Green weren't only at work on *Out of This World* as 1950 dawned; they were also in discussions about a new show with Bernstein and producer Oliver Smith. The piece was to be inspired by a bastion of Bohemia that had sprung up in Brooklyn in the early 1940s, the famed "February House" at 7 Middagh Street. Established by *Harper's Bazaar* editor George Davis with several friends, the home was a sort of commune for artists, ranging from composer Benjamin Britten to writer Carson McCullers, as well as stripper Gypsy Rose Lee, who wrote a mystery novel there. Another resident at one time had been Smith himself. In a letter to Bernstein in May 1950, Comden described the piece as "the show we all want so much to happen." During the spring she and Green met with

Jerome Robbins to discuss the project, and in the same letter to Bernstein she wrote, "He got interested in the idea."[12]

As their discussions continued they allowed their thoughts about what the show would be to evolve freely. At times it would be a piece that was akin to the classic George S. Kaufman and Edna Ferber play *Stage Door*, centering on a group of hopefuls all living under the same roof. At other times it took on a different tone and felt something more akin to a modern *La Bohème*. Ultimately, though, Comden wrote, "We find it hard to think of 'number' [*sic*]—the musical expression of what the show should be. We cannot hear it. We sometimes feel it is more a play—and not suited to musical theater at all."[13] A few months later she would wryly close the door on the project, writing Bernstein that "the Middagh Street opus bore no edible fruit and we are happy to hear you are not what they call married to the idea."[14] (Sixty-two years later the Public Theater would produce the musical *February House*, by writer Seth Bockley and composer Gabriel Kahane, based on a 2005 nonfiction book by Sherrill Tippins about the denizens of 7 Middagh Street, to decidedly mixed critical and audience response off-Broadway.)

But even if the Middagh Street musical had proven viable for Comden and Green, they would have had to put it aside for some time, because a new assignment had come up at MGM. As May of 1950 ended, they found themselves hurrying to California to find out what Arthur Freed had in mind.

UNBURNED BRIDGES

The fact that George Abbott wasn't involved with the movie version of *On the Town* didn't diminish his respect for or desire to work with Comden and Green. A November 25, 1949, letter from Abbott in Nigel Simeone's *The Leonard Bernstein Letters* finds the director telling Bernstein about a new project, a musical version of Betty Smith's turn-of-the-century novel *A Tree Grows in Brooklyn*. Abbott hoped that "maybe if you were interested in this we could get Betty and Adolph to do the lyrics." Abbott would end up collaborating with composer Arthur Schwartz and lyricist Dorothy Fields on the musical the following year.

CHAPTER 7

Turning Back the Clock

S tarting in February 1949, MGM would include in its listings of upcoming plans a movie titled *Singin' in the Rain*, which, of course, was also the name of a hit song that Arthur Freed and Nacio Herb Brown had penned twenty years before. Details other than a title weren't provided in these slates of future pictures, nor were they offered a couple of months later when Ann Miller was being touted as the movie's star (even in features about her recent segue from supporting roles to starring ones).

Mentions of both the movie—and Miller's involvement in it—disappeared from view for the balance of 1949 and through the first months of 1950. But then the notion of a picture with the title *Singin' in the Rain* resurfaced in July 1950, when reporter Thomas F. Brady announced in the *New York Times* that "Adolph Green and Betty Comden have been engaged by Metro to write the scenario for 'Singin' in the Rain,' a projected Arthur Freed musical production."[1]

The matter-of-fact nature of the *Times* announcement belies the thorny path that Comden and Green took with Freed to reach an agreement about the film, which was to use the catalog of songs he had written with Brown over the years. Difficulties started when Comden and Green rushed to California at Freed's request at the end of May. When they got to the studio the place was empty, with employees enjoying a six-day Decoration Day (the precursor to Memorial Day) holiday.

When they finally met with Freed, he called them into his office and, as Comden recalled during an interview for the Winter 2002 edition of the *Michigan Quarterly Review*, said, "Well, kids, your next movie is going to be called *Singin' in the Rain*, and it's going to have all of my songs in it."

It was a hefty proposition given the producer's body of work as a songwriter, but there was a further complication. Comden and Green had sped to Hollywood under the impression that they would be writing a new musical with an original screenplay and their own lyrics. They were also working under another assumption. They had been told, as Green would later relate, that "it was in our contract that we would always write our own lyrics, unless they were using songs by Irving Berlin, Cole Porter, and a few others."[2]

As disappointment combined with a belief that their contract was being violated, they refused to accept the project. Hugh Fordin, in his book *The Movies' Greatest Musicals*, quotes them as saying, "We sneered imperiously, skulked out of the office and went on strike." It wasn't long, though, before they decided to have Irving "Swifty" Lazar, the Hollywood super agent who had recently begun to represent them, examine their agreement with the studio.

After reading through the contract, Lazar informed them that it had no such provision. They had requested that there be some sort of stipulation about movies with songs by other writers, but the clause never made it into the final, signed document.

Comden and Green returned to Freed and informed him that they would begin work on the project immediately. At this juncture they had no concept for *Singin' in the Rain* beyond its using the title song. As Comden would later often joke, "All we knew was, that at some point in the film, someone would be out in the rain and singing about it."[3]

Their first step was to meet with Roger Edens. With him they spent hours playing through the Freed catalog of songs, which included both well-known numbers, such as "You Stepped Out of a Dream," "All I Do Is Dream of You," and "Broadway Rhythm," along with lesser-known tunes, such as "The Moon Is Low," "I'm Feeling Like a Million," "My Wonderful One, Let's Dance," and "A New Moon Is Over My Shoulder." They allowed their imaginations to wander as they listened to the numbers, and for a while they wondered whether the tunes could fit into some sort of cowboy-western musical. It seemed possible, but not necessarily the best choice.

Eventually, Comden and Green began to think about the Hollywood era in which the songs were written. They realized that many of Freed's best-known tunes were penned just as sound came to the moviemaking business, and so the team started to wonder, "What if *Singin' in the Rain* were to take place during that time?" The idea clicked.

It helped that they had both witnessed Hollywood's first, awkward forays into talking pictures as teenagers. Green, in particular, distinctly remembered two important film experiences. One was John Gilbert's performance in *His Glorious Night*. The movie, widely believed to have ended the silent film star's career, featured him repeating the words "I love you" to his leading lady to ludicrous effect. Green, as an adult, could recall the hilarity the moment caused, as well as his disappointment that Gilbert, whom he admired as an actor, "didn't sound like him—or at least what I expected him to sound like."[4]

Similarly, Green remembered seeing MGM's early movie musical *Hollywood Revue of 1929*, which had included "Singin' in the Rain," and finding the picture amateurish. The studio pulled together all of its stars for this cinematic revue. The movie actually functions like a stage performance, complete with curtains opening and closing between acts. It also boasts two emcees who introduce the stars, such as Joan Crawford, who sang and danced, and Stan Laurel and Oliver Hardy, who did magic as they desperately strove to add dialogue to one of their routines, which previously had been wordless.

Beyond giving moviegoers the chance not only to see but hear their favorite performers—and it's difficult today to understand exactly what that must have felt like for people who had had only silent movies or radios as entertainment media—MGM attempted to demonstrate technical innovations in *Hollywood Revue* as well. Technicolor was sporadically used, most notably in a bit of meta-theatrics involving Norma Shearer and the previously mentioned John Gilbert in a scene from *Romeo and Juliet*. Trick photography also played a role in the movie. Bessie Love gets "miniaturized" so she can fit in the breast pocket of Jack Benny's tuxedo, only to magically grow to full size on screen before performing her routine.

Interestingly, in both of these sequences the picture's screenwriters and tunesmiths view their industry through a satirical prism. Shearer and Gilbert find that they have to re-shoot their big balcony scene after a letter arrives from the New York office telling director Lionel Barrymore that they can't use Shakespeare's dialogue. Love's number, "I Never Knew I Could Do That," opens with the announcement that "these crazy sound effects have made a mess of me." It continues by allowing Love to kid herself a bit, as she sings about her "vocalizing being kind of weak" and how it all seems "to have a certain squeak."

A little more than 10 years after this movie was released Comden and Green would pick up the baton when they developed a Revuers sketch about this very period. The sequence included performers' mouths being out of sync with their recorded dialog and the unevenness of sound based on the performers' proximity to unseen microphones. These details would eventually surface in their screenplay for *Singin' in the Rain*.

After the Revuers disbanded, Comden and Green continued to offer the sketch up at parties in California and New York. Indeed, a year before they began work on *Singin' in the Rain*, *Los Angeles Times* columnist Edwin Schallert chronicled an impromptu performance they gave at a party at screenwriter Harry Kurnitz's home. In the February 22, 1949, edition of the paper, Schallert wrote: "Betty Comden and Adolph Green put on as good a show as one could imagine with their satires on scenarists at work, light operas, actors in early talkies etc."

Comden and Green, having decided on the silent-to-talkies era for the aborning movie, began working on the screenplay, and various drafts were completed between August and October 1950. In all of these the arc of the picture as we know it today was established. Don Lockwood and Lina Lamont are Hollywood darlings of the silent era who find the transition to talkies difficult. The shift proves particularly troublesome for her because of her voice: a nasal screech with a heavy "New Yawk" accent.

After their first picture with sound disastrously previews for a test audience, it's decided that reworking it as a musical might save the day for all concerned, particularly if Lina's vocals are dubbed by someone with a more dulcet voice. Don knows exactly who would fit the bill: a young actress named Kathy Summers (a surname later changed to Selden) who also interests him romantically. She agrees (because the feeling is mutual), and their ruse is a success. The movie debuts to great acclaim, and though there are some bumps along the way for Don and Kathy's relationship, they also manage to triumph in love.

Reports vary about whether or not Comden and Green knew who the star of the movie would be as they were writing during the late summer of 1950. They would often claim not to have known that it was meant to be a vehicle for Gene Kelly and point to their thoughts about the possibility of its being a singing western. If the script had gone in this direction, it could have been a movie suited to Howard Keel, for instance.

Stanley Donen, who co-directed and co-choreographed *Rain*, would relate the movie's origins differently. "The picture was always going to be for Gene, always—never for Howard Keel, never for Van Johnson, which has also been mentioned, and never for anyone else," biographer Stephen M. Silverman quotes Donen as saying in *Dancing on the Ceiling*.

Donen also recalled, "One idea was to adapt the Jean Harlow picture *Bombshell* or some other early talkie. We screened a lot of pictures from that time, literally dozens, but Betty and Adolph said no, they have this other idea."[5]

ALWAYS A HELPFUL SPOUSE

Comden's husband Steven Kyle had a hand in helping shape *Singin' in the Rain*. She and Green were so inspired by the comedic possibilities for the picture that they developed three ways in which it could begin. Comden, when talking with William Baer for the Winter 2002 edition of the *Michigan Quarterly Review* recalled, "We read our opening sequences to Steven and he laughed hugely and said, 'Why don't you use all of them?' Which is exactly what we did. It seems so insanely simple now, but it was maybe the best idea anybody ever gave us."

As they wrote, Comden and Green were aware of one performer whom Freed had intended for the film: Oscar Levant. The actor-pianist was a favorite of the producer, and Green told Levant biographers Sam Kashner and Nancy Schoenberg that "Arthur Freed would have cast Oscar Levant as Huckleberry Finn if he could've gotten away with it."

Comden and Green, as they had for *The Barkleys of Broadway*, in which Levant appeared, crafted a role suited to his varied talents: a man by the name of Cosmo Brown, Don's oldest and best friend, a pianist who had come up through the entertainment ranks with him. To give Levant an opportunity to demonstrate his skill at the piano, they created a sequence in which he pitched the idea of a follow-up movie musical, called *The Piano-Playing Pioneer*. As Cosmo described it to the head of the studio, a fantasy sequence unfurled in which Levant, playing the hero of the movie, subdued a murderous group of Native Americans with his rendition of a classical piece of music.

Another moment tailor-made for Levant's dour screen person came as Lina emerged from her on-set trailer in opulent 18th-century French regalia. Comden and Green's stage directions noted that her appearance would be accompanied by Cosmo snidely playing "The Old Gray Mare" on the piano.

Beyond these details suited to Levant, Comden and Green integrated a subtle through-line, present in both the original drafts and the final version, that underscores the blithe and often hilarious comedy and the sweet romance. From start to finish, *Singin' in the Rain* sparks with glee as it repeatedly reveals the facts behind Hollywood's fictions. They start with Don's revisionist history of his youth, in which his trips to the theater are seen in flashbacks as having really been visits to schlocky silent horror films. Next they expose the venom that drips between Don and Lina as they film *The Dueling Cavalier*; he makes love to her while berating her for having gotten Kathy fired, calling her a "reptile." Duplicity even extends into the characters' realities, as Kathy lies to Don about her lack of knowledge of his screen work.

The biggest deception, of course, becomes the dubbing of Kathy's voice to Lina's performance. Given that Comden and Green meticulously integrate the divergence of fact and fiction into the screenplay as a whole, there's an even stronger comedic payoff in the film's climactic moment, when the world at large learns the truth about the bit of cinematic trickery in the talkie.

As 1950 drew to a close, Kelly's involvement with the picture became official, and after he enjoyed a post–*An American in Paris* vacation, he and Donen began collaborating with Comden and Green on revisions to the screenplay.

THE CLOSENESS OF THE COMDEN-GREEN-KELLY-DONEN COLLABORATION

As Comden and Green often noted, they had a "shorthand" with Kelly and Donen because of their long-standing friendship. Kelly's wife, Betsy Blair, remembers in her book *The Memory of All That*, how closely they would collaborate when working on a film. One day Comden and Green arrived at the home she shared with Kelly: "Adolph, as always, was irrepressible. There were jokes and laughter. They went into the study to work." Later, Blair was leaving for an appointment and she recalled, "They were all in the living room, with Roger at the piano. I closed the red front door as they played the introduction to a song."

Beyond finalizing what songs would be part of the picture (Comden and Green generally only indicated ideas for what tunes might be used where in their drafts), the quartet slotted where dance numbers could be placed in the movie. One of the most significant changes during this period was the reworking of how the title song would be incorporated into the film. In the original drafts the song was to be sung by Don, Cosmo, and Kathy after they had come up with the idea of turning the dismal *The Dueling Cavalier* into *The Dancing Cavalier*. It was a joyous expression of their belief that they had sidestepped disaster.

After their working sessions with Kelly and Donen, the song—and accompanying dance—became a solo for Kelly's Don. And instead of it being a musical expression of the group's joy over their solution to their professional worries, it allowed Don to revel in the blossoming of his relationship with Kathy.

Even as Comden and Green were effecting these changes, they had to contend with an issue of recasting. In March, Levant withdrew from the project, and in his place a very different actor, Donald O'Connor, was cast as Cosmo.

While Levant would have brought an elegant sardonic demeanor to the role, O'Connor, a former vaudevillian whom MGM "borrowed" from rival studio Universal-International, came to the movie with a goofier and more impish quality. It was a drastic change in type, and Leonard Lyons, in one of his March 1951 syndicated columns, hyperbolically described how

O'Connor's casting would affect Comden and Green. He opined that the work lying ahead of them would be "the strangest rewriting job ever tried in Hollywood."

Comden and Green, no strangers to quickly developing new ideas, revised accordingly. In the process, and as was their wont for having songs that meshed with a piece's overall stories, they created one moment that required a number other than what was available from Freed's existing catalog. In their original draft, the elocution work Don did in preparation for his first speaking role was accomplished in private as he listened to recordings of tongue twisters. As they reworked the script they incorporated a vocal coach for Don and had Cosmo interrupt. It became an apt moment for Kelly and O'Connor to hoof it up together, and so they wrote the lyric for "Moses Supposes," for which Roger Edens provided an appropriately jaunty melody.

For Levant, Comden and Green said they had also "painfully wedged into the script"[6] the Freed-Brown song "The Wedding of the Painted Doll." It was to be used as a number in which Cosmo attempted to cheer Don out of his doldrums over Kathy. This moment was ultimately replaced with a second new tune, one penned by Freed and Brown, "Make 'Em Laugh," which unintentionally used the melody for Cole Porter's "Be a Clown." Porter, always the gentleman, graciously let the plagiarism go.

This latter change came as shooting of the film approached, and after Comden and Green had returned to New York, being, as they put it, "pioneers in bicoastal living."[7] They had a new Broadway show to attend to, a musical revue called *Two on the Aisle.*

RETROFITTING AT MGM

To bring the studio world of 1929 back to life for *Singin' in the Rain*, MGM dusted off its own past. It reopened an old soundstage that had been used for filming early talking pictures. The space's primary feature was a booth with a large glass window that separated the director, crew, and cameras from the playing area, which had been key to ensuring that the sound of cameras rolling was not captured by microphones. Further, according to a July 8, 1951, Associated Press wire story, the studio filled the space "with antiquated movie equipment that [had] lain almost forgotten in an underground vault for twenty years."

Comden and Green's new stage show was the brainchild of Arthur Lesser, who had just presented Les Ballets de Paris on Broadway to great acclaim. As a follow-up to this success, he envisioned presenting a revue, *Two on the*

Aisle, on Broadway, and as the writers finished the drafting process on their movie script, Lesser announced that he had lined up the revue's two stars. Bert Lahr, who had an impressive stage résumé—and would continue to build on it through the early 1960s but of course will be forever remembered as *The Wizard of Oz's* Cowardly Lion—would be the male headliner. The female star of the show was to be Lena Horne, the now-legendary vocalist who had been slowly amassing Hollywood credits and was enjoying a successful career at the time as a nightclub performer.

As Lesser heralded the casting, he also announced that he was hoping to secure Harold Arlen, who had written the music for the movie *The Wizard of Oz* and for such Broadway shows as *Bloomer Girl* and *St. Louis Woman,* as the revue's composer. But—as would become a habit with Lesser as the show was in preparations—he made the announcement prematurely, and several weeks later Jule Styne was named composer of *Two on the Aisle.*

Styne, like Comden and Green, enjoyed a bicoastal career. He and Sammy Cahn were the authors of six Academy Award–nominated film songs, including "It's Magic" and "I Fall in Love Too Easily." They had also collaborated on such stand-alone hits as "Saturday Night (Is the Loneliest Night of the Week)" and "It's Been a Long, Long Time." Styne also had a pair of Broadway successes to his name, *High Button Shoes* and the breakthrough hit for Carol Channing, *Gentlemen Prefer Blondes.* Lesser's teaming of Styne with Comden and Green turned out to be inspired, and it was a decision that had a profound impact on the careers of all three. They would continue to collaborate on musicals through the mid-1970s.

As 1950 turned into 1951, the writing team—along with Lahr—proved to be Lesser's only constant for the show. First, just as rehearsals were supposed to begin, Horne withdrew from the production in order to "return to M-G-M to make a film with Billy Eckstine."[8]

Lesser scrambled and turned to a less-well-known performer to fill Horne's slot on the bill: Dolores Gray. At the time, Gray had only a pair of minor Broadway credits, but she was riding a crest of popularity in Europe thanks to her work in the title role of Irving Berlin's *Annie Get Your Gun* when it debuted in London in 1947. After finishing her run, she remained overseas to launch a nightclub act. Just before Lesser approached her about returning to New York, Gray opened at the Society in London.

As he informed the press about Gray's addition to the company, Lesser also announced that rehearsals for the show would start at the end of March, even though no director had been officially named. This date came and went, and as it did Lesser hosted auditions for the show. At the beginning of April he added Kaye Ballard, a comedienne just at the beginning of her career who would go on to great acclaim on both stage and television, to the revue's roster of talent. Lesser concurrently named William Hammerstein, son of Oscar Hammerstein II, as the director, but his involvement lasted barely a month. At the end of April, Hammerstein departed after accepting a movie deal, and Lesser replaced him with Abe Burrows.

Burrows, who joined the production at Styne's suggestion, enjoyed a successful career as a radio writer and host throughout the 1940s and transitioned to television in 1950 with *Abe Burrows' Almanac*. Coincidentally, two of his guests on the show's premiere were Comden and Green. Burrows's work in the theater began just months before the program's debut when he had helped to make Frank Loesser's *Guys and Dolls* a Broadway smash by revising Jo Swerling's original book for the classic, and he had just completed similar (although uncredited) work on the Styne-produced musical *Make a Wish*, which was in tryouts just as Lesser was working to sort out the details of his aborning show. It was because of this association that Styne felt Burrows should direct *Two on the Aisle*. Burrows jokes about his transition from writer to director in his memoir *Honest, Abe*: "[Jule] asked me if I would like to direct [*Two on the Aisle*]. That's how I became a director. Simple."

With Burrows's arrival the production picked up momentum. Other cast members were announced, including Colette Marchand, a principal dancer with the ballet company Lesser had brought to Broadway, and Elliot Reid, a member of Orson Welles's Mercury Theatre company who would go on to enjoy a healthy career on both the big and small screen, notably playing Jane Russell's love interest in the film version of Styne's *Blondes*.

Two on the Aisle also was able to set a relatively firm schedule at this juncture. It would play tryouts in New Haven and Philadelphia in June before opening at the Mark Hellinger Theatre on Broadway in July.

The sketches that Comden and Green developed for the show combine tropes of vaudeville and burlesque with their satirical sensibilities. One sequence takes on serials about outer space as it imagines Captain Universe (Lahr) with his space brigade exploring Venus in hopes of finding an element that will wipe out the scourge of penicillin poisoning. Their mission is interrupted by the arrival of the Queen of Venus, the granddaughter of an earthman who arrived on the planet years before with an interplanetary touring company of *Oklahoma!* In this sketch Comden and Green segue from playing with pop culture to burlesque as the captain falls hard for the queen.

The theater itself gets lovingly spoofed in "Triangle," a three-part sketch that imagines an unfaithful wife attempting to rendezvous with her lover. Comden and Green first deliver the scenario as it would have been performed in a burlesque house; then they imagine how it would have unfolded at the hands of poet-playwright T. S. Eliot, whose opaque *The Cocktail Party* was then a hit among New York's cognoscenti; and, finally, they offer it up in a mini-musical in the style of Cole Porter.

Contemporary life also gets skewered in the revue with "There Never Was a Baby Like My Baby," in which a couple who've amply read trendy parenting books worry about what effect taking a rattle away from their six-month-old will have on his future. Will it contribute to future teen delinquency, or perhaps even drug abuse? The perils that the couple foresees in the simple decision are dire.

Two other sequences, a sketch by Burrows himself and a monologue written and performed by Reid, were also up to the minute as they tackled, respectively, the burgeoning of television sports coverage and the broadcasts of the Kefauver hearings into interstate crime.

Along with their sketches, Comden and Green developed a variety of songs with Styne. In some instances, such as the opener "Show Train," Styne puts a high show-biz gloss on the team's "Reader's Digest" mode of distilling classic literary works into three rhymed comedic lines. In this number, however, Comden and Green don't deliver barbs on great books; instead, they lovingly rib current Broadway hits, such as Burrows's own *Guys* and Styne's *Blondes*.

Elsewhere, Styne's pop stylings take Comden and Green's humorous lyrics into new bluesy terrain, such as in Gray's "There Never Was a Baby Like My Baby." The writers' (and particularly Green's) familiarity with "highbrow" music can be felt in both "Catch Our Act at the Met," in which a push toward a more popular sort of opera gets lampooned, and "The Clown," a solo for Lahr about the dramatic aspirations of a comic. In this latter number Styne masterfully blends an almost balletic quality with both Latin rhythms and traditional British pomp, while Comden and Green's lyric cum scenario affords him the opportunity of morphing from a sad-sack persona into a mock Rudolf Valentino and then Queen Victoria.

In *Two on the Aisle* Lahr almost got to reprise (in a way) his most iconic role in the unused "Leo the Lion" sketch, in which Comden and Green imagined that MGM's trademark roaring beast decides to play hardball with his contract renewal. Tired of being limited to opening pictures or being given token—and clichéd—opportunities to appear in films, such as one in *Quo Vadis* where he was supposed to devour the heroine in Rome's Coliseum, Leo demands more from his bosses. As funny as it sounds, the sketch never made it to the show's first performances in New Haven.

The sequence wasn't removed because the writers had a change of heart about spoofing their Hollywood bosses or even because Lahr decided that he didn't want to once again don a lion's suit, as he had in *Oz*. Quite the contrary, the comedian relished the idea but had one demand: "I'll do it, but the most important thing is my face. You have to get me the same face I had at MGM for *The Wizard of Oz*."[9] Lesser assured Lahr that he would secure the appropriate costume.

By the time performances began in New Haven, however, Styne remembered going through the costume list and thinking, "Lesser was dressing his show with a Safeway shopping list. All stock stuff."[10] When it came time for Lahr to don the lion outfit he was outraged and announced, "I'm not doing the goddamned thing."[11] And that was the last of "Leo the Lion" for *Two on the Aisle.*

Lesser's lack of attention to such matters also meant that one day in Philadelphia Comden and Green found themselves scurrying through a Woolworth's looking for straw hats and other items, and Green recalled, "Most of those hastily improvised outfits stayed with the show through the entire run."[12]

As if the problems created by Lesser's producing were not enough for the creative team to contend with, there were also serious issues within the company. Gray became jealous of Ballard's material, particularly the number "If (You Hadn't but You Did)," in which, as a kind of precursor to "The Cellblock Tango" ("he had it coming") from Kander and Ebb's *Chicago* some 25 years later, a woman recounts all of the slights that led to her murdering her boyfriend. Gray eventually took over performing this number. Ballard saw her parts in other portions of the show slowly whittled away until finally she realized that "all I had left to do in the show were two little walk-ons."[13] And even though she was still earning $550 per week for this minimal work, Ballard left the company before it concluded its New Haven engagement.

Worse still was the flare-up that happened over *Aisle*'s running order just before its first preview. Traditionally, a revue's primary star first appears in its third segment, and Burrows assigned this to Lahr. However, as Burrows recalled, "[Gray] insisted on appearing in the number three spot. Bert Lahr, of course, wouldn't accept that. Comden and Green, Jule Styne and I all agreed with Bert."[14]

Nothing would appease Gray, and Burrows departed the theater, returning shortly later in a suit and tie. One of the show's backers—Tony Farrell, the owner of the Mark Hellinger, the Broadway house into which *Aisle* was booked—saw him and asked why he was so dressed up, and Burrows informed him that he was quitting. Burrows describes in *Honest, Abe* what happened next: "Tony gave me a long look. Then he turned to the cast and said, 'If Abe goes back to New York, I'm going to close the show.'" Gray quickly agreed to appear in the number two slot.

When *Two on the Aisle* opened in New Haven, the trade papers *Variety* and *Billboard* gave it distinctly diverging reviews. In the former, on June 13, "Bone." wrote, "[It] will be a producer's headache before it can be a ticket broker's dream," while 10 days later Sidney Golly's review in the latter publication began: "[It] shows every indication of shaping into top summer fare."

Tinkering and restructuring began, and the company moved to Philadelphia, where it received a rave from *Philadelphia Inquirer* critic Henry T. Murdock on June 21: "'Two on the Aisle' took Philadelphia show business out of the summer pastures with a resounding hey-nonny-nonny at the Forrest Theatre last night." Audiences concurred with his assessment. Ticket demand (and the creators' desire to hone the production further) warranted a week's extension and a slight delay in the show's Broadway bow.

ANOTHER KIND OF OUT-OF-TOWN REWRITE

In their introduction to the published version of the *Singin' in the Rain* screenplay, Comden and Green describe a call they got while *Aisle* was in tryouts. A revision to the movie's first love scene was needed. The sequence had originally used several songs and featured Gene Kelly and Debbie Reynolds strolling through different backlot sets. Kelly wanted a single song and dance. He hoped Comden and Green could do a quick rewrite. "We wrenched our minds from the great Bert Lahr...and time-machined ourselves back to *Singin' in the Rain* long enough to fill the order. It worked." The sequence, of course, is the magically filmed "You Were Meant for Me."

Comden, Green, and *Two on the Aisle* returned to New York for the show's newly scheduled opening on July 19, and the following morning they found that the show and its stars had received a bounty of love notes from the critics. Ward Morehouse in the *New York World Telegram* announced that the team "brought a lively and funny revue into the Hellinger Theater, the kind of show that just isn't supposed to come in until all the fashionable people are back in town," and in the *New York Times* Brooks Atkinson, who interrupted his vacation specifically so that he could write about Lahr, noted, "Thanks to Bert Lahr and Dolores Gray, the rest of the summer is going to be mighty pleasant on Broadway." As for the show, he deemed it "an excellent, light revue," praising Comden and Green for writing "the pithiest material any revue has had in these parts for a long time."

The show was meant to have been a theatrical amuse-bouche for the summer, but audiences, like the critics, fell in love with it, and the revue ended up continuing into the new year. It ultimately played 276 performances before closing on March 15, 1952.

During the course of its run Comden and Green were able to celebrate a first in their career. *Two on the Aisle* was preserved in their first released cast album, and in the September 29 issue of the *Saturday Review*, Bill Smith told readers that it was "the most entertaining show album to come our way since 'Guys and Dolls.'"

Styne's knowledge of promoting songs also meant that Comden and Green saw a greater number of popular artists releasing versions of songs from the show than they had with their previous Broadway outings. Among the notable cover versions were two from Ella Fitzgerald and one from Peggy Lee, who released a tune that had been cut from the show, "So Far, So Good."

With *Two on the Aisle* successfully opened, both Comden and Green took time to travel, even as Kelly finished filming on *Singin' in the Rain* and Arthur Freed began planning what would become their next movie project. With the opening of *Rain* on the horizon and a musical that they had not even contemplated not far behind, 1952 was gearing up to be a busy, successful—and at times stressful—year for the team.

COMDEN: THE WORKING MOM

A great indication of how Comden was juggling her role as a working mother comes from a feature by Elizabeth Lips in the *Brooklyn Eagle* on October 17, 1951, just after *Two on the Aisle* began its run. The interview, Lips told her readers, took place in "the living room of [Comden's] remodeled three-story brownstone, which has been converted into a compact, modern triplex apartment by her husband, Steven Kyle." In addition to covering Comden's career, Lips made sure that the article contained details about her personal life: "She has been married 10 years and upstairs in the nursery the Kyles' small daughter, Susannah [*sic*], was taking her afternoon nap."

CHAPTER 8

Theatrical Adventures
On Screen and On- and Offstage

Just as Comden and Green were taking some much-needed time off after the stresses leading to the opening of *Two on the Aisle*, Arthur Freed started the rollout for a new slate of films for MGM. One was to be a vehicle for Fred Astaire, who would be joined by Broadway's Nanette Fabray (the star of Jule Styne's first Broadway show, *High Button Shoes*, as well as *Make a Wish*, which he later co-produced), and one would be for Dolores Gray, who was co-starring in *Aisle*.

As Freed made these announcements, he also indicated that he had tapped Comden and Green to write the film that would feature Gray. His plans changed quickly, though, and in short order he put them on the Astaire project, which had gotten both a title and plot. The movie, tentatively known as *The Strategy of Love*, would be based on an original story by Peter Viertel and center on a TV writer (Astaire) who uses a fourteenth-century French tome about romance to woo the woman he loves.

Freed also decided that in the tradition of *Singin' in the Rain* and *An American in Paris*, the movie would use a preexisting song catalog, specifically that belonging to composer Arthur Schwartz and lyricist Howard Dietz. They were a team whose work Freed had always wanted to showcase. Beyond writing with Schwartz, Dietz also happened to be a vice president heading up publicity at MGM and the man credited for creating the studio's leonine mascot and its slogan, "Ars gratia artis" (Art for art's sake).

The collaboration between Dietz and Schwartz began with the Broadway revue *The Little Show* in 1929. The two men continued to work together, providing material for such shows as *The Band Wagon*, which starred both Astaire and his sister, Adele, *At Home Abroad*, and *Revenge with Music*. The men's substantial body of songs included such classics as "Dancing in the Dark" and "You and the Night and the Music."

Shortly after the Dietz-Schwartz aspect of the project was announced, the movie began to be promoted with the title *I Love Louisa*, which happened to be the title of a number from *The Band Wagon*, and additional members were added to the creative team. Vincente Minnelli, the Oscar-nominated director of *An American in Paris*, would helm the project. Further, Michael Kidd, who created the dances for *Finian's Rainbow* and *Guys and Dolls* on Broadway, was brought in to choreograph. Freed also hired Comden and Green's friend and sometime producer Oliver Smith to design the movie and announced that Oscar Levant would be featured in it.

After spending the holidays in New York, Comden and Green made their way to California in early 1952 to begin discussions about the project. As the idea of using the Viertel story had been put to the side, they needed to develop some sort of scenario that could integrate the existing tunes. As Green later recalled: "We had all these elements...Astaire and Oscar Levant, an old friend of ours, and songs by Schwartz and Dietz which weren't exactly the latest thing...and we couldn't figure how to put all these things together."[1]

Eventually, Comden and Green opted to pay tribute to the theater and the stage experiences—and traumas—that so many of the principals on the movie, which was eventually known as *The Band Wagon*, had known. Astaire would play Tony Hunter, a one-time Broadway star who had gone on to make it big in Hollywood. As the movie begins Tony's big-screen luster has faded. He is selling his belongings at auction, has put his home up for sale, and is returning to New York. There, two old friends, the husband-and-wife musical comedy writing team Lester and Lily Marton, have a new project they have written just for him. It will be the perfect vehicle to relaunch his stage career, particularly as they're hoping to get Jeffrey Cordova, a man with three simultaneously running hits, to direct.

Cordova, currently starring in his own production of *Oedipus Rex*, does come on board, but he doesn't see their story about a children's book author who begins writing crime fiction on the side as a light and fluffy entertainment. Instead, he sees the tale as being a modern-day *Faust* and begins to shepherd the team toward rewriting it so that it can become, as the character puts it, "a modern musical morality play with meaning and stature."

From here Comden and Green unspool a satire on the making of a Broadway failure as creative pressures mount. Cordova hires a beautiful ballerina, Gabrielle Gerard, as Tony's leading lady, and her choreographer boyfriend to do the show's dances. Her classical dance background makes Tony nervous, while his show-biz acumen unsettles her. The ill ease the two stars feel with one another only makes the difficult birthing process of the show even more fraught, as it spirals toward heavy-handed allegory and spectacle under Cordova's guidance.

After the show bombs out of town, Tony takes over. He returns the piece to its frothy roots, in the process transforming it into a hit and solidifying the romance that has developed offstage between him and his leading lady.

Green would later say of the story, "We wanted to show all the clichés... how the troubles out of town can happen... how it happens that friends can turn to you and ask, 'How can you smart people get together and turn out such a mess?'"[2]

As with *Singin' in the Rain*, the arc of *The Band Wagon* that moviegoers know from the completed picture—as well as most of its major plot developments—was present in the screenplay as Minnelli and his company began their rehearsal process in August 1952. The only element absent from the early version is the movie's climactic ballet.

There are, however, some notable differences between the script that was used for preproduction and the final cut. In some instances they involve numbers that Comden and Green thought might become part of the film. For instance, they indicated that Schwartz and Dietz's "Sweet Music" could be used in the moments after Cordova has secured the funding to bring the show to Broadway. They also suggested weaving "Got a Brand New Suit" into a series of scenes depicting the frantic New York rehearsals for the show and used "Never Marry a Dancer" as an ensemble number that follows Tony's announcement that he will take over and fund the floundering musical by selling his exquisite art collection.

It's interesting that in the rehearsal draft Comden and Green beautifully set up Tony's largesse. In the final cut of *The Band Wagon*, the paintings are seen only once before Tony decides to sell them to fund the new version of the show-within-the-movie. The French impressionist works appear, rather surprisingly and incongruously, in a scene in his New York hotel suite. When Gabrielle comments on them, he uses them as a punchline of a self-deprecating joke about his age, and in that moment the paintings seem to have fulfilled a singular purpose until he opts to part with them.

As Comden and Green originally wrote it, however, *The Band Wagon* included one other scene with the paintings. It came at the very beginning of the picture in a sequence that takes place in the California house Tony is selling. In it a potential buyer announces that she will not consider purchasing the home if Tony intends to leave the artwork. The scene simultaneously sets the stage for an ever-evolving joke about the collection and also starts the film with gentle satire about lowbrow artistic sensibilities.

Similarly, moviegoers are most likely familiar with the scene in which Lily and Lester squabble in a theater alleyway during rehearsals, and it is the single time when audiences glimpse the impact that the rehearsal period rewrites are having on their marriage. But in the rehearsal version of the screenplay, Comden and Green made certain to show the slow, corrosive effect that Cordova's tinkering and adding such lines as "Have you ever tried spreading ideals on a cracker?" has on them individually and as a couple. Lily and Lester have a comic argument in their bedroom, they spar a bit more seriously in the theater, and then, finally, there's the blow-up in the alley.

The resolution to their problems—and the payoff for Cordova's classic bit of spur-of-the-moment rewriting—fascinatingly also arrives in the sequence in which Tony decides he can rework the show. Comden and Green have Tony take to the piano and sing "Spreading ideals on a cracker" to the melody of Schwartz and Dietz's "You and the Night and the Music." The utter inanity of what he's done spurs Lily and Lester to understand how unnecessary their squabbling has been; they quickly mend fences with each other.

As they carefully laid out their story, Comden and Green also channeled their own experiences into the script and drew from realities surrounding the picture. For instance, the moment when Tony arrives at Grand Central Station and is greeted by Lily and Lester as his "fan club" echoes how Comden welcomed Green back to New York after their first disastrous trip to Hollywood a decade earlier.

In a similar vein, the premise that Tony has hit the skids in Hollywood magnifies the position that Astaire himself was in. The star came to *The Band Wagon* after the release of the disastrously received movie *Belle of New York*, and though Astaire was not nearly in Tony's dire straits, the picture and its reception had been a disappointment. But almost in the same optimistic fashion with which Tony takes over the musical in *The Band Wagon*, Astaire, in his memoir, *Steps in Time*, segues between the two pictures with a joke: "There's one thing about having a flop movie at a major studio that has it all over a stage flop. You do get paid." Astaire further compliments producer Freed, noting, "He didn't hold anything against anybody because of a situation like [*Belle*]."

Comden and Green even went so far as to use Astaire and his co-star Cyd Charisse's height discrepancy to humorous effect in the script. It was a move that Dietz described as "ingenious," because it "converted a handicap into an asset." The lyricist related, "Cyd was an inch taller and had longer legs, and her long legs made her look streamlined like the Chrysler Building. Fred was General Motors."[3] It made Astaire nervous, and so when Tony and Gabrielle first meet by the grand staircase in Cordova's townhouse, Comden and Green include a moment in which he sizes up her height and his relation to it by alternating between steps until he discovers the one that puts him at eye level with her.

ALSO DRAWN FROM THEIR PAST?

Comden and Green often said that José Ferrer had served as their inspiration for the character of Jeffrey Cordova. As they were writing, Ferrer did indeed have a trio of shows on Broadway, including the drama *The Shrike*, in which he was starring. But they might also have been thinking about Irving Caesar, who was behind the disastrously received *My Dear Public*. Caesar had written book, lyrics, and music; directed; and produced the show. Dick Vosburg reported in a December 19, 1996, London *Independent* obituary for Caesar that after *Public* opened to contemptuous notices, Caesar called Ira Gershwin and during their conversation confusedly asked, "Why is everybody blaming me?"

As winter turned into spring, Comden and Green continued with their writing in consultation with Minnelli, who relates in his autobiography, *I Remember It Well*, "I discussed every inch of the script with Betty and Adolph. Neither one of us let go of it until we were all satisfied." At the same time, Dietz and Schwartz had an assignment for one new number. Freed requested a paean to the entertainment industry like Irving Berlin's "There's No Business Like Show Business." The result was a song that would become not only a centerpiece of the movie but also an anthem of equal stature to its precursor: "That's Entertainment."

Concurrent with these artists' work on the new picture were MGM's preparations for the premiere of *Singin' in the Rain*, which bowed in New York at Radio City Music Hall on March 27, 1952. Given the stature the movie has acquired since its debut, the mixed and tepid notices it received at the time may surprise. In the *New York Times* the following day, Bosley Crowther wrote: "Betty Comden and Adolph Green may have tossed off the script with their left hands, but occasionally they come through with powerful and hilarious round-house rights." Otis L. Guernsey Jr. in the *New York Herald Tribune* echoed this sentiment: "The book is less a narrative than a series of skits.... These incidents are blithe, breezy, and disrespectful, and they provide the show with a solid foundation of humor."

As the movie opened in other cities across the country and ultimately Los Angeles in April, critics could be even less generous. In the April 10 *Los Angeles Times* review, Philip K. Scheuer wrote that the writers "have been fairly murderous in administering their kicks, the poor old silents haven't a leg to stand on.... It is rather like the pot, just because it has learned to talk, calling the kettle black."

Green himself once looked back on the reception *Singin' in the Rain* had when it opened and remarked, "It was just considered another picture then.

The reviews were good, but nobody considered it exceptional. It came and went."[4]

MGM RETROFITS AN OPENING

Just as it had when *Singin' in the Rain* was filming, MGM turned back the clock for the opening of the movie in Los Angeles, ensuring that there were both A-list names and others from the silent era at the picture's premiere at the Egyptian Theatre. According to a report in the April 2, 1952, edition of the *Los Angeles Times*, the studio invited "outstanding marquee names during the hectic change-over from silent to sound movies" to the opening. Everyone from Gloria Swanson, Spencer Tracy, and Charles Chaplin to Joe E. Brown, Ramon Navarro, and James Gleason attended.

Minnelli also used the summer of 1952 to finish one crucial piece of casting for *The Band Wagon*. Originally, the MGM brass offered the role of Cordova to Clifton Webb, but he declined, preferring instead to appear as John Philip Sousa in the biopic *Stars and Stripes Forever* for 20th Century Fox. Webb did, however, suggest someone for Minnelli to consider: British stage and screen star Jack Buchanan. In his memoir *I Remember It Well*, Minnelli says, "We sensed Jack could supply the impulsive, scatter-brained explosiveness we were looking for," and the part was offered and accepted.

With Buchanan in place alongside Astaire, Fabray, Levant, and Charisse (in her first starring role), rehearsals for *The Band Wagon* began in August 1952, and Minnelli started shooting six weeks later. As he moved through the movie's preproduction and production process, one major addition was made to the script: the full scenario for the final "Girl Hunt Ballet." In their original screenplay Comden and Green merely indicated that there would be some sort of "Murder Mystery number" as the film reached its climax. When Freed saw a large feature in *Life* magazine on writer Mickey Spillane and the enormous popularity of his pulp crime novels, he suggested to Minnelli that the phenomenon might be ripe for parody. Minnelli dove into a stack of Spillane's novels and agreed with Freed's assessment, although as the director notes in *I Remember It Well*, "Applying the term satire to a ballet based on this school of fiction was actually a bit redundant, for in practically every page the writing contained the seeds of its own parody."

After Minnelli formulated a plot for the dance, Roger Edens took themes from the Dietz-Schwartz songbook and created the score. As for the storyline heard during the course of the number, Minnelli recalled, "Since Comden and Green had returned to New York before the ballet was fully plotted, I wrote Fred's voice-over narration for the action."[5]

Minnelli's recollection in his memoir, though not accurate, does retain the spirit of the agreement that was made with regard to the words that accompany the dance. In actuality, the voice-over dialogue was written by Alan Jay Lerner, who was at the studio working on the movie version of *Brigadoon*. As Hugh Fordin relates in *The Movies' Greatest Musicals*, Lerner was having lunch with Minnelli and Freed, and Minnelli asked the book writer-lyricist to pen the narration. "Lerner at first was very reluctant; after all this was Comden and Green's picture." The producer and director persisted and eventually Lerner agreed. "'No conditions, no money—I'll do it for fun,' Lerner said. Minnelli even promised he would claim to have written it himself."

The question of credit for authorship of this section of the film continued even after its release. According to Minnelli biographer Mark Griffin, Minnelli went into a rage when MGM released an abbreviated soundtrack recording for the film that included a credit for Lerner and Edens for "The Girl Hunt Ballet." "Minnelli demanded that Metro recall the soundtrack and redistribute the record with his own name replacing Lerner's on the album jacket."[6]

Indeed, Comden and Green were back in New York while the narration for the dance was being written, and on the East Coast they were contending with more serious issues than the birthing pains of a Broadway show. Green focused on issues in his marriage to Allyn McLerie, which, according to columnists, was beginning to founder. Their dual careers meant that they were separated more often than not, either by the span of a continent or even across the Atlantic. For instance, she spent several months in England filming the movie version of *Where's Charley?* and then followed that with a brief run in a West End show.

For the balance of 1952 and into the spring of 1953, the two were separated, but at times they did attempt reconciliation. Eventually, in May 1953, McLerie filed for divorce in Alabama and was granted one. The reason she turned to the southern state was that laws regarding residency there were particularly lax; one had only to demonstrate some intent of living there. For the balance of their lives and into their subsequent marriage, both Green and McLerie said that they had parted amicably and maintained a friendly relationship.

Issues regarding the marriage might have been one reason that Green kept an uncharacteristically low profile during 1952. As for Comden, she was equally quiet. One reason for both of them to have been relatively reclusive after returning to New York was perhaps because they had seen friends and colleagues—two of the five Revuers, Judy Holliday and Alvin Hammer—being called to testify in the Senate's investigation of communist infiltration of the entertainment industry and saw no reason to attract undue attention.

When Hammer was summoned, he refused to appear. Holliday, on the other hand, endured a grilling by the Senate committee on March 26, 1952. During the course of questioning, the nature of appearances that the Revuers had made arose, and Holliday—with counsel Simon Rifkind, the noted trial attorney and a former federal judge, at her side—carefully explained that they had either not happened at all or that she had had no knowledge of the sponsoring organizations.

Eventually, the questions turned to Comden and Green specifically. Richard Arens, the committee staff director, inquired: "Adolph Green and Betty Comden, with whom you were associated in The Revuers, have Communist Front records, do they not?" Holliday answered, "No. I am as sure of that as I can be of anybody that isn't me."[7]

Arens also drilled Holliday about the writers' alleged support of a one-time New York City mayoral candidate, Benjamin Davis, who had also at one point worked as an editor for a communist paper targeted to African Americans, *The Negro Liberator*. With regard to Comden, whom Arens asserted had been a sponsor for Davis's campaign, Holliday managed to make a joke of the idea, quipping, "I never knew that and I really doubt it."[8]

Interestingly, there was cordiality to the proceedings even though Holliday, along with Comden but not Green, had just five years earlier signed an open letter protesting the activities of the House Un-American Committee and its investigation of artists. The letter had appeared as an advertisement in papers such as the *New York Herald Tribune* on October 27, 1947, bearing the headline "Who's Un-American?" Underneath came the text of the letter, which stated, among other things, "We hold that these hearings are morally wrong" and that any attempts "to set arbitrary standards of Americanism, are themselves disloyal to both the spirit and the letter of the Constitution."

RED-BAITING WITH ERRORS

Indications of how zealous and overreaching some were to smear suspected communists during the early 1950s comes from one of Walter Winchell's syndicated columns in September 1952. The legendary gossip columnist and prominent red-baiter was eager to tout his foreknowledge of what would be in the McCarran Commission's report when it would be released. He announced that the artists it would name as communists were "Alvin Hammer (and Sickle?) whose commy card was 11810 in 1945 [and] Betty Comden and Adolph Green." Ironically, Winchell went on to undermine himself by announcing in the case of the latter two that "[They] are no longer wed."

Holliday was never placed on the career-ending blacklist. The subcommittee also failed to demonstrate that she had been a "fronter" for the Communist Party, and Comden and Green were never summoned to defend themselves in Washington. During the coming years, however, their lives would continue to be touched by the Red Scare, as other artists whom they knew or worked with were called to testify. The taint of communism also brushed up against a new stage project that was about to become a very sudden part of their lives: a musical adaptation of the hit play *My Sister Eileen.*

The show was based on Ruth McKenney's autobiographical stories that started appearing in the *New Yorker* in 1937. In them the author wryly recounts events from her and her sister's teenage years in Columbus, Ohio. McKenney also wrote stories about their lives together after moving to New York, where they rented a small, cramped apartment near Christopher Street in the heart of Greenwich Village.

The stories, which quickly gained popularity among the magazine's readers, were collected and published by Harcourt, Brace in book form under the title *My Sister Eileen* in 1938. In short order the book was on bestseller lists around the country. Concurrently, theatrical producers began to eye McKenney's work—both sly and sweet—as ideal for the stage. There were false starts by both McKenney and others before the playwriting team of Joseph A. Fields and Jerome Chodorov took the property and gave it theatrical viability.

The Fields-Chodorov adaptation was announced in September 1940, and before the year was up Broadway producer Max Gordon, a different man altogether from the Max Gordon who gave the Revuers their first gig at the Village Vanguard, opened the play on Broadway. Starring Shirley Booth, an actress who had been steadily working on Broadway since 1925 and who will most likely be forever associated with such roles as Lola in *Come Back, Little Sheba* and television's *Hazel,* the production immediately garnered both critical and popular acclaim, going on to run for more than two years. Screen rights for Fields and Chodorov's work went to Columbia Pictures, which released the film version—with a screenplay by the writers and starring Rosalind Russell—in September 1942, a full three months before the original Broadway production had shuttered.

In the years that followed, the allure of Ruth and Eileen never abated. In 1950, television producers began to contemplate creating an early sitcom based on the young women's adventures, and the play's original Broadway producer, Gordon, had begun to think about a musicalization of the piece. Neither project moved beyond discussion stages, but the concept of *My Sister Eileen* as a musical continued to surface. In many instances when reporters described progress on a potential *Eileen* tuner, Russell was mentioned as the star who would play Ruth. Unfortunately, timing and creative differences stalled any movement on the idea until a young maverick of a producer, Robert Fryer, came on the scene.

Fryer, who had worked as an associate producer with George Abbott on the musical *A Tree Grows in Brooklyn*, announced in late June 1952 his intention to bring a musical version of the play to Broadway. He signed Fields and Chodorov to adapt their original work and hired Abbott to stage the production. Within a span of six weeks Russell made a commitment to appear in the production he was assembling. For the show's music, Fryer engaged composer Leroy Anderson, who was the Boston Pops Orchestra's arranger and had penned works such as "Sleigh Ride" and "The Syncopated Clock." Anderson's songwriting partner was to be Arnold Horwitt, who had contributed both sketches and lyrics for the Broadway revue *Make Mine Manhattan* and was also in the process of writing sketches for another upcoming Broadway revue, *Two's Company*, which was to star another screen icon, Bette Davis.

By the beginning of October, a first rehearsal date of December 8 was set and a trio of tryout engagements scheduled. Now known as *A Likely Story*, the musical would play stints in New Haven, Boston, and Philadelphia during the first two months of 1953 before premiering on Broadway on February 18. Sam Zolotow, in the October 8, 1952, edition of the *New York Times*, announced all of this and went on to note that Russell had yet to sign a contract for the production but was still its presumed star. According to Zolotow, she was due in New York the next day to meet with Fryer, Abbott (who was on board as director), and the quartet of writers. The reporter also informed his readers that Russell had "read the first draft and is said to have recommended some changes."

A significant part of the meeting was to be Anderson and Horwitt playing their score for Fryer, Abbott, Fields, Chodorov, and Russell. As Russell recalls in her autobiography, *Life Is a Banquet*: "Since I don't know one note from another, I watched Fryer and Fields' faces. They looked despondent, so after the composer had left, I shook my head. 'It wasn't very good,' I said." Given that she had been on the fence about the project, she used the Anderson-Horwitt audition as an excuse to bow out of the production, telling the assembled group, "I really must be excused. The music is no good, and I cannot do the play."[9]

Abbott, in his memoir, *Mister Abbott*, writes: "In this dilemma I turned to my old friends, Betty Comden and Adolph Green. They read the book and liked it, and they suggested getting Leonard Bernstein to write the music."

Bernstein, it turned out, was interested and free, and so Fryer returned to Russell with news of the new songwriting team. She still wasn't sure, and in her book, Russell says that it wasn't until he asked her, "If we put this show on with you for just three months, would you do it?" that she was swayed. She knew that it would be impossible for him to see a return of his investment in such a short period of time, but his reasoning that he "could get it off the ground" with her and then "keep it flying with someone else" both made sense and touched her as a gesture of friendship.

Russell was on board, and Comden, Green, and Bernstein had just over a month to write a complete score for a new Broadway musical.

Interestingly, Fields and Chodorov were not convinced that the musical needed to stay rooted in its original 1930s milieu, but Comden and Green disagreed. "Greenwich Village today and the Village of the thirties are quite different," they wrote in an article for the August 1953 issue of *Theatre Arts* shortly after the musical opened. Of course, they knew this from their firsthand experiences in the area in the days leading up to their lives as colleagues.

Even more important to the songwriting team was "what the thirties meant musically. It gave us an approach to the entire score." To Comden, Green, and Bernstein the era encompassed "the big-band sound of Benny Goodman, the nervous delicate saxophone 'doo-doots' of Hel Kemp, [and] the characteristic Eddy Duchin vamp."[10] Their arguments swayed Fields and Chodorov, and the musical remained in the original time period of McKenney's experiences and stories.

To meet what would seem to be an almost impossible deadline, the trio holed up in Bernstein's apartment. As Bernstein's sister, Shirley, vividly related, "They worked 18 hours a day, shut away in Lenny's dark, gloomy studio. . . . I remember many an evening during these weeks when I visited with Felicia. We would be sitting chatting in the living room, not far from the closed door of the studio. There would be no sign of the threesome, only an occasional concerted shriek of laughter and the sound of the piano dimly heard."[11]

Of course, they were not only writing the entire score for the musical in the span of weeks but also having to craft songs that would fit Russell's voice. The star recalled delaying the moment when she would first sing for the composer, dodging out of meetings alongside Abbott. The star recalled, "Finally Bernstein said decisively, 'Please don't leave today, Roz, when the others do. I can't continue writing the score until you sing for me. I have to know your range.' 'Mountain range? . . . Gas range? . . . Firing range?'" I quipped. I continued my delaying tactics for several days."[12]

Russell couldn't avoid the inevitable, and she did finally sing for the composer, as well as Comden and Green. "They heard me sing a couple of times," she said after she had opened in the show, adding, "Then they said that they weren't worried any more, that they were sure my singing could be heard to the limits of Yankee Stadium."[13]

The songwriting team completed the score by their deadline, and in that five-week period they penned more than a dozen numbers, the majority of which would be heard when the show opened on Broadway only three months later. Bernstein, working for the first time on writing a period show, let his musical imagination fly, and from the Western-sounding "Ohio" to the Cab Calloway–esque sections of "Swing!," his melodies evoke a gamut of styles that would have been popular in the mid-1930s.

Comden and Green, in turn, outfitted the songs with lyrics that could move audiences with unexpected simplicity, such as Eileen's short outbursts of "It's so/I don't know/I'm so/I don't know" in "It's Love." Elsewhere, their work amuses with references to boldface names of the era, such as Charles G. Dawes, a prominent businessman who was both no stranger to scandal and vice president under Calvin Coolidge as well as an ambassador for Herbert Hoover; and Warden Lawes, who would have been head of Sing Sing at the time the musical takes place. These references, along with one to an old friend, Mitzi Green, crop up in the climactic Act One "Conga!" number as Ruth attempts to interview a group of Brazilian navy cadets.

Beyond their work as lyricists, the writers lent their satirical bent to the show by penning a trio of vignettes that brought to life Ruth's short stories that she was shopping around to various New York magazines. These contributions parodied styles ranging from Noël Coward's rarified drawing-room works to Clifford Odets's gritty urban dramas. In these, Comden and Green mirror the revised tone that Fields and Chodorov gave McKenney's stories in their first adaptation. From the play through the film through the musical, the two men freely changed details from the original stories, most often in a spirit of making it seem as if both Ruth and Eileen were unsophisticated naïfs from the Midwest.

In point of fact, McKenney was anything but a wide-eyed rube when she arrived in New York, and on some levels her stories about her childhood echo Comden's own. Just as Comden encountered Coward's film *The Scoundrel* while still in her teens, McKenney took in the playwright's then-scandalous work *The Vortex* when it toured to her native Ohio. Further—and just as Comden does in her memoir—McKenney writes about her teenage impressions of the play with insight.

Given the similarity between the two women, it might have been understandable if Comden had fought to undo some of Fields and Chodorov's revisions, but instead she and Green helped to sustain Ruth's unsophisticated air in their book vignettes. In the process they echoed their Revuers' parodies of hackneyed genres—Ruth gives one of her tales the title of *For Whom the Lion Roars*—all the while reinforcing the sense that Ruth needs to grow as an author before she will be able to attain success.

Interestingly, and despite Comden and Green's adherence to this aspect of Fields and Chodorov's book, Abbott recalled in his memoir, *Mister Abbott,* that the writers bristled at the satire the lyricists were injecting into the show. This led to a rehearsal period that Abbott characterized as having "more hysterical debate, more acrimony, more tension, and more screaming" than "any other production [he] was ever involved with."

Just before Christmas and just before the difficult rehearsal period, the show was christened *Wonderful Town* and Abbott finalized casting, notably choosing Edith Adams (who had yet to adopt the more casual "Edie" as her professional moniker) to play Eileen. At the time she was an actress-singer at the start of her career with a handful of television credits, including an appearance on television opposite her future husband, Ernie Kovacs. Other members of the company included George Gaynes, formerly George Jongeyans, who had distinguished himself in opera roles and played Jupiter in *Out of This World* (the Cole Porter musical that for a while had a Comden-Green book), who played a magazine editor Ruth develops a personal interest in; and Cris Alexander (from the original company of *On the Town*), who was playing Frank, Eileen's sweet Walgreen's manager beau. The cast even boasted a member of the original *My Sister Eileen* company: Joseph Buloff was slated to reprise his performance as Ruth and Eileen's landlord. The show also featured one notable future Broadway luminary in its ensemble: Joe Layton, who would go on to distinguish himself as a director-choreographer on Broadway and beyond. And the production's stage manager, and the understudy for the role of Frank, was none other than Harold Prince.

As an indication of how the material was evolving during the final weeks of 1952, both Buloff and Beverley Bozeman, who was to play one of the young women's neighbors, departed the company before 1953 dawned because their roles had significantly changed. Taking their places were Henry Lascoe, who came to the show from the original company of *Call Me Madam,* and Michele Burke, another Broadway vet, whose most recent credit was Abbott's *Where's Charley?*

On January 19, less than two months after Comden and Green began work on the project, *Wonderful Town* played its first performance at New Haven's Shubert Theatre as producer Fryer had originally planned. In this fabled spot for Broadway-bound shows the musical received positive notices, including what could be construed as essentially a rave in the January 21 issue of *Variety*. Critic "Bone." noted that even though audiences were familiar with the material, the show "engenders plenty of laughs" and that "lyrics of a couple of good comedy songs add to the general merriment."

Despite such praise, Abbott and the writers knew that the show needed work, but they had to wait before they could make certain changes. The *Variety* critic did forecast one potential pitfall, noting that the production might be in danger due to "the loss of [Russell's] voice or complete exhaustion." In these words there appears to have been some prescience. On the day the review ran, Russell had a temperature of 101, necessitating the cancellation of that evening's show. The following day Patricia Wilkes played the role with only a day's rehearsal. Russell returned to the show on January 23 and played the rest of the New Haven run, which ended the next day.

When the show opened two days later at Boston's Shubert Theater, the creators had made two major cuts to the production. The first was the excision of a ballet that opened the second act. Lehman Engel, *Wonderful Town*'s musical director and conductor, described it as "an excellent and complex jazz piece," and yet from the moment he heard it he said, "I knew it was wrong for a second-act opening to so light a play."[14]

The second trim was to one of Adams's numbers, "Let It Come Down." In her autobiography, *Sing a Pretty Song*, Adams describes the diegetic number as "a sophisticated throbby dirge." She also notes that she wasn't sorry to have it taken away, saying, "Even as a newcomer, I realized that this bluesy minor-key number wasn't going to work seven minutes from the end of the show." While the song was cut, the music itself remained in the show as "Ballet at the Village Vortex," a dance sequence that leads into the musical's climax. The complexity of Bernstein's work on this number can be heard in recordings, and one can understand why Robert "Red" Ginzler, when invoicing for the orchestration for this section, wrote that the fee was for "twenty-seven pages of blood."[15]

Reviews on January 27 in Boston again were for the most part positive. Cyrus Durgin in the *Boston Globe* called it "a gay and winning show," but Edwin F. Melvin in the *Christian Science Monitor* that day was less enthusiastic, noting that the show gave "the impression of being a repetition of the play with some added music and dances rather than an integrated work in its own right."

During the production's two weeks in Boston, the creators continued to tinker with it, most notably the beginning. In New Haven, the show's second number had been "Lallapalooza," which was delivered by Mr. Appopolous, the man who becomes Ruth and Eileen's landlord. In Boston the number was performed on some nights and not others, as indicated by inserts for the theater's playbill.

By the time *Wonderful Town* reached its final tryout engagement in Philadelphia, the song had been cut from the show entirely. Ironically, it wasn't the first time that Bernstein had seen this piece of music fall to the wayside from a show on the road. He originally wrote the melody in 1950 for *Peter Pan*, which starred Jean Arthur, and there too the number was cut prior to its Broadway opening.

Beyond excising "Lallapalooza," the authors also replaced the show's first number, "Self Expression," which introduced the zeitgeist of the Village in the mid-1930s. From the outset Engel felt that it was wrong for the musical, characterizing it as "complicated, argumentative, and too 'special' for so simple a comedy as *Wonderful Town*."[16]

Despite the fact that the creators and Abbott made two wholesale cuts between New Haven and Boston, they were initially reticent to do anything but attempt to revise and rework "Self Expression." Eventually, Russell delivered an ultimatum, according to Engel; it was that number or her.

In light of this, Bernstein, Comden, and Green huddled together. They were joined by Jerome Robbins, who had been called in to help Abbott and choreographer Donald Saddler, a veteran Broadway hoofer who was getting his first chance at creating dances for a show. From their working sessions the team developed "Christopher Street." Green recalled that the new opening started *Town* "in exactly the right way [and] made a tremendous difference." He added, "Jerry staged it perfectly,"[17] and Engel recalled that "after its introduction into the show in Philadelphia the entire act glowed."[18]

Themes of "self-expression" remained in the replacement, but this new tune expanded the song, so that it provided theatergoers with both a lighter and less angry context for the sensibilities of the time as well as the neighborhood itself. Interestingly, "Christopher Street" became one of the numbers that *Philadelphia Inquirer* critic Henry T. Murdock singled out in his February 10 review, which exclaimed, "The musical comedy the season's been waiting for is now at the Forrest."

Still the creators were at work on the piece, and before *Wonderful Town* departed Philadelphia it acquired a hilarious new number for Russell's Ruth: "One Hundred Easy Ways to Lose a Man." In a feature the actress wrote for the *Saturday Evening Post* in September 1962, she recalled its genesis: "When *Wonderful Town* was in its tryout period on the road, before the Broadway opening, I suggested the trio write me a number about the fact that I couldn't get a man. 'It will help the audience understand the character.'"

The writers asked her if she meant a kind of blues number, and as she remembered explaining in her *Life* story: "Not a blues song, that's when you've had a man and he's done left you. Maybe it will help if I tell you something about me. When I was a girl, I'd go to a football game with a boy and say, 'The next play is going to be an end run,' and he'd say 'You're crazy. It'll be a forward pass.' Then, they'd run an end, and I'd never see him again."

Comden and Green embellished on this story and created others, and Bernstein penned a properly staccato and slightly edgy melody for the lyric, resulting in a song that was inserted into the show during its second week in Philadelphia.

Abbott and the writers continued to tinker with the show, and before its February 25 opening at Broadway's Winter Garden Theatre they had shifted this song's placement and recast the role of the man who opened the show as "the Guide" in "Christopher Street."

On February 26 the cast and creative team were able to savor raves such as Brooks Atkinson's in the *New York Times*, which described *Wonderful Town* as "the most uproarious and original musical carnival we have had since 'Guys and Dolls.'" He went on to write that Comden and Green "have written some extraordinarily inventive lyrics in a style as unhackneyed as [Bernstein's] music."

Similarly, in his review for the *Daily News*, John Chapman noted that Bernstein, Comden, and Green might expect some numbers such as "A Quiet Girl" and "It's Love" to become jukebox hits and then went on to praise them for writing beyond popular appeal. "Their principal aim has been to make songs and music fit the show. This finesse is what gives *Wonderful Town* a superior score."

THE PITFALLS OF SUCCESS

Even before it opened, *Wonderful Town* was playing, according to a report in the March 4, 1953, edition of *Variety*, to "standee houses at all performances." After the reviews appeared it became the hottest ticket on Broadway. As with any hit show, a paucity of tickets caused grumblings among those who were unable to get in, but in the case of *Wonderful Town* resentment poured onto the "Letters to the Editor" pages of New York's papers where writers also complained about ticket brokers' prices and the sightlines at the Winter Garden. As an indication of what a tough ticket the show was, Ethel Merman reportedly paid $85 (or nearly $770 in 2017) for a ticket to see it one week after it opened.

For New Yorkers unable to secure tickets and for Americans unable to reach New York to see the musical, a cast album was in stores by the beginning of April. Before that, two cover versions of "Ohio," from Bing Crosby and Lisa Kirk, had reached stores, and by the end of March it was among the top 30 songs on radio, according to *Variety*.

Comden and Green were able to savor their success with this musical they hadn't planned on writing even as they were being lauded for their work on *Singin' in the Rain*. Just weeks after *Wonderful Town* opened they received a Screenwriters Guild Award for their screenplay for the movie. This honor was followed in short order with their first Tony Award, which they received when *Wonderful Town* was honored as best musical.

For Comden the spring held an even more significant reason for celebration, as she and her husband, Steven Kyle, welcomed their second child into the world. On May 23 she gave birth to a boy, whom the couple named Alan.

These happy events were, however, tempered by some bittersweet happenings during the spring of 1953, but with summer's arrival they would find additional acclaim coming their way, as well as new projects for both stage and screen.

CHAPTER 9

Serious Screen Fare,
but Flying High on Stage

Just before Comden's son was born, she and Green witnessed an unfortunate series of events unfolding around *Wonderful Town*. As with many highly anticipated shows, groups bought blocks of tickets to use as fundraising events. One charity was the Speyer Hospital for Animals, which purchased some 300 tickets for the evening performance on April 8, 1953. The *National Guardian*, an independent weekly with a left-leaning editorial policy, scooped up another allotment of tickets for that same performance.

Word of this latter group's use of tickets to raise money that would help it continue operations reached the press, in particular *New York Daily News* columnist Ed Sullivan, whose writing was syndicated nationally. After he learned of the *National Guardian's* intent, Sullivan railed at the publication in a March 9 column for "forever raising money to trumpet the party line" and exhorted Russell in print to "step out of this April 8 job for the Kremlin."

Producer Robert Fryer debated for a week about what he should do regarding the situation. He even explored whether it would be feasible to schedule an additional performance later in the week to accommodate ticketholders in the event he cancelled the show for the night of the April 8. In the end, an extra performance was not possible, and Fryer had no choice but to cancel and hope that the show would not be tainted by it all. As he did, the *National Guardian* issued a statement that retaliated against a writer like Sullivan, who "with a few blows on his typewriter, can close a Broadway theater."[1] In short order, Fryer's decision was condemned by artists such as playwright Elmer Rice and debated in letters sent to newspaper editors.

These unpleasant events faded almost as quickly as they developed and, as was the case with Judy Holliday's testimony in Washington just over a year earlier, the brouhaha did not taint Comden and Green's reputation; it only served as an all-too-vivid reminder of how dangerous the times were.

Though not as unpleasant, Allyn McLerie's divorce from Green came shortly after the storm over the April 8 *Wonderful Town* performance, but even though this was not a happy moment, there were no recriminations to be heard from either party as the marriage ended. In fact, Green had a hand in McLerie's remarriage. One night at *Wonderful Town* he introduced his former wife to the show's male lead, George Gaynes. He and she began dating and before 1953 ended they were engaged.

A few years later columnist Leonard Lyons ran into Green and McLerie at a nightclub. When they married, Lyons had suggested that Judge Ferdinand Pecora officiate. The columnist also assured the couple that all of the weddings that this particular judge conducted ended in total happiness. On the evening in question, Lyons admitted to feeling guilty about having made such a promise. To which McLerie replied, "But you were so right. All parties involved are happy now." She went on to reiterate why, ending with, "I'm happily married to George Gaynes,"[2] and it was a union that lasted until his death in 2016.

But well before McLerie's trip to Alabama for her divorce from Green, and as Comden spent time at home with husband Steven Kyle and their daughter and newborn son, Green headed to England for a working vacation: to discuss a UK production of *Wonderful Town* with potential producers. The overseas jaunt also allowed him to be on hand to celebrate the coronation of Queen Elizabeth II. In a June 2 column Earl Wilson reported about the royal doings, noting that not only was Green in London but so too were producer David Selznick, theater owner and producer Lee Shubert, and writer Nunnally Johnson, among others. Wilson lamented that he would not be seeing these celebrities for 12 hours while he was in his seat on the Mall to watch the procession to and from Buckingham Palace. The columnist then noted, however, that he would be enjoying the company of all of them that evening at a ball hosted by Perle Mesta, the socialite-ambassador who inspired the central character in *Call Me Madam*.

Green returned to the states shortly after these festivities and just in time for the premiere engagement of *The Band Wagon* at Radio City Music Hall on July 8. With this film, more so than any they had previously written, Comden and Green's contribution was thoroughly championed. Bosley Crowther recognized them in the opening sentence of his *New York Times* review on July 9: "That wonderful talent for satire which Betty Comden and Adolph Green possess and which was gleefully turned upon the movies in their script for last year's 'Singin' in the Rain' is even more gleefully let loose upon the present-day musical stage in their book for Metro's 'The Band Wagon.'"

Otis L. Guernsey Jr. in the *New York Herald Tribune* that same day also opened with praise of the writers. He stated that they had "written another sparkling musical" that was "nudging the modern theater with the same pointed satire as in their story of early sound pictures." Both writers would further laud the film and Comden and Green's work in thought-piece assessments later in July, and then, in August, as *The Band Wagon* began to play in cities around the country, new paeans to the film began appearing. One was Richard L. Coe's in the *Washington Post* on July 25, in which the critic stated that *The Band Wagon* "is probably the best movie musical I've ever seen." Coe said that it was "on a par with *An American in Paris* and some people will like it more."

It's hardly surprising that on the heels of this success there would be speculation about what Comden and Green's next MGM project would be. Starting in August there were rumors. Hedda Hopper announced that Freed had them working on a screenplay for a picture that would reteam Astaire and Charisse. It would, she said, "be named for a song."[3] By the end of the year any notion that the writers would be working on such a project vanished; columnists around the country began discussing the next Comden and Green movie, described by Thomas M. Pryor in the December 28 edition of the *New York Times* as one with "a cavalcade of Cole Porter music." The picture was to be Gene Kelly's follow-up to his then-current project, the movie version of *Brigadoon*. In fact, the new film would fall to the wayside as Comden and Green began to work on another piece for the actor-dancer-director, but a film with music by Porter would continue to be on their docket for the next several years.

The movie that became a reality for the writers and Kelly was *It's Always Fair Weather*. As Thomas M. Pryor explained to his *New York Times* readers on May 8, 1954, "In figuring out the course of out [sic] a story framework for the Porter musical they hit upon another idea and after discussing it with Mr. Kelly and Arthur Freed, the producer, agreement was reached to proceed first with the picture called 'Fair Weather.'"

In point of fact, *It's Always Fair Weather* wasn't a new idea for Comden and Green. The story about three servicemen who reunite years after their tour of duty together had come to them while they were taking their three-day cross-country train ride to California when Freed summoned them for *Singin' in the Rain*.

In a letter to Bernstein, Comden described their idea. It had "a post-war theme, capturing, we hoped some of that Age of Anxiety feeling."[4] Specifically, they imagined four men who had been comrades-at-arms during the war and who discovered as civilians that the differences between them, which were leveled while they were fighting, reasserted themselves. Ultimately, she felt that the idea wasn't right for the time, and she and Green set it aside.

With the storyline back on their minds, they completed a rough draft by April 1954 and sent it to the principals involved, including Frank Sinatra, as they hoped he would consider appearing in the film. At that juncture, even though Sinatra and Kelly would be reuniting in roles similar to the ones they played in the *On the Town* movie, Comden and Green had not written a strict sequel. The character they envisioned Sinatra playing was that of Angie, a sweet guy who, after his service, settles into a quiet life in upstate New York with a wife and kids.

Sinatra, however, would not be able to do the movie because of another commitment at Warner Brothers: *Young at Heart*, which was inspired by a song penned by composer Johnny Richards and lyricist Carolyn Leigh, the latter being someone with whom Comden and Green would soon be associated. Further, given the upswing that Sinatra's career had taken after winning the Academy Award for *From Here to Eternity*, MGM brass, in the process of implementing austerity measures, worried that he might demand too high a salary for the film. Ultimately, the picture, which Kelly would once again co-direct and co-choreograph with Stanley Donen, came to feature Dan Dailey, who had just wrapped *There's No Business Like Show Business* for 20th Century Fox and came to MGM on loan from that studio, and Michael Kidd, the man who choreographed *The Band Wagon*, in a rare onscreen role.

It's Always Fair Weather focuses on a trio of army buddies who, on the first night they are back in New York as civilians, vow to meet 10 years later on October 11, 1955. They believe that the friendship and camaraderie they developed and enjoyed while serving together will endure, even after they've gone their separate ways.

After the 10 years elapse, however, the guys find that they are virtual strangers to one another; the disappointments they have faced individually have changed them from carefree young lads just released from the service into disillusioned and slightly bitter men approaching middle age. One of them, Doug (Dailey), had aspired to being a great painter, but in the intervening years he has settled into a comfortable—and highly lucrative—career as an advertising illustrator, specifically for animated television commercials. And while his success in his field has allowed him to amply provide for his wife, it has also meant he has been frequently absent from home, and as the picture begins, his unseen spouse has begun divorce proceedings.

As for Angie (Kidd), his dreams of life as a great chef have gone to the wayside in favor of family life upstate. There he channels his culinary aspirations into something less grand than he ever imagined. He cooks at a roadside diner he owns, the Cordon Blue Burger.

The third, Ted (Kelly), took a blow on his first day back stateside when he received a "Dear John" letter from his fiancée. During the 10 years that have passed he has existed as a gambler-playboy, sometimes living the high life and sometimes a down-on-his-luck "bum." When Ted meets up with

Doug and Angie, his life is on an upswing. He has begun managing the career of a small-time boxer (whom he won in crap game), and as Ted and his friends reconnect, the kid, deliciously named Mariacchi as if for the Mexican music genre, has earned eight consecutive knockouts in the ring.

To lighten what would otherwise have been a maudlin musical look at veterans' lives, Comden and Green concocted a lighter-than-air scenario involving one of the television properties sponsored by a product that Doug represents. The show, *Midnight with Madeline*, is part variety hour and also part *This Is Your Life*, thanks to one segment on it: "Throb of Manhattan," which spotlights a heartwarming—theoretically—human-interest story. The program's hostess (played by *Two on the Aisle* co-star Dolores Gray), who on screen is saccharinely sweet and who off screen is a ruthless diva, likes these pieces to simultaneously inspire her viewers to tears (for the guest) and adoration (for her).

Early in the film she pitches a fit when she learns of a last-minute change in the guest for her evening program. No longer will she be talking with a man who successfully battled alcoholism (he has fallen off the wagon). Instead, she will chat with a man from Queens who has always dreamed of traveling to the Far East, but as he's unable to afford it, he is building a model of the Taj Mahal out of chewing-gum wrappers.

After Madeline's tantrum about this substitution and her announcement that she won't do the show, her program director, Jackie (Cyd Charisse), who's been casually introduced to the three vets, suggests that they be the surprise guests that night. Madeline, figuring she can capitalize on looking like some sort of stellar patriot, eagerly agrees.

Comden and Green fill this aspect of the screenplay with zestful, satirical humor about the television industry. From the zany animated commercials for Klensrite that Doug has created to the ditzy spiel the *Midnight* emcee gives for H2O Cola, a beverage "that's pure as water, as unfattening as water— but boy oh boy, that Cola taste zooms you to the skies," Comden and Green go for the jugular. The caricatured character they create for the show's hostess, Madeline, proves equally cutting. As the broadcast opens she tells the live audience (whom Comden and Green mock, indicating they go madly wild each time some US town is mentioned) that she wants to sing them a song from her new recording, adding, "I hope you just love it. But even if you don't—I don't really care as long as you love me."

The team even manages to inject humor into the three guys' disillusion-ment with one another after they first reconnect. Since they began working together, Comden and Green had a penchant for putting new words to a preexisting melody, which they did when they wrote the lyric for "I Get Carried Away" in *On the Town* to the tune of Rodgers and Hart's "You Mustn't Kick It Around," from *Pal Joey*. At other times they would even mash up two incongruous pieces. Their ability to deliver "La Marseillaise" to the tune of "Take Me Out to the Ball Game" was often heard at benefit performances and private parties.

In *It's Always Fair Weather* they do something similar, and to extremely comedic effect, when the three men are lunching at a very posh restaurant. As a string quartet plays Johann Strauss II's "The Blue Danube Waltz," the men's thoughts are sung in a voice-over with the words set cunningly to the familiar 3/4-time tune. Doug's internal monologue, for instance, begins with "This thing's a bad dream" while Ted's starts "I shouldn't have come." Both phrases lilt with Strauss's rhythm before the familiar "bomp bomp— bomp bomp." Similarly, and once again satirizing television advertising, Madeline pitches Klensrite with a lyric about its cleaning power to the opening chords of Liszt's *Second Hungarian Rhapsody*.

SPOUSAL ASSISTANCE

In early 1954, Carol Channing succeeded Rosalind Russell in *Wonderful Town*, playing Ruth on Broadway until the show ended its run and then on the national tour. Comden and Green were on hand for some rehearsals, as was Comden's husband, Steven Kyle. Channing recalled how he helped her when he saw she was being directed to play the role as Russell had. For a May 17, 1973, story in the *Washington Post*, she told Tom Donnelly that Kyle had said, "Carol isn't Roz, and she shouldn't try to be so brittle and flip. Let her do it her own entirely different way." As a result of this advice, she said, "We ran a year in Chicago."

Beyond their work as the screenwriters for *It's Always Fair Weather*, Comden and Green provided the lyrics for the picture's songs, which had music by André Previn, who had been with MGM for nearly 10 years working as composer, music director, and conductor. With Previn they developed more than a dozen numbers that range from the Sousa-esque "March, March" that underscores the movie's opening montage, a kaleido-scope of the men's wartime experiences, to the razzmatazzy "Music Is Better Than Words," a number for Madeline on her show, to "Time for Parting," a gentle ballad that echoes the team's "Some Other Time" from *On the Town*.

Beyond these familiar-sounding numbers were several others that pushed the boundaries for the sort of music that one would associate with a major MGM movie musical. For instance, there was the jazzy "Situation-wise," a song-and-dance number that Doug delivers while having a mini-breakdown at a posh party with his corporate colleagues and their wives. Beyond its driving jazz sound, it ironically samples tunes such as "I Dream of Jeanie with the Light Brown Hair" and "Be My Love." Lyric-wise, Comden and Green outfit the song with a satirical litany of corporate doublespeak as Doug compounds words with an ending of "-wise." The team had also written one tongue-in-cheek romantic song, "Love Is Nothing but a Racket," which begins as if it were an English madrigal only to transform into something more contemporary, a percussive and lyrically complex round for Ted and Jackie.

After they completed work on the score, Previn recalled how he, Comden, and Green were summoned to studio head Louis B. Mayer's office to play what they had written, and after they finished, Previn remembered Mayer as musing, "What happened to the songs of yesteryear?"[5]

At this, according to Previn, "Adolph reacted instantaneously and sprang into action.... 'Where did I put them? Betty, André, where did we put those songs of yesteryear, can you remember?'" Once Green had finished rifling through desk drawers and shuffling through papers, "Betty murmured something about 'Oh God, Adolph, one step too far,' and we managed to back out of the place."[6]

It's interesting to note that not all of the numbers were written specifically for character or situation, as was Comden and Green's habit when writing for the theater. For instance, Madeline's "Music Is Better Than Words" was originally slotted as a number for Angie, who was to sing it in a restaurant as he attempts to calm a group of unruly kids who are having a meal out with their beleaguered parents.

Such lack of specificity in some of the songwriting does ultimately undermine the team's ambitions for the film. They wanted to explore a serious theme on screen, using a movie musical vernacular. In some instances the team's intent and the final cut of the movie do beautifully meet, most notably in Kelly's solo "I Like Myself," when Ted comes to realize that he has overcome a decade of depression and self-loathing by allowing himself to become emotionally available to Jackie.

But elsewhere the writing team's intent and the demands of being an MGM production prove to be mutually incompatible. This is seen clearly in the way the song "Love Is Nothing but a Racket"—which was filmed but ultimately excised from the final cut—was handled. Knowing that a love duet for Kelly's and Charisse's characters should be part of the equation of the film, Previn, Comden, and Green crafted a song that musically echoes the moment when sparks first fly between the characters as he corrects her on a quotation from Shakespeare she has used. After its provocative opening, Previn transforms the melody into something sultry and modern while Comden and Green create an intricately interwoven lyric.

Kelly and Donen resisted the number but eventually did choreograph and film it, though it was not delivered as the writers originally envisioned.

The song's tempo was speeded up and the overlapping verses were eliminated. Any unique qualities that it had in relation to character or story disappeared in favor of brashness. The sequence was ultimately cut, and while Comden, Green, and Previn may have been relieved that moviegoers did not see this incarnation of the song they had so carefully developed, Comden would later ruefully comment, "Who ever heard of a musical where the lovers don't sing a duet?"[7]

Comden and Green's final draft for *It's Always Fair Weather* carries a date of August 23, 1954, and Kelly and Donen began shooting in October. But before Comden and Green finished their last-minute ministrations to the screenplay and while preproduction was progressing, there was also a new and very sudden theatrical project on their docket: They were abruptly called in to provide material for a new production of *Peter Pan* starring Mary Martin.

KEEPING PACE ARTISTICALLY WITH THE LATEST TECHNOLOGY

For *It's Always Fair Weather*, Gene Kelly and Stanley Donen contended with creating visuals that would take advantage of (and accommodate) MGM's recently introduced Cinemascope format. Artists, however, weren't the only ones dealing with studios' efforts to make films more spectacular visually. Movie theaters had to adapt as well. *Variety* reported on June 10, 1953, that Radio City Music Hall execs held private screenings "at midnight and later" to determine what screen size would best showcase each upcoming film being shown there. Comden and Green eventually skewered Cinemascope in a sketch for the 1960 television special *The Fabulous Fifties* that looked back on the highs and lows of the decade.

Much like *Wonderful Town*, the new *Peter Pan* had been in development as Comden and Green were working on their most recent film. In January 1954, Edwin Lester, producer of the San Francisco and Los Angeles Light Opera Associations, announced his plans to present a new production of *Peter Pan* during the summer in California, with audience fave Martin in the title role and staging by Jerome Robbins. As time passed, Broadway and television producer Leland Hayward—who among other things was the man behind the famed *Ford 50th Anniversary Show*, which featured a lengthy duet for Martin and Ethel Merman staged by Robbins—became involved with this new venture. With Hayward's addition to the production, speculation grew that these West Coast engagements were essentially lead-ins to an eventual Broadway run.

In March, a pair of neophyte songwriters was added to the production. This *Peter Pan* would feature songs by Carolyn Leigh, whose lyric for Sinatra's hit "Young at Heart" had impressed Martin, and composer Mark "Moose" Charlap, with whom Leigh had just begun collaborating. The two would ultimately come to outfit the show, which was using an adaptation of Barrie's original script created by Robbins, with nearly a dozen songs.

As the spring progressed, the cast grew to include, among others, Cyril Ritchard, an Australian-born performer with a long string of Broadway credits, both dramatic and musical, as Captain Hook and Mr. Darling; long-time Robbins dance associate Sondra Lee as Tiger Lily; a Broadway new-comer, Kathy Nolan, as Wendy; and in the role of the Darlings' maid, Martin's daughter, Heller Halliday.

Peter Pan opened its first California engagement at San Francisco's Curran Theatre on July 19. Reviews were supportive, and the production was playing to capacity, recording-breaking crowds. Nevertheless, it was a troubled show. As *Variety* reviewer "Soan." noted on July 21, "[It] would be a little difficult for anyone unfamiliar with the Barrie story to understand just what it is all about." Further, the critic observed, "Miss Martin is in the rather curious position of functioning as a subordinate player." In his July 20 *Oakland Tribune* review, Wood Soanes was blunter: "'Peter Pan,' as it stands, is a musical that is sorely in need of a play doctor and director."

At this juncture Robbins put out a call to Comden and Green, with whom he'd created *On the Town* and for whom he had just done some out-of-town show-doctoring himself just a year before, and Jule Styne, with whom he had worked on *High Button Shoes*. All three were in southern California, and they traveled north to take a look at the show. Green remembered what happened once the curtain was down: "We all told Jerry afterward that the show could be saved."[8]

Robbins and the producers were willing to allow Styne, Comden, and Green the opportunity to write a score from scratch, but they didn't want to oust Charlap and Leigh, who had, in Comden's opinion, "written some very nice things." She went on to say, "They were young people with their first show. We certainly didn't want to push them out." The problem in her mind was that they had "the play with songs," rather than a full-scale musical.[9]

The producers announced the addition of the trio to the *Peter Pan* team on August 5, a little more than a week before the production was slated to end its San Francisco engagement and move to Los Angeles's Philharmonic Auditorium for an August 17 opening. Given the timing and Comden and Green's other commitments, large-scale changes and additions couldn't be made, but by the time *Peter Pan* hit Los Angeles, they had contributed one new song, the piquant ode to the title hero's home, "Never Never Land." Comden recalled why they added this song: "The first thing we said was it needs an overall theme, a big song that expresses Barrie and expresses the feeling of *Peter Pan*," and, as Green added, "expresses Mary Martin, the star of *Peter Pan*."[10]

This lone addition inserted before the Los Angeles opening belies the myth—created by or at least endorsed by Comden, Green, and Styne—that the trio wrote all of their material for *Peter Pan* in eight days.

The single tune from the team wasn't enough to sway the *Los Angeles Times*'s Albert Goldberg. In his August 18 review he echoed his Bay Area colleagues, writing of the Charlap-Leigh score: "It is good show music in its fashion but its melodies are not outstanding nor are the lyrics of Carolyn Leigh the kind to match Barrie's fanciful prose." Goldberg didn't even mention the Styne-Comden-Green contribution. This was not the case in a follow-up review from *Variety*, which ran a week later. In this write-up, critic "Scho." mentioned the tune by name, but only after pointing out that Leigh and Charlap "had failed to provide a single outstanding song." "Scho." also informed readers that more new songs were to be written and inserted as *Peter Pan* continued in Los Angeles.

To facilitate their work on the musical, Comden and Green got a deadline extension for their final version of the screenplay for *It's Always Fair Weather*. Eventually, they wrote an additional seven numbers for *Peter Pan*, including the comic, Eastern European–tinged "Mysterious Lady," in which Peter teases Captain Hook. The writers infuse this tune with some delightful meta-theatrics as Peter, being played by a woman, pretends to be one, giving Martin, as the boy who won't grow up, the chance to display her coloratura soprano.

Styne later recalled the impetus behind the number, explaining that Charlap and Leigh "missed the boat you know. They didn't have a duet for the two stars."[11] The show had, in fact, opened in San Francisco with a number for Martin and Ritchard, "I'm Hook," but the tune had either been cut by the time Styne saw the production or had simply failed to register with the veteran tunesmith. Curiously, Leigh wrote this song not with Charlap but with Roger Adams, the show's assistant conductor.

The addition of the Comden-Green-Styne team to the production was enough to convince Martin to move forward with taking it to New York, and by the end of August the opening date and theater for *Peter Pan* had been confirmed. The show would bow at Broadway's Winter Garden Theater (recently home to *Wonderful Town*) on October 20. Hayward, however, had to bow out as the show's producer for health reasons, and in his stead Martin's husband and manager, Richard Halliday, stepped in, presenting what was billed as "Edwin Lester's Production."

As *Peter Pan* continued its run in Los Angeles, Robbins implemented more changes. By September 19, just a month after the show's opening there, Lewis Funke reported in the *New York Times* that six new songs had been integrated into the show, and among the newest additions were "Wendy," "Ugg-a-Wug," and "Captain Hook's Waltz." The last is a Viennese confection from Styne that's worthy of the Strausses, and Comden and Green set a lyric to it that contains the sort of wordplay found in Gilbert and Sullivan's patter songs, that Green had so hungrily committed to memory as a child.

Comden and Green also collaborated with Robbins on revisions to the show's book. "Jerry was quite worried about the book being too long or too wordy. So we did some work with it, more or less cutting, trimming, or rearranging it."[12] One specific sequence the writers added involves the scene in which Wendy tells the Lost Boys the all-too-similar ends of various fairy tales before relating the end of Shakespeare's *Hamlet*. After hearing about all of the characters who die in the tragedy, the boys still want to know what happened. Wendy says, "Well, the rest of them lived happily ever after!" It's quintessential Comden and Green humor that beautifully mirrors the dryness found in Barrie's original script and stories.

Peter Pan played to record-making capacity crowds (despite the reviews) during its Los Angeles engagement, which ultimately was extended by three weeks until October 9. After this the company headed east and settled into the Winter Garden, giving two preview performances before the show's official opening.

When the reviews ran on October 21 there was little doubt that *Peter Pan* was a personal triumph for Martin, who had, as she told *Oakland Tribune* reporter Wood Soanes just before the production opened in San Francisco, "dreamed of doing a musical version of 'Peter Pan' for 12 years." Brooks Atkinson in the *New York Times* extolled her: "Miss Martin, looking trim and happy, is the liveliest Peter Pan in the record book." Robert Coleman in the *Daily Mirror* went a step further: "She is nothing less than magnificent." And Walter Kerr in the *New York Herald Tribune* wrote, "Miss Martin and her musical-comedy version of 'Peter Pan' are sky-high with joy."

Among the cheers that Martin—as well as Ritchard and the flying effects—received, however, were less charitable comments. Kerr didn't believe that the show's music and lyrics were "all that Sir James Barrie's indestructible fantasy deserves," and in the *Daily News*, John Chapman stated simply, "The songs will do."

Still, the sense of whimsy that Martin (and Robbins's production overall) delivered instilled delight in audiences. And given the crowd-pleasing nature of the musical, along with Martin's popularity from touring productions of *South Pacific* and *Annie Get Your Gun* and numerous special musical presentations on television, there was soon considerable speculation about whether she would bring this *Peter Pan* to television, as had been the plan when Leland Hayward was the show's producer.

Eventually, the executives at NBC and all of the parties involved with the show, from the star through the writers and director-choreographer, were able to agree on terms, financial and otherwise, for a live broadcast. After the production ended its limited engagement at the Winter Garden on February 26, work and rehearsals began almost immediately for a March 7, 1955, air date. As Jo Coppola noted in a glowing review in *Newsday* the following day: "The production marked the first occasion that a Broadway play, right from a successful run, was transported intact—the cast, director, full orchestra, scenery and costumes—from a theater to television."

It was a broadcast event that attracted some 65 to 75 million viewers, which represented, according to a *Variety* report two days later, "up to 21,000,000 homes...or about two-thirds of the television sets in circulation." *Peter Pan* on the small screen also prompted columnists to write hopefully about the future of this nascent medium. In his March 8 review in the *New York Times*, Jack Gould wrote, "Last night's treat makes us hungry for more." Five days later he championed the idea of similar transfers: "The theatre and television need each other, artistically and economically. Happily, they already are complementary, not competitive. As the years go by many ways will be found in which they can cooperate."

And though efforts to bring theater to audiences electronically would prove only fitfully successful for the next 40 years, the success of this broadcast prompted NBC to schedule a second presentation, also live, in January 1956.

A WEST END BOW

By 1955, Comden and Green's film work had been hailed in the UK by critics and savored by moviegoers, but their stage musicals had yet to be seen there. *Wonderful Town* changed that, and just days before *Peter Pan* had its nationwide airing in the United States, the show opened at the Prince's Theatre. The musical excited some critics, such as Kenneth Tynan, who, in a February 27 review in the *Observer*, remarked that it "is head and shoulders above anything of its kind since 'Guys and Dolls.'" The production failed, however, to excite British theatergoers and folded after only 207 performances.

Comden and Green celebrated one last opening in 1955: the premiere of *It's Always Fair Weather* at Radio City Music Hall on September 15. Roughly two weeks before the film opened, *Variety* critic "Holl." heralded it in an August 24 review as "[a] topnotch musical satire," saying it had "sock entertainment value for family trade with excellent b.o. outlook."

Once the newspaper critics began to weigh in on it, the trade paper's assessment was reiterated by the likes of Bosley Crowther in the *New York Times*, who, in the September 16 edition of the paper, cheered how Comden and Green's script was "howling with derision at such recognizable idiocies of TV as singing and slobbering commercials, audience-participation shows, [and] give-away plugs for mundane products."

That same day, Paul V. Beckley in the *New York Herald Tribune* looked at the film in a deeper manner, recognizing that the team had tackled "a subject pungent enough to strike a chord with several million now de-khakied chests." At the same time he understood how the story was "tossed about in the oil and vinegar of sprightly lyrics and crisp dialogue," all of which amounted to "unquestionably one of the best musicals turned out by the motion picture industry."

As the picture rolled out across the country, critics reveled in both the film's seriousness and its comic bite, but, unlike their previous films, *It's Always Fair Weather* failed to click with moviegoers. Years later the team would reflect on the picture, with Green remembering, "It got great reviews but I don't think the MGM management understood [it], and audiences weren't going to musicals any more because of, withering pause, television." Comden added that in developing the story, "We did write it dark, definitely, definitely," to which Green added, "*Fair Weather* wasn't written to be up."[13]

Regardless of the film's reception at the box office, the picture did linger in the memories of Academy Award nominators, and in February 1956 Comden and Green received their second Oscar nomination for an original screenplay. By that point, however, they had moved forward, working concurrently on both a film and a stage project, and just over a year after the premiere of *It's Always Fair Weather* they were celebrating a theatrical success that lasted almost until the dawn of the 1960s.

CHAPTER 10

Hollywood Passes,
Broadway Says "Yes"

Almost immediately after the opening of *It's Always Fair Weather* in 1955, a new slate of pictures from MGM included the film that had been put to the side in favor of it: the "Cole Porter cavalcade," which originally was announced in late 1953. Beyond being back among the movies MGM was committed to producing, the project now had a title: *Wonderland*. By the end of 1955 Comden and Green were actively promoting their screenplay, telling the *Washington Post*'s Joe Hyams, "We told [the story] to Arthur Freed, our producer; and he loved it. Gene Kelly loved it, so now we think it's a lovely idea."[1]

MGM first slated the picture for a February 1956 production date but eventually delayed that as Comden and Green honed their script, and managerial and philosophical changes continued to evolve at the studio. In the December interview with Hyams, Green made it a point to note that it would be "our last picture for M-G-M under our current contract," indicating that he and Comden were aware of how tenuous long-term commitments in Hollywood were becoming.

Comden and Green turned in the screenplay in February 1956, and in the process of developing the project they opted to spoof themselves (or at least screenwriters in general). They centered *Wonderland* on a pair of Hollywood scribe-producers, Johnny Benson and Hal Conway, who find themselves writing a cinematic musical compendium similar to *Singin' in the Rain* or *The Band Wagon*. Johnny and Hal have convinced their studio to spend a small fortune on the song catalog of the fictional tunesmith Noel Waters (whose canon would be composed of Porter's work). The guys believe that they'll be able to quickly churn out a biopic about Waters based on their assumption that he's had a standard-issue "rags to riches" life. Unfortunately, at their first meeting with him they discover that he's gone from a privileged childhood to an even wealthier adulthood.

Hal and Johnny then have to develop some sort of project that will justify the studio's purchase of the songs and contend with a British stage star, Iris Fielding, who has been brought over to headline the movie. Her presence only complicates the guys' lives further, because, having read too many dime-store novels about the dangers lurking for young women in Tinseltown, she feigns a chilly exterior as she remains ever-vigilant about preserving her virtue.

Comden and Green spin some of their funniest and most satiric material for the fantasies that these three principals have. As Hal and Johnny furiously scramble to develop a scenario that might serve to showcase Waters's songs, they imagine ones ranging from a movie about Henry VIII to a science-fiction escapade. In the former, the guys envision the king delivering "Just One of Those Things" as Anne Boleyn heads to her death. The latter features aliens, who, offended by Earthlings' treatment of the planet, arrive to destroy it but only after singing "Please Don't Monkey with Old Broadway." Beyond their giddy use of Porter's work, Comden and Green jab at the MGM trademark roaring lion: Johnny and Hal's imagined films are preceded by their studio's signature opening, a roaring tiger.

Iris's fertile fantasy life includes one dream in which she's abducted by Hal and Johnny and put through a giant machine that turns her into a cookie-cutter starlet. Comden and Green musicalize the nightmare by having it culminate with Iris and the young women singing Porter's "Give Him the Ooh La La" from *DuBarry Was a Lady*.

In the end, Comden and Green have Johnny and Hal take a meta approach to the story. They develop a screenplay about a British performer who comes to Hollywood with such groundless fears and eventually finds herself romantically involved with the men who are penning the picture she's to star in. Ironically, Hal and Johnny become the bitter rivals that they are writing about as both of them fall for Iris. The only thing that saves the day for all three is that her affections lie elsewhere, making for a happy end for all concerned. The picture can finally go in front of the cameras, and the men's personal and professional relationship is restored to its collegial jocularity.

After they turned their script in, the project languished at MGM. As of June 1956, it remained on Arthur Freed's docket of forthcoming movies, but Freed himself, like Comden and Green, was winding down at MGM. He had been notably absent during the filming of *It's Always Fair Weather*. Further, as Comden recalled, "It wasn't Arthur who had the final word anymore," and Green added, "Arthur was answerable to Dore Schary the way he hadn't been with Louis B."[2] Additionally, MGM and Freed had another Porter movie musical in the works: *Silk Stockings*.

For the studio to stall on one of their scripts was unusual. Comden and Green had seen everything else they turned in go into production almost immediately. But it couldn't have been too bothersome to the writers. They were also at work on a new musical project during the same period, and after they turned in the *Wonderland* draft they were able to concentrate on it fully.

This new stage musical had been part of their lives at least since May 1955, when reports ran that they were at work on a new musical for Leland Hayward, who had been one of the original producers of *Peter Pan*. There were no details about what the show might be about, only that it was to have music by Jule Styne and that Hayward hoped to have it on the boards in the spring of 1956. In addition to having the writing team in place, Hayward also had the show's director-choreographer, Jerome Robbins

STYNE'S OWN *WONDERFUL TOWN*

A movie of *Wonderful Town* was not in the cards because of the tangled issue of rights surrounding Ruth McKenney's stories. A movie musical based on them did, however, hit the screen in late 1955. With five songs featuring music and lyrics by Jule Styne and Leo Robin, *My Sister Eileen* starred Betty Garrett and Janet Blair as the sisters and also featured Bob Fosse as both its choreographer and Eileen's soda fountain–working beau, and while critics all reminded readers about the stage musical, they left comparisons out of their reviews. And much in the way that the film version of *On the Town* never soured Comden, Green, and Leonard Bernstein's friendship, this *Eileen* did nothing to undermine the fruitful collaboration between the writers and composer Styne.

As 1955 progressed, the writers moved forward with Styne on their new project. By October the show had been given the provisional title of *The Bells Are Ringing* and a star. The production would bring Judy Holliday—Comden and Green's old Revuers colleague—back to Broadway. It would be Holliday's first major Broadway appearance since her breakout turn in *Born Yesterday* a decade before. Holliday, who won an Academy Award for her appearance in the film version of the Garson Kanin play, had appeared on the Main Stem in between but only in a brief limited engagement of a revival of Elmer Rice's *Dream Girl*.

With the announcement of Holliday's involvement, the show's basic story line was shared with the public. As Lewis Funke colorfully told his *New York Times* readers on October 16, "The story is about one of the unsung heroines of our time . . . an answering service girl." He also informed readers that the character's "zeal and concern for each of her many subscrib-ers carry her beyond the anonymous realm into their lives."

The idea for the show came to Comden and Green during one of their daily meeting sessions, when they found their productivity was at an ebb. "We were staring at the back of the Manhattan telephone book. I saw an ad for a telephone answering service," Comden recalled. She asked Green about his service, and he said he had never visited it and knew nothing about it. They decided to pay a call on the women who were taking mes-sages for him while he was out, and as he remembered, "We expected a busy, modern place, but instead there was this dilapidated little cellar room and one enormously stout lady at an enormous switchboard."[3]

For the first few months of 1956 the team worked on *Bells* and *Wonderland* concurrently and were even able to use a trip to California in January to confer with Holliday on the former and MGM execs on the latter. By April an outline for the stage musical was in good enough shape to convince Holliday to sign a contract with the Theatre Guild, which, having brought such musicals as *Oklahoma!* and *Carousel* to the stage, had taken over the role of producer of the show.

Working on this new Broadway musical didn't give Comden and Green a break from their bicoastal work habits. In June they—along with com-poser Styne—were back in California discussing the project with Holliday and also auditioning actors for other roles in the show. At this juncture the Guild announced a schedule for *Bells*. It would go into rehearsal in September, followed by tryouts in New Haven, Boston, and Philadelphia. The show's Broadway opening would come at the end of November.

Over the course of the summer various A-list names were mentioned in the press as possibilities for Holliday's leading man, including Lloyd Bridges, Gordon MacRae, Alfred Drake, and John Raitt. Ultimately, the role went to a relative unknown, at least in theater circles: Sydney Chaplin, the son of Charlie Chaplin.

In mid-1956 the younger Chaplin had only a handful of minor movie roles and some stage work in California on his résumé. He had been, how-ever, a good friend of Comden and Green since he was in his teens. In addi-tion, Chaplin and Holliday had met, and by some accounts she had become romantically interested in him. All three felt he had genuine potential for the show and encouraged him to audition for Robbins.

By his own account Chaplin was "horrible"[4] when he read, and yet the writers and star insisted he had potential. Robbins, however, was concerned that Chaplin would never be able to rise to the challenges of being the ro-mantic lead in a new musical. His worries were only magnified by the fact that neither Chaplin nor Holliday considered themselves singers, and both had expressed reservations about the sort of material they would be willing to perform in the show. Holliday, for instance, "insisted she could not sing a straight ballad and would not try."[5]

Robbins reluctantly agreed to casting Chaplin, but with one condition: If he did not prove himself during the first week of tryouts in New Haven, Robbins would be able to replace him.

Even as Robbins was coping with this central casting issue, he also had to deal with another problem—the writers had yet to finish the show's script and score. In early June, with just three months until the start of rehearsals, Robbins approached Raoul Pène Du Bois about designing the production and was able to send only a rough draft of the first act. The director-choreographer took extreme measures to address the issue. He told the writing team, "I'm locking you in my house, then I'll know you're writing. I'll serve you lunch and you can go home at the end of each day."[6] The composer and book writer–lyricists complied, and a script and score were completed in time for the mid-September rehearsals.

It was during this time that the team wrote what would become the musical's stand-alone hit songs, "Just in Time" and "The Party's Over." The melody for the former had been in Styne's "head for years,"[7] and the composer hoped that it would make its way into *Bells*. Unfortunately, Comden and Green could find neither a suitable title nor lyric for the tune. Styne, desperate for advice about the potential song, reportedly turned to Frank Loesser, who told him "keep on rolling it and the words will come up."[8] Styne shared this wisdom with Comden and Green, and in short order they had a title: "Just in Time."

"The Party's Over" came from a title suggestion from the lyricists, and in this instance the title itself inspired Styne instantly. According to the composer's biographer, "Within an hour, Jule had set the beginning of the melody."[9]

The earliest outlines of the show and the roughest drafts of *Bells* all contain the basic arc of the musical that eventually opened on Broadway. Ella Peterson (Holliday) works for her cousin Sue's answering service, Susanswerphone, and Ella takes her job, and the lives of the clients, quite seriously. In addition to relaying messages to them, Ella will, for instance, pretend to be Santa for one mother whose son is particularly unruly. Madame Grimaldi, an opera singer who also subscribes to Susanswerphone, struggles with a cold, and so Ella provides her with a mustard-plaster recipe that gets the singer back in voice.

These helpful perks are relatively unobtrusive, particularly when compared with the ways in which Ella works to help three men who are also Susanswerphone clients. With Blake Barton, a Marlon Brando–wannabe actor, she disguises herself as a fellow beatnik in order to convince him to go to an audition dressed in a suit. With Dr. Kitchell, a dentist who dreams of being a songwriter, she uses information from another client to get the tunesmith to a club where he can audition his work.

And then there's playwright Jeff Moss (Chaplin), who, after a breakup with his longtime writing partner, fills his life with women and alcohol, ignoring his producer's deadlines for a new script. Ella has fallen for Jeff and takes it upon herself to get him back to his typewriter. When she appears at his apartment with a surprising (at least to him) knowledge of his problems, he thinks she has some sort of special gift of insight and promptly falls in love with her. He also gets back to writing in earnest. Jeff finishes his play during a retreat in the country, and his producer, overjoyed with the results, throws a celebratory party in Jeff's honor. It's a fete where Jeff wants to show off Ella, but she feels out of place at the celebrity-filled affair. This fact, combined with her growing realization that he has fallen for her under false pretenses, leads her to bolt. When Jeff goes in search of her, he runs into the two other men she's helped, and they all come to realize that the woman who has aided them is Ella.

Comden and Green weave two other plots into the musical, and both of these stories serve to up the ante on the show's zaniness. The first involves Sue and the man she's dating, a bookie named Sandor, who romances her and promises to help her expand her business. In actuality, Sandor schemes to use the answering service as a cover for his bookmaking operations. His ruse is that Susanswerphone will be taking orders for the classical record company he supposedly owns. Sandor's system replaces track names with composer names, while a symphony number and an opus number represent race and horse number, respectively, and the speed of the recording (33 1/3, 45, etc.) specifies the sort of bet being placed. Comden and Green also weave into their plot the story of an overzealous police detective. This character, convinced that Susanswerphone is nothing more than a cover for some sort of call-girl operation, tails Ella throughout, attempting to gather evidence about her illicit assignations.

It all conspires to create a vision of New York as some sort of fantasy place, not unlike the one found in their first show, *On the Town*, where lives of total strangers perfectly intersect, romance triumphs despite all odds, and even the most curmudgeonly of Manhattanites turns into a softie by someone extending the simplest of friendly gestures on the subway, such as saying "Hello."

If the team's vision of the city harkened back to *Town*, this latter detail, which became an ensemble number, "Hello, Hello There!," dates to the Revuers' radio show. On an episode that aired in April 1940 they performed a sketch in which riders—and the train conductor himself—are reduced to tears by a stranger who utters the two-syllable greeting.

Even if Comden and Green reached into their own trunks of urban sketch material for this number, the remainder of the score for *Bells* brims with zesty originality, particularly Sandor's "Simple Little System," a kind of *schnitzelbank* that outlines the code for the betting system ("Puccini is Pimlico"), and "Drop That Name," another ensemble number in which Ella finds herself snowed by Jeff's celebrity friends as they chat about their famous friends.

COMDEN AND GREEN DROP NAMES

In an early draft of *Bells Are Ringing*, Ella answers the phone for Gloria Vanderbilt's residence. In fact, the heiress was a friend of the writers, and just as they were working on their script Comden took her to Ebbets Field to see a Dodgers game. According to a Leonard Lyons column from May 1956, it was Vanderbilt's first trip to Brooklyn, and as they were driving over the Williamsburg Bridge, she asked Comden where they were. Comden pointed north toward the Gracie Square neighborhood her companion called home, and said, "I'll tell you where we are. We're right in the middle of your view."

Beyond these numbers and the two ballads, Styne outfitted the show with songs that had the sounds of the day, such as "Mu Cha Cha," which capitalized on the cha-cha dance craze of the time, and "You've Got to Do It (On Your Own)," a jazzy tune for Jeff as he works to start on his new play that sounds as if it might have been intended for a swinging nightclub performer of the day. Other tunes work in a more traditional theatrical vein, such as "The Midas Touch," a cheesy diegetic ditty written by the tunesmith dentist, and "Is It a Crime?," a showy solo for Ella as she questions the sanity of not becoming involved in other people's lives. Regardless of a song's style, Comden and Green graced the melodies with sly and smile-inducing gems, such as Jeff's litany of things he could make without a helping hand. He starts with the natural-sounding "martinis" before riffing off to "wienies" and "blinis."

Robbins finalized casting during August and September, and the company came to include Jean Stapleton, who was coming off a stint in *Damn Yankees* and who would go on to immortality as dingbat Edith Bunker on television's *All in the Family*. She was hired to play Ella's boss and cousin, Sue. For the other central male roles Robbins turned to relative newcomers to the Broadway scene. For years Eddie Lawrence had been making a name for himself as a comic monologist in clubs. Having recently embarked on a recording career, he was cast as Sandor. For the two other men whom Ella helps, Robbins chose Bernie West to play the dentist and Frank Aletter as the Brando-esque actor. As with the team's last New York–centric musical, *Wonderful Town*, the show also featured one future choreographer of note in the company, Peter Gennaro, playing a neighborhood delivery boy whose fondness for and knowledge of classical music inadvertently brings down Sandor's betting scheme.

Robbins, who had Bob Fosse at his side as co-choreographer, rehearsed the company starting in mid-September, while Styne was working with the principals on the music. With Holliday he had to resort to some trickery with one number: "The Party's Over." Because the actress had firmly stated she would not sing a ballad in the show, he, as well as Comden and Green, were not sure how to approach her about this tender number. Then Comden and Green remembered how fond Holliday was of singing harmony. Styne taught her the song's melody, telling her that she would be singing it in counterpoint to the chorus. After a few days she asked him what the primary melody was, and Styne said, "You should know. You've been singing it for the last week."[10] Holliday wasn't happy about being duped; nevertheless, she continued to rehearse and eventually introduced the now-classic song on stage.

Once the company got to New Haven they began their final run-through, and during it Holliday stumbled hard into a piece of scenery and braced herself with one hand. Nothing was broken from the accident, but she was advised by a doctor to have her arm in a sling for a couple of days. She fashioned one out of a scarf, and on October 15 played the first public performance of the show with the arm semi-immobilized. The following morning "T.H.P." in the *Hartford Courant* made mention of the injury in a largely negative review and wrote that *Bells Are Ringing* came across as a "very muted chime." Further, the critic characterized Comden and Green's book as "hardly more than a series of skits with a nodding acquaintance." T.H.P. went on to describe Holliday's performance as "just vaguely cute."

The *Variety* review the next day was more encouraging. "Bone." wrote that the show's title was "a tipoff on the action in store for the box office," and after praising the production, from the script through performances, the critic did note that it would benefit from "some 20 minutes of required cutting."

Chaplin, whose job was on the line based on the reception he got in New Haven, proved himself with audiences, critics, and Robbins himself, so he was off to Boston with the rest of the company after the week of performances in Connecticut. The show's second tryout engagement opened on October 23. Once again reviews were tepid overall, and at this, tempers began to flare. One post-performance meeting among the writers, Robbins, and Holliday ended with Styne and Green "snarling at each other, screaming about 'shitty music' and 'shitty lyrics.'"[11] Comden later recalled that she took issue with the scenery, calling it "clumsy and unattractive" and saying, "Jerry should have changed it."[12]

Du Bois's scenery may not have gotten changed, but Comden and Green were working to recalibrate the book, particularly the show's initial scenes, as *Bells* played Boston. They were notably attempting to soften some of the harder edges of Jeff's character, who in initial drafts was portrayed as an extreme womanizer. They had already achieved some of their goal by the time the show reached performances, as the opening scene no longer featured Jeff waking up after a one-night stand with a woman—whose name he's forgotten—still in his apartment.

For performances in New Haven and Boston they had not, however, cut one early blues-y number, "Oogie, Woogie, Shoogie," that Jeff used to forestall dates. He dictated it to Ella over the phone, and she was then to relay it for him. After the opening in Boston, the creators did take the number out, and this helped audiences more readily empathize with the romance between the couple. He became less of a cad, and her infatuation no longer seemed quite so masochistic.

But the roots of the tension that was simmering between the creators ran deeper than their knowledge that the show, so intricately plotted, needed careful recalibration. They were also painfully aware that the show was missing something critical to its success.

From the first performance, Holliday's final number in *Bells* was "The Party's Over," a beautiful song no doubt but also something of a downbeat moment for a star toward the end of a musical. Green would recall that he and Comden both knew that the show needed a big, upbeat number for her at the end, but "we were too pooped to write it."[13]

After the New Haven opening, Holliday mentioned that she, too, felt the show and she needed something toward the end, but again the writers were stymied. It wasn't until *Bells* moved to Boston that Comden, inspired by a novel by François Sagan, finally thought of a potential title for an eleven o'clock number for the star: "I'm Goin' Back to the Bonjour Tristesse Brassiere Company." She shared it with Green, who immediately liked it, and then they took the idea to Styne in his hotel suite. After hearing it, "he began to play an old soft-shoe rhythm."[14] It was a perfect fit, and the trio completed the number, with Robbins staging it in time for the Philadelphia opening.

In the same way that the addition of "Christopher Street" had buoyed *Wonderful Town* when that musical shifted from Boston to Philadelphia, "I'm Going Back" proved to be the number that changed overall perceptions of *Bells Are Ringing*. The morning after the show's November 14 bow, the *Philadelphia Inquirer's* Henry T. Murdock delivered the production's first rave, calling it "a fast and funny musical comedy." He spread accolades evenly among the creative team and cast and then noted that Holliday's "finale number, 'I'm Going Back,' had the customers cheering."

The Revuers: Adolph Green, John Frank, Betty Comden, Alvin Hammer, Judy Holliday. (Photofest)

Writing *On the Town*: Leonard Bernstein, Adolph, Betty, Jerome Robbins. (Photofest)

Publicity for *Singin' in the Rain*: Adolph, Betty, Gene Kelly. (Photofest)

The *Wonderful Town* family: Adolph, Leonard Bernstein, Robert Fryer, John Bruno (back row); Rosalind Russell, Betty, Edie Adams (front row). (Photofest)

Rehearsing *Bells Are Ringing*: Adolph, Betty, Judy Holliday, and Jule Styne. (Photofest)

In performance, 1950s: Betty and Adolph.

Rehearsing *Do Re Mi*: Adolph, David Merrick, Phil Silvers. (Photofest)

Rehearsing *Subways Are for Sleeping*: Sydney Chaplin, Betty. (Photofest)

Striking a familiar pose for *Fade Out–Fade In*: Adolph, Carol Burnett, Betty. (Photofest)

At *Applause* rehearsals: Betty and Adolph. (Photofest)

Publicity shot for *Lorelei*: Adolph, Carol Channing, Betty.

In performance, 1970s: Betty and Adolph. (Photofest)

Candid at *On the Twentieth Century*: Adolph, Larry Fuller, Imogene Coca, John Cullum, Betty, Madeline Kahn. (Photofest)

A Grammy win for *The Will Rogers Follies*: Pierre Cossette, Adolph, Cy Coleman, Betty.

In performance, 1990s: Betty and Adolph.

With the addition of this song the writers provided Holliday with the moment both she and audiences were craving. There was, however, still one problem with *Bells*: the opening. From their first drafts, Comden and Green had begun with a pitchman offering a tongue-in-cheek promotion for Susanswerphone. After this, audiences were introduced to the reality of the business that had been made to sound so terribly chic in the ad.

Bells didn't get under way musically until later in the opening scene, when Holliday sang "It's a Perfect Relationship," a warm-spirited number in which Ella describes her infatuation with Jeff. This song was followed by the show's title song, delivered by Ella, Sue, and another woman who works for the service. It was a bittersweet moment as they all commented that while they were tending to their clients' messages about parties, dates, and other social events, they, themselves, were not going out. This meant that *Bells* was beginning with a rather somber picture of its heroine and her life.

To address this, and spark the show, the songwriters gently re-crafted the number, changing a word here and there. Robert Russell Bennett gave it a different orchestration, and the new version was used to open the show, delivered by the chorus as a buoyant ode to what life can be for women if they subscribe to Susanswerphone.

It took a while, but the team had finessed *Bells Are Ringing* in time for its opening at New York's Shubert Theatre on November 28. When the dailies' reviews began appearing, they were, for the most part, odes to Holliday and Chaplin and the show overall. For instance, John McClain in the *Journal-American* wrote, "It has style. It is never labored. It is always amusing," and in the *New York Post*, Richard Watts Jr. praised both show and star, noting, "The outstanding virtue of *Bells Are Ringing* and its star is a warm-hearted friendliness that is wonderfully endearing." A voice of dissent came from Brooks Atkinson in the *New York Times*. Although he lauded the performers, he also noted, "There have not been so many surprised hellos, inept song cues, and dance signals since 'Oklahoma!' drove hackneyed musical comedy out of business."

Despite this and other concerns about the writing, *Bells* was clicking with audiences and began playing to capacity houses instantly. The show, which ultimately received a Tony nomination for best musical but lost to *My Fair Lady*, ran 924 performances. Holliday, who had had concerns about being in the musical, actually bested Julie Andrews in the Tony Award race for best actress in a musical and stayed with the show until it closed. Interestingly, during one vacation Chaplin and she were replaced by Larry Parks and his real-life wife, Betty Garrett, who had starred so memorably in two of Comden and Green's films.

WHAT MIGHT HAVE BEEN

The Tony Award race between *My Fair Lady* and *Bells Are Ringing* carries a certain irony, because the Theatre Guild had, in the early 1950s, approached Comden and Green about turning George Bernard Shaw's *Pygmalion* into a musical. In response they watched the play's 1938 film version. Years later Green was quoted in the June 12, 1983, edition of *Newsday* about the response he and Comden had given the Guild: "Don't touch this masterpiece. You're mad." He then added, "Indeed, we were very mad afterwards."

With the success of *Bells* and no immediate film prospects, Comden and Green had, for the first time in more than a decade, a chance to settle into their lives in New York. For Comden it meant that for a while she wouldn't be jetting off, leaving husband and two children, now aged three and seven, at home. Throughout the past 10 years or so she always made sure to schedule time with them. When working on a film in California, she would devise ways to fly back to New York for a day or two. Similarly, while a new musical was in its tryout stages, she would work to return to New York for a day's visit.

Comden's efforts to mitigate her absences while working had mixed results. On one level, Susanna and Alan were able to enjoy some moments of normalcy with their parents and extended family. In notes from the period kept by Comden's secretary, an assistant shared with Green, as reminders of business calls and social engagements are mingled with attempts to arrange dates for Alan and Susanna to visit and play with their cousins.

And while such get-togethers remained private, the children also discovered that they were "boldface names" by virtue of their mother's celebrity and even enjoying an ice cream sundae was not outside the realm of being written about. In a September 17, 1956, *Philadelphia Inquirer* column, Douglas Watt informed his readers: "In Maxfield's ice cream parlor the other day: Judy Holliday's kid, Betty Comden's two kids, Herman Levin's kid, Lori March's kid and Lee Strasberg and his daughter Susan." Similarly, Susanna's difficulties with having a working mom could even crop up in the newspapers. Syndicated columnist Leonard Lyons reported in one of his October 1958 columns that Susanna had complained to Comden about the bus continually dropping her off at school late. When Comden asked how others were getting there, "the girl replied, 'They come by mother.'"

Comden was unaware at the time of any difficulties Alan might have had with her before he was a teenager. Years later, however, she did learn of his unhappiness. In her book *Off Stage* she admits, "The mother of one of Alan's friends told me that Alan had said he wished I would either come home and stay or not come home at all." And in hindsight Comden did realize that the trips she made to be with the family while working on the coast "had a feeling of unreality about them."[15]

As for Green, who had been a bachelor now for several years, columnists were eager to write about the women he was seeing; among them were Carol Marcus Saroyan, who had been married to the Pulitzer Prize–winning playwright and later would become Mrs. Walter Matthau, and singer Marti Stevens. Walter Winchell in a March 1957 column colorfully told readers that Green and Stevens being seen together was "another sign of early spring." Not surprisingly, there was always special attention made to his being out on the town with his ex-wife, Allyn McLerie, and generally they were in the company of her new husband, the one-time *Wonderful Town* star George Gaynes.

The notice that columnists were taking of both of their lives indicates the level of celebrity that Comden and Green had achieved by the mid- to late-1950s. Their national news value was only enhanced by their increasing presence on television, and as personalities their activities were worthy of ink. One of the more amusing stories from the period involves Comden and Humphrey Bogart, who found themselves in a heated argument over dinner at her house; the subject was Judy Garland's television debut. According to a Dorothy Kilgallen column from October 1955, "[He] loved the show, and Betty, who had gone out to see it on a color set, thought it was terrible."

This new level of fame, combined with their dedicating less time to working on both coasts, meant that Comden and Green could also take part in an ever-growing number of charitable events, and their appearances as philanthropic writer-performers would remain a constant for the balance of their lives. In some instances, they took the time to pen specialty material for the fundraising events, such as a fashion show for the March of Dimes in early 1955.

At times the team would go to great lengths to be on hand for a good cause. One of the most notable from this period came in December 1956, a cavalcade of entertainment created to both raise awareness of and money for refugees fleeing from the 1956 Hungarian revolution. This event, carried concurrently on all television and radio networks on Christmas Day of that year, featured, along with Comden and Green, such stars as Julie Andrews, Sammy Davis Jr., and Danny Thomas, as well as Mary Martin, who appeared with her family from their home in Connecticut. For Green, the hastily scheduled program meant rushing back to New York from Newfoundland, where he had been appearing in a special holiday-time show to entertain servicemen.

Green almost didn't make the Christmas Day televised special because the plane in which he and his fellow entertainers were flying back to

New York skidded across the runway during takeoff. The passengers were taken off the plane, and at this juncture Green launched into an impromptu routine to amuse his fellow travelers about "swine-raising in ancient Britain," beginning, "The problem in this course is to find the derivation of the Hampshire swine. Did it come from Hampshire?"[16]

At the same time and taking a cue from collaborator Jule Styne, Comden and Green began to concentrate their energy on being businesspeople. The process began as early as the summer of 1952, when, not long after their first show together, *Two on the Aisle*, Comden, Green, and Styne wrote "The Girls Are Marching." A piece of specialty material intended as a recruiting anthem to attract women to the US Air Force, it was their first step outside the realm of writing for the stage and screen. The peppy military march tune carries a gently humorous lyric, particularly when it promotes the idea that "the uniform is glamorous," and the song had such a crossover appeal that it received several pop recordings, including covers by Vic Damone and the Mariners. It is interesting to note that this patriotic tune was written and released at almost the same moment that Holliday was testifying in Washington, DC, about alleged communist ties.

Four years after this, while they were working on *Bells*, the trio deepened their business relationship with the composer, forming Stratford Music. The company assured them both a level of control over the songs they wrote together and a business umbrella for other activities, such as producing other writers' shows.

It was under the auspices of Stratford and thanks to Styne's song-plugging acumen that songs from *Bells Are Ringing* were on the airwaves even before the show opened in New York. Styne hoped to get Frank Sinatra to record the first single of "The Party's Over," but the singer had no interest in it. Styne then turned to Tony Bennett and offered him "Just in Time." The singer recorded it, and the 45 was available just as *Bells* started its first out-of-town engagement in New Haven. Before the musical opened in New York, Bennett's disc was charting in *Billboard*, while singers ranging from Doris Day to Carmen McRae recorded "The Party's Over."

Styne's savvy business sense also led to Comden and Green's next theater project. The show had its genesis in early 1957, when Styne purchased the rights to *Say, Darling*, a new novel from Richard Bissell, who had also written *7 ½ Cents*, which ultimately was transformed into the musical *The Pajama Game*.

In his new book Bissell fictionalized and skewered his experiences on that musical, turning out a story that was not just for Shubert Alley insiders but also for the general reader. In his March 24 review in *Newsday*, William K. Zinsser wrote, "It is funny by any standards, and so are its characters." For those in the business, the temptation to figure out which Broadway luminaries Bissell was mocking in his book was irresistible. After all, artists such as George Abbott, Harold Prince, and Bob Fosse were principals in the success of *The Pajama Game*.

Styne scooped up the rights to the novel in April, when the book was hitting the *New York Times* bestseller list, and by the summer of 1957 got *Two on the Aisle* director Abe Burrows to commit to directing its stage adaptation. The piece wasn't conceived of as a musical but rather as a comic play that would also feature songs. These would be diegetic, meant to be the ones that were being rehearsed and performed for *The Girl from Indiana*, the show-within-the-show.

Styne, knowing that Comden and Green's lyric sensibility perfectly matched the tone of Bissell's book, convinced them to provide the lyrics for his tunes, and the results ranged from genuinely felt ballads to silly nonsense songs. The writing team for the show also grew to include director Burrows himself, who eventually assisted Bissell and his wife in adapting the novel.

With rehearsals set for the end of January 1958, Burrows completed casting during the final weeks of 1957. To play Jack, the Midwestern first-time playwright who finds himself navigating the tricky waters of New York show business circles, Burrows turned to David Wayne, for whom Comden and Green had tailored the role of Mercury in their version of *Out of This World*. Vivian Blaine, who was the leading lady of *Greenwich Village*, the movie that brought the Revuers to Hollywood, and who more recently had indelibly originated the role of Adelaide in *Guys and Dolls*, was hired to play Irene, the one-time big Hollywood star who's trying to make a comeback. Johnny Desmond, a high-profile recording artist and sometime screen actor, was cast as Rudy, Irene's ex, a hot-shot pop composer who's hired to write the score for *The Girl from Indiana*.

Among others in the company were Robert Morse, just a couple of years away from his star-making turn in *How to Succeed in Business without Really Trying*, who played the aggressive young producer who's bringing Jack's show to the Great White Way, and Broadway vet Jerome Cowan, who played the senior producer-director who's co-writing and staging the show. In these characters, audiences couldn't help but think of their real-life counterparts, Prince and Abbott, respectively.

The songs for this rollicking journey backstage echo the satiric tone of the show in general. "Chief of Love," which is meant to be one of Rudy's big pop hits, mocks the inanities typical of the era's most dimly conceived hits: "Chief of Love/You're my thief of love." Other numbers, such as "The Husking Bee," the cornball ensemble number that's intended as the big opener for *The Girl from Indiana*, and "It's Doom," which is meant to be sung by the musical's title character, are caricatures, a pop songwriter's notion of what musical theater sounds like.

The team didn't write all of the music for *Say, Darling* with a tongue-in-cheek tone. Both the title song and "Dance Only with Me" are satisfying ballads that would have been respected in most any musical of the period. In fact, for a while there was even a song in the production that had been intended for an actual musical: "My Little Yellow Dress," which Styne, Comden, and Green wrote originally for *Bells Are Ringing*.

The New Haven tryout engagement for *Say, Darling* met with tepid responses. On February 26, *Variety* reviewer "Bone." characterized the production as "sometimes sock, sometimes slump," and the following day in the *Hartford Courant* T.H.P. wrote, "If not newly invented, it is extremely professional in the treatment and engaging in the doing."

The show got a much warmer reception in Philadelphia. Henry T. Murdock in a March 6 *Philadelphia Inquirer* review pronounced it "fresh and witty," and he shrewdly acknowledged that "since some of the songs are destined to be thrown out of [the show-within-the-show], they are lilting if undistinguished." Murdock even recognized that the best numbers came at the end of the production, signaling that occasionally a musical "can be saved during a New Haven tryout."

Say, Darling came to Broadway on April 3, and the critical response was decidedly mixed. On the positive side in the daily reviews on the morning after the opening were ones such as Walter Kerr's in the *New York Herald Tribune*, which deemed the show "light, random, affectionate, and very, very cheerful," and Richard Watts Jr.'s in the *New York Post*, which called it "an enormously engaging and likable show." On the negative side were reviews such as Brooks Atkinson's in the *New York Times*, which said, "This one is hardly more than a clever college show," and John Chapman's in the *Daily News*: "I think 'Say, Darling' could be fixed up."

At least there were accolades for some of the tunes. Robert Coleman in the *Daily Mirror* took time to recognize that the songs managed to be "easy on the ears and yet make satirical points." And almost all critics praised the rousing "jubilee tune" that closed the show. This number, "Something's Always Happening on the River," plus several others, received high-profile cover versions from pop artists ranging from Perry Como and Dinah Shore to Cy Coleman and Annie Ross.

AN AURAL DECEPTION

Because of the Styne-Comden-Green pedigree, *Say, Darling*, which boasted 10 full numbers plus several incidental musical segments, had record labels competing for the rights to a cast album months before it began rehearsals, and RCA Victor emerged as the winner of the bidding war. Interestingly, the original cast recording provides listeners with a false impression of what happened on stage. It features full orchestrations from Sid Ramin, though in the theater the songs were performed with just a two-piano accompaniment. The album even features an overture written especially for the recording.

Despite the lukewarm critical response *Say, Darling* received, it had legs, as the saying in the business goes, and the production continued a run that lasted into January 1959. What was important about the show for Comden and Green was that it allowed them to continue writing for the theater even as they devoted their attention to their next film project, the first they'd ever done for a studio other than MGM. Interestingly, as was the case with *Say, Darling*, it was also a book to stage (and now to screen) adaptation.

CHAPTER 11

Throwing a Stage Party
and a Cinematic Revel

B efore *Bells Are Ringing* had reached its three-month anniversary on Broadway, word of its national tour was already beginning to circulate. In an early March 1957 column, Dorothy Kilgallen even ascribed its acclaim to the reason that Comden and Green were staying put in New York to consider "fabulous offers from the networks as well as movie producers."

Indeed, they were being courted for myriad projects after the opening of *Bells*. For a brief moment it looked as if they might serve as the lyricists for a project that their friends and collaborators Jerome Robbins, Arthur Laurents, and Leonard Bernstein had been developing for a number of years: *West Side Story*. Stephen Sondheim had been working as co-lyricist, with Bernstein, for this show that Robbins would be doing immediately following *Bells*, but in spring 1957 there were rumors that dissent had arisen among the writers.

Shortly after this, a story in the May 29 issue of *Variety* about touring productions slated for Washington, DC, noted that that city's National Theatre would reopen in August with a tryout engagement of *West Side Story*. In this piece Comden and Green were named as the lyricists for the aborning musical. In short order, all announcements about *West Side Story* once again named Sondheim as the lyricist.

In the years that followed, stories about the groundbreaking show would mention that Robbins and Bernstein originally discussed the idea of Comden and Green working with them as potential collaborators, and an early draft of a treatment for the show in Comden and Green's papers indicates that they were approached about it. Further, Laurents always indicated that they had been talked to early on, although he would ultimately say, "This show wasn't for them"[1]

In all the years that followed the premiere of *West Side Story*, none of the principals involved ever mentioned that during the months just before its premiere Comden and Green were approached, leading to a different conclusion about the *Variety* story. It was, most likely, the ruse of a sly press agent hoping to restore equilibrium to the existing team's working relationship. It appears that the idea of Comden and Green reteaming with Robbins and Bernstein unexpectedly had enough credibility to accomplish this goal.

Concurrent with this news about *West Side Story* were announcements of another new musical. This one was being assembled by David Merrick, who was rapidly becoming one of Broadway's most prolific and profitable producers. Merrick had won a bidding war for the stage rights to a forthcoming memoir from Gypsy Rose Lee. Her life story, from a career as a child performer in vaudeville to her work headlining in burlesque, seemed ripe for musicalization.

The same May 27, 1957, announcement that Merrick had obtained the rights to Lee's book carried news of the team that would transform it into a musical: Jule Styne would write the score and Comden and Green would supply the book and lyrics.

Comden and Green had, indeed, agreed to do the show, but as the year progressed "they could not find a suitable approach to the adaptation," Styne remembered. "Obviously they'd cooled on it. So did I at that time. I'd worked with them long enough to know that if they really felt strongly about something they'd move along with it."[2]

For the remainder of 1957, any mention of the musical that would ultimately become *Gypsy* would include Comden's and Green's names, but then, on December 21, *New York Times* theater journalist Louis Calta announced that the team had to "reluctantly drop out" of the project. One reason cited was their commitment to songwriting for *Say, Darling*, which would be starting rehearsals just after the start of the New Year. The other reason concerned delays on their most recent film project, which also came their way in that very busy May of 1957.

The movie was not one for MGM, the studio for which they had worked exclusively for a decade. Instead, it was for Warner Bros. Jack Warner himself wanted them to write the screenplay for the movie version of the hit play *Auntie Mame*, which was to feature its original Broadway star, Rosalind Russell.

Auntie Mame, like *Say, Darling* and *Gypsy*, began life as a book, this one written by Patrick Dennis, a pseudonym for author Everett Edward Tanner. In it he chronicles what life was like for 10-year-old Patrick, who after the death of his father is raised by his flamboyant aunt. A raucous journey through the 1920s, 1930s, and 1940s as Mame attempts to instill her lust for life in her nephew, the book was a bestseller in 1955 and arrived on

Broadway as a play a year later. Rosalind Russell played the fabulous title character, and the show, which followed *Wonderful Town*, was another stage triumph for her.

Unfortunately, while critics were cheering her work, there were sharp complaints about Jerome Lawrence and Robert E. Lee's adaptation of Dennis's book. In his November 1 *New York Times* review, Brooks Atkinson carped, "They have pasted this skit together but they have not been able to develop a narrative coherently. . . . This is a pretty shabby job."

It was at Russell's insistence that Warner brought Comden and Green in to write the stage-to-screen adaptation. Comden recalled, "She was so anxious for us to do it." Further, Comden remembered that although Russell wanted to keep the portions of the play that were working, at the same time "she actually said she wanted us to change it a lot."[3]

Comden and Green worked on the screenplay during the summer of 1957, and a draft from October demonstrates that they were allowing themselves the freedom to invent and embellish both Dennis's original and the play it inspired. The addition about which they would remain most proud is the conception of the furniture that Mame installs before she entertains Patrick's future in-laws, the stuffy Upsons from Connecticut. "We invented the rising and falling chairs for the last sequence," Green recalled, with Comden adding, "There were the chairs going up and down, and other things to discomfort these prejudiced people and show Patrick the right road."[4]

Another significant alteration for the screenplay involves a revision to Mame's life philosophy: "Live. Live. Live. Life is a banquet and most poor sons-of-bitches are starving to death." Lawrence and Lee kept the expletive in their play, but for film audiences, and no doubt to placate the Hollywood Production Code, Comden and Green opted for the gentler "suckers."

While these two changes made it into the final version of the movie, other Comden and Green embellishments did not. One of their most amusing involved an additional career for Mame during the Depression, after her fortune was wiped out. In between her attempts to work as a law firm's receptionist and a saleswoman at Macys, they made her a door-to-door representative for a cookware company. As with her other attempts at joining the workforce, this one ends disastrously as she destroys a kitchen of a Queens home while demonstrating the marvels of a multifunction pressure cooker.

One other substantial change that thankfully did not make it into the picture involves Dwight Babcock, the haughty trustee from the Knickerbocker Bank, who handles Patrick's money and also tries to shape his character. In their draft version of the screenplay, Comden and Green imagine this stuffed shirt succumbing to both Mame's charms and her worldview, and by the end of the picture the two characters were married and enjoying a free-spirited life together.

In a similar vein Comden and Green also revised what has proven to be one of the most memorable moments in the film, the terribly unfunny story Patrick's fiancée tells about a ping-pong match at a country club. Lawrence and Lee created the tale for the play, and in the screenplay Comden and Green retained the moment in which Gloria tells a boner of a story. However, in their early draft they imagine her trying to tell a yarn about being mistaken for a worker when she and some school chums are on a field trip to a factory.

All of these revisions, however, did not address the central complaint about the stage adaptation—that it was too fragmentary. As Comden and Green developed their version of the story for the screen, they attempted, in subtle ways, to forestall any similar complaints about the film. They did this with delicate plot-related constructions that helped to create fine threads of continuity between what could otherwise be considered unrelated scenes. In one instance, when Mame returns from an overseas jaunt during which she mourned the loss of her husband, Comden and Green wrote a casual aside for Mame about seeing and hearing cellist Abraham Epstein playing aboard a ship she was on. The few lines didn't make it to the film, and yet had they been included there would have been a sensible connection to Mame's knockout punch at Patrick's engagement party, when she announces that she has purchased property adjacent to the Upsons' abode for the Epsteins to use as a home for refugee Jewish children.

Similarly, during an early montage meant to show audiences what Patrick's life becomes immediately after moving in with Mame, Comden and Green invented a scene in which she's seen talking about Picasso's work at an art gallery, following it with one in which Patrick explains to the Irish maid Norah that the new décor in Mame's apartment has been inspired by the artist's cubist period. Seemingly the moments are throwaway, but they lay the groundwork for Patrick's own artistic endeavors. Attempting to cheer his aunt up when they are broke at Christmas just one year later, he hangs an abstract painting of Santa, clearly inspired by the Spanish artist, over the fireplace in their home.

Comden and Green's October draft, which shows signs of being a genuine working document, with passages of dialogue stapled onto some pages, huge excisions of text, and smaller handwritten changes to individual lines, indicates that as 1957 was drawing to a close they still had significant work to do on the screenplay for a movie that was set to start filming in early 1958. Their decision to pass on *Gypsy* was a necessary one.

BELLS CHIMES IN THE WEST END

Just a month after they finished a draft of their *Auntie Mame* screenplay, the West End production of *Bells Are Ringing* opened at the Coliseum. Starring Janet Blair (who had played the title character in the movie musical *My Sister Eileen*) as Ella and George Gaynes as Jeff Moss, the show, which also featured Gayne's wife and Green's ex Allyn McLerie as Sue, received slightly better reviews than *Wonderful Town* had when it debuted in London. Kenneth Tynan, in an *Observer* review on November 17, called it "enchanting," but acknowledged that "it is written in a vein of highly allusive wit." Nevertheless, the production lasted 292 performances.

Comden and Green finished the *Auntie Mame* screenplay at the top of 1958, just as *Say, Darling* was going into rehearsal. As the year progressed, Morton DaCosta filmed *Auntie Mame,* and *Say, Darling* settled into its run at Broadway's ANTA Theatre, while the two writers began tending to their lives outside the theater. For Comden, the first order of business was a trip to Europe. Even on holiday, however, Comden was at work as she checked in on *Wonderful Town* in London and traveled to Brussels to discuss a forthcoming production that was to be headlined by Mitzi Green, the former star of *Billion Dollar Baby.*

As for Green, there was a new woman in his life, actress Phyllis Newman, who was Judy Holliday's standby in *Bells Are Ringing.* Born and bred in New Jersey, Newman had been performing since she was a child. One of her first big breaks came when her mother finagled an audition for her daughter in front of Belle Baker, a popular singer in the first half of the 20th century who toured extensively. Baker took a shine to Newman and her vocal talents and put the girl into her act, billing her as "Baby Phyllis Baker."

After high school graduation, Newman made her Broadway debut in the ensemble of *Wish You Were Here* and then traveled to Hollywood to play a couple of small roles in films, including the movie of William Inge's play *Picnic* and a starry version of the operetta *The Vagabond King.* She then returned to New York and, in addition to landing a few gigs on television series, secured the role in *Bells.*

In her memoir, *Just in Time,* Newman recalls that she was attracted to Green early on. At the same time, she writes, "I was intimidated by his age, his reputation as an intellectual, his success, and most of all his mind-boggling eccentricities." As for Green, she remembers that after a while he started paying attention to her and eventually asked her out.

Green recalled that evening and where they went: the famed caricature-lined eatery on 44th Street, Sardi's. He would later relate: "We sat up front

under a portrait of Alfred Lunt and Lynn Fontanne. We were very impressed with each other."[5] Newman, who spent days leading up to the
dinner memorizing the titles of weighty books and their authors in order
to impress Green, committed several gaffes, such as mentioning that she
had recently read something by Andrew Gide rather than André Gide. She
characterized the evening by rating it "Terror: ten. Sparks: three and a half.
Interest: seven." After the date Newman described the state that she and
Green found themselves in as "reconnoitering each other"; eventually, he
came to be, as she put it, "taking me out from time to time and then from
time to time to time."[6]

The Green-Newman courtship would continue for another 12 months
or so. During this period she moved on from *Bells* to the Styne-produced
First Impressions, a musical version of Jane Austen's *Pride and Prejudice,* and
not surprisingly Green had projects to attend to. One of them arose quite
unexpectedly for him and Comden as 1958 was drawing to a close.

A DRESS WORTHY OF AUNTIE MAME?

For her *Wonderful Town* and *Auntie Mame* costumes, Rosalind Russell turned
to some of the country's leading couturiers. For the musical her wardrobe
was designed by Mainbocher. She used Travis Banton (of Marusia) for *Auntie
Mame* on Broadway, and after Banton's unexpected death in early 1958 she
turned to Orry-Kelly for her outfits for the television version of the musical
and the film of the comedy. Comden was equally astute when it came to fashion, and sometimes just as "out there" as Mame might have been. In a
September 1958 column Dorothy Kilgallen noted that Comden had recently
sported a "black dinner dress and matching hem-length coat [that] are made
entirely of crocheted straw. The ensemble is a souvenir of Florence, Italy."

As fall descended on the city, Comden and Green received an invitation
that was too delectable for them to pass up: the opportunity to return to
performing. It came from Gus Schirmer Jr., who had created a special series
of Monday evening performances at the intimate Cherry Lane Theatre in
Greenwich Village.

Schirmer, who worked as a stage manager and performer on Broadway
and who had also staged an acclaimed revival of Sandy Wilson's *The Boy
Friend* that played at the Cherry Lane, had devised a special series that made
use of the space when its regular productions were not in performance. He
started the series, called "Mondays Nights at Nine," by presenting for several performances chanteuse Mabel Mercer, a toast of the New York cabaret
scene in the early 1940s.

In this same spirit he invited Comden and Green to offer some of their material, much as they had as Revuers, at the theater. Comden recalled, "It happened very suddenly. . . . I ran into him most casually on Fifty-seventh Street and he said why don't you come down and do some of your material on Mondays when the Cherry Lane was dark?"[7] For two artists who admitted to the *Los Angeles Times*'s Philip S. Scheuer in early 1952, "We're frustrated hams . . . always wanted to be performers,"[8] Schirmer's invitation couldn't have been more alluring. Naturally, they said yes.

Since their last regular stint on Broadway in *On the Town* in 1945, Comden and Green had had their chances to perform. They both did brief appearances as last-minute stand-ins for ill performers in *Billion Dollar Baby*, and Green was, of course, featured in the aborted *Bonanza Bound*. But beyond these opportunities, which occurred in the late 1940s, they had not been able to return to the stage. They hadn't even been able to write the show for themselves that they would frequently mention in interviews; there were just too many other projects on their docket. The closest thing to professional acting that either had done since the 1940s fell to Comden, who provided a voice-over in *It's Always Fair Weather*, reading the "Dear John" letter that Gene Kelly's character receives during an early scene in the movie.

Nevertheless, they were able to keep sharp as performers by giving what Green characterized as a "wild performance"[9] of a just-completed screenplay for producer Arthur Freed and the stars of whatever film they were working on or entertaining at social events. Further, they embarked on a short but lauded recording career in 1955 courtesy of the Heritage record label. The small company had success in releasing albums featuring noted writers, such as Alan Jay Lerner and Harold Rome, delivering their own material. Comden and Green followed in these men's footsteps with a pair of LPs.

The first, titled simply *Comden and Green* (indicating how much of a "brand" the team had become), hit stores in May. For this LP they chose selections from their musicals, including two numbers from the unrecorded (as of then) *Billion Dollar Baby* and their contribution to the film *Good News*, "The French Lesson." It was a highly personal album, one that captured the depth of personality that Comden and Green put into each of their songs.

Reviews in both trade publications and general press touted the LP and the style that Comden and Green possessed as performers. A May 25 *Variety* review noted, "They've still got the bistro bounce and an exuberance that adds up to a lot of fun." And in his June 26 *New York Times* review, John S. Wilson commended the "raucous vehemence" that the performers brought to the material.

The label released the second Comden and Green album before the end of the year. It was made up of all of the songs they had written with André Previn for *It's Always Fair Weather*. Again, the recording displayed the pair's unique performance style. It also allowed them to share with the public a pair of numbers that had not made it into the film: "I Said Good Mornin'," a chipper tune that ends on an amusing curmudgeonly note that became something of a signature for the two of them, and "Love Is Nothing but a Racket," which they performed as they and Previn had originally conceived it.

Beyond allowing them to flex their muscles as performers, the LPs helped provide them with a sort of outline for the show they would offer at the Cherry Lane. They structured the evening chronologically, working through their careers in three different segments: "The Performers," in which they offered some of their Revuers material; "The Performer-Writers," which consisted of material they wrote through the first part of the 1950s; and then "The Writer-Performers," which covered their work from *Wonderful Town* through *Bells*. Even in their titles for the show's three segments Comden and Green could invoke a smile, with the last one indicating that they had had to accept the fact that they were more writers than performers.

Schirmer scheduled them for a single performance on Monday, November 10. It quickly sold out, and even before appearing they agreed to do a second one a week later.

After their first show there were reports about the throngs that had rushed to the Village to see them. Eugenia Sheppard, in the November 12 issue of the *New York Herald Tribune*, told her readers that "Cadillacs were three deep and there were as many chauffeurs as autograph hounds" on Cherry Lane's tiny curved section of Commerce Street in the Village on the 10th. Getting to see Comden and Green's return to performing became one of the city's hottest tickets, and they agreed to add two additional performances, one on Sunday, November 23, at midnight and another the following night at the usual time.

Given the rampant success of this hastily scheduled and assembled piece, it's hardly surprising that rumors of a Broadway transfer began circulating quickly, and exactly one month after they offered their first performance in Greenwich Village, the *New York Times*'s Sam Zolotow told readers that the show would move to the John Golden Theatre on 45th Street, presented by the Theatre Guild and Schirmer. Performances were set to begin on December 23, and "for the Broadway stand, the program has been dubbed 'A Party with Betty Comden and Adolph Green.'"

WONDERFUL TOWN TAKES TO THE AIRWAVES

Comden and Green found their lyrics reaching into American living rooms and dens on November 30, 1958, when CBS broadcast *Wonderful Town* featuring its original star, Rosalind Russell. The critical reaction to this televised musical was not nearly as enthusiastic as it had been for *Peter Pan* three years earlier, and Comden and Green's contributions were generally not mentioned. The triumph of this small-screen outing belonged to Russell, as well as to composer Leonard Bernstein. As *Variety* critic "Rose." noted on December 3, "It was, in fact, Bernstein Day on CBS right down the line, with the composer-conductor also inaugurating his own Lincoln-sponsored series earlier in the day."

While Comden and Green were still packing them in at the tiny Cherry Lane in the Village, their work was also being showcased at the gargantuan Radio City Music Hall in Midtown, where *Auntie Mame* opened as the holiday picture on December 4. The following morning Russell received, not unexpectedly, critical bouquets. The screenplay, however, was buffeted at almost every turn. In a November 26 *Variety* review, critic "Powe." noted, "There isn't much difference in the picture's final version . . . from the play." More stinging was Paul V. Beckley's December 5 review in the *New York Herald Tribune*. He derided a "bumptious air of satire that hangs over everything" and an increased "accent on slapstick." Particularly troubling to the critic was the climactic scene, with its flaming cocktails and adjustable-height furniture. In the *Saturday Review* on December 27, Arthur Knight also took exception to the final scene, noting that it had done nothing to leaven what was often a "disturbingly static picture.'"

Nevertheless, in the week following its opening *Auntie Mame* did record-making business in New York and continued to do so during its run there. Critical reaction in the new year, when the film began to play in cities around the country, was similar to what it received in New York, and yet audiences flocked to the picture, which went on to accrue six Academy Award nominations and a considerable following.

As *Auntie Mame* settled into its Christmas-time run at Radio City, Comden and Green put the finishing touches on their *A Party With* Broadway transfer, and the show opened as scheduled on December 23. Due to a newspaper strike, reviews the following morning were limited to the one that ran in that day's abbreviated edition of the *New York Times*. Brooks Atkinson raved: "They are just about good enough for any civilized corner of the world." In his assessment the critic also proclaimed, "Miss Comden and Mr. Green are ideal performers. They have the expertise of the professional although they have not lost the enthusiasm of the amateur." Atkinson went on to say that theatergoers would find "two brilliant minds" at work in the revue.

As the year wound down and 1959 dawned, similar accolades came. On December 27 in the *Christian Science Monitor*, critic J. B. lauded the production, writing, "Nothing lighter, gayer, or more fetching has been deposited under the Broadway Christmas tree," while Robert Coleman's review for the *Daily Mirror*, printed on January 7, noted, "They know what to do with smart material, and they are lucky enough to have themselves as their own scripters."

The reviews were enough to warrant a one-week extension of the show's original three-week engagement. The production might have been able to continue even longer, but Comden and Green had to get to California. There were changes they needed to make to the screenplay for the movie that would become their final picture for MGM, which had changed significantly since they arrived to write *Good News* in 1947.

Not only had the studio been forced to separate its moviemaking business from its theater-owning side because of the government's enforcement of antitrust statutes, but television had also eaten into its profits. It was a different beast. Comden would later recall being among a throng of studio employees at a luncheon where these changes were discussed. "There was ice cream served in the form of small chocolate 'Leos,' the M-G-M lion. We watched them melt before our eyes and it seemed so symbolic. But no one caught on."[10]

The world of Broadway and its audiences' tastes and expectations had changed as well during this time, and while Comden and Green were about to end the 1950s and hit the 1960s with no less energy than they had at the start of the decade, they would discover that they, too, would have to find ways to evolve as writers.

CHAPTER 12

A Movie, Some TV...
and Jukeboxes

A s 1959 dawned and Comden and Green were basking in the success
of *A Party With*, they were also coping with the significant work they
had to do on the screenplay for the movie version of *Bells Are Ringing*. The
picture, being produced by Arthur Freed, who had shepherded all of their
movie musicals to the screen, was a long time in the making. MGM acquired the rights to the musical in mid-1957 after protracted negotiations
with both the writers and the star. According to a report from Thomas M.
Pryor in the August 7 edition of the *New York Times* that year, "Irving Lazar,
who negotiated the sale, said the terms call for a payment of $500,000
[roughly $4.1 million in 2017], plus 25 percent of the profits from the
screen version." Because Holliday was to star in the film, work could not
begin on it until after the musical had wrapped up its Broadway engagement, as she had a run-of-the-show contract.

Nevertheless, Freed worked to move the project forward while *Bells* continued its Broadway run. In January 1958 he selected Vincente Minnelli,
who had brought the team's *The Band Wagon* to the screen and who subsequently helmed the movie musicals *Brigadoon* and *Gigi*, to direct the picture. At this juncture, production for the new movie was slated to begin
sometime during the middle of the year, but the show's success on Broadway
meant that filming had to be delayed. Still, Comden and Green headed to
Culver City in July to start discussions with Freed and Minnelli about the
picture and the new songs they would write for it.

By the end of the year, Comden and Green finished a draft of the
movie, but what they turned in was far longer than what had been agreed
to in their contract. Further, they had not provided any new songs. The
draft contains only one provisional new title, a tune called "Where in
the World?" Freed told the writers that the draft was unacceptable and

could have turned to other writers. Yet because of their long-standing professional—and personal—relationship, he granted them an extension to their original deadline. Freed also agreed to their delaying any work on revisions to the script until after they had concluded the run of *A Party With*.

From this draft through to the final rehearsal and production script for the *Bells Are Ringing* movie, Comden and Green attempted to address certain complaints that were leveled at their script for the stage show, such as its sketch-like structure, and to strengthen the psychological and emotional arcs for the two principals, Ella and Jeffrey. To accomplish the former, they gently magnified the role that Inspector Barnes played in the story, providing a slender thread linking each of Ella's in-person encounters with the Susanswerphone clients.

As for Ella and Jeffrey's through-lines, the most interesting of the additions the team made was a scene in which Ella goes out on a blind date arranged by her cousin. This scene, first included in their second draft and then seen in the final cut, establishes how uncomfortable she is with men face-to-face and one-on-one. Another scene, which they ultimately decided against, was between Ella and her co-worker Gwynne, in which Ella worries about the way that she's deceived Jeff. This latter addition laid important groundwork for Ella's eventual Cinderella-like departure from the society party she attends with him. For a brief period the writers also toyed with the idea of having the opera singer who gives Ella one of her costumes recognize the gown at the same party, both establishing continuity between two unrelated aspects of the script and providing Ella with further impetus to leave.

As for Jeff, Comden and Green reverted briefly—and after the casting of Dean Martin—to their portrayal of the character as it was in their first drafts of the stage musical. In an early version of the screenplay they revealed him at his apartment in the middle of a raucous, alcohol-fueled party. The scene effectively established the character as a playboy playwright. Ultimately, though, they opted to downplay the debauched lifestyle from which Ella rescues him, removing this scene and curtailing references to his dependency on alcohol. In many regards they simply made him a manchild, not unlike the hero for another musical to which they had contributed, *Peter Pan*.

Among the other embellishments they made to their original script that did not make it to the final draft or final cut was a lengthy sequence about the ruses that Ella employs to gain access to Jeff's apartment building for the first time she meets him. Their stage directions for this portion of the film have Ella ultimately disguising herself to fit in among a group of United Nations delegates from India, and it brings to mind the sort of shenanigans Lucille Ball's character would employ on a weekly basis on the television series *I Love Lucy*. Similarly, as they drafted the screenplay they also added and then cut a large-scale wedding scene during the final moments of the picture.

As they moved through the various drafts of the *Bells* screenplay, they made two substantial cuts to the original score. "Salzburg," the schmaltzy comic duet that Sue and her bookie boyfriend share toward the end of the show, was left out starting with the first draft, and by their final version "Hello, Hello There!" was also gone.

Their contract had called for a trio of new songs for the movie version, but early in their drafting process Comden and Green slotted only the previously mentioned "Where in the World?" They, and Styne, never wrote this number, and by the time Minnelli was ready to start shooting they had added three songs, which while adhering to the letter of the agreement didn't necessarily match its spirit.

One was "Do It Yourself," a lackluster revision to the number that had been used on stage. Also newish was "Better Than a Dream," a duet for Ella and Jeff during their first meeting, but this song had been added to the Broadway production mid-run, though after they had signed their contract with the studio. Finally, the team developed and completed the number that had been slotted for late in the movie and known as "Where in the World?" The song, "My Guiding Star," is a generic ballad for Jeff as he searches for Ella late at night in Brooklyn Heights. Minnelli filmed the sequence, but it was removed from the final cut.

From Minnelli's biographers to those writers who chronicled Holliday's life, reports are rife that the director was never happy with the screenplay that Freed ultimately accepted. Yet Minnelli appears to contradict this in his memoir when he writes that he felt the original book for *Bells* "was nearly perfect," adding, "their main challenge in adapting the picture to the screen was to rephrase it in cinematic terms."[1] Yet he never openly says whether or not Comden and Green achieved everything he felt was necessary, and the director's politic politeness, on many levels, simply excuses the slim alternations that the duo made as *Bells Are Ringing* moved from the stage to the screen.

Comden and Green had repeatedly demonstrated their ability to rewrite quickly and create new scenarios on the fly for nearly 20 years. Given this, their reticence to change *Bells* and the relative slowness in their writing process is surprising. Ultimately, it's difficult not to wonder if they were attempting to avoid what had happened when their first musical, *On the Town*, came to the screen and ended up bearing only a slight resemblance to what had been so dynamic and groundbreaking on stage. It could be, too, that they had simply grown weary of the Hollywood grind. In September 1959 they declined the opportunity to script a new picture when they were offered $150,000 (about $1.2 million in 2017) to adapt Truman Capote's successful novel *Breakfast at Tiffany's* for the screen.

BRINGING SOME REALITY TO A MUSICAL FAIRY TALE

For all of its quirky coincidences and Cinderella-like story, Vincente Minnelli's *Bells Are Ringing* pulses with a certain reality, thanks to how he portrays New York in the film. The sense of Manhattan transforming from a metropolitan wonderland with small-town values into a sterile concrete-and-glass world becomes apparent during the movie's opening sequence as images of demolitions of older buildings making way for skyscrapers whisk by under the movie's credits. And, in fact, the Susanswerphone offices are located in a single brownstone that has been left standing amid debris from its former neighbors. Minnelli discovered the building after seeing its picture in a *Life* magazine article about how Manhattan was transforming.

After Minnelli began filming *Bells* in October 1959, Comden and Green traveled to the coast once to check in on the movie. But they were becoming increasingly New York–based, as evidenced by the time they spent there while writing the screenplay. They simply had too many other matters and new projects for them to attend to.

In fact, during the spring Green had not only been in New York but also Philadelphia. His jaunts to this city were inspired, according to columnists, by his desire to be near Phyllis Newman during the tryouts of the musical she was appearing in, *First Impressions*. Of course, his presence at the show's previews might also have been professional. Abe Burrows, who staged *Two on the Aisle* and *Say, Darling*, was directing the production, and it featured a score that was being published by the company Green, Comden, and Styne had formed.

With the arrival of summer, and though there was some work still to be done on the *Bells* screenplay, Green took his first overseas trip in more than two years. His reasons for going abroad were both personal and professional. During his time away he visited with producers in England to discuss a possible stint for *A Party With* in London, and according to a *Variety* story on July 15 he was in Paris to savor "the local atmosphere for a book show he will write with Betty Comden." The story went on to say that the unnamed piece would be a vehicle for the team as performers. Also on Green's agenda was a trip to Vevey, Switzerland, to spend some time with his childhood screen idol and now adulthood friend Charlie Chaplin.

Newman, coincidentally, was also vacationing in Europe during this time, taking a break after the brief Broadway run of *First Impressions*, and she had a London-to-Paris itinerary that was similar to Green's. Newman would later recall that they "made the vaguest nonplan to meet, maybe," and that despite the dates that they had shared, "I wasn't even remotely sure how I felt about him." As for Green, Newman's recollection was that "he was only really sure he was serious about me when my ambivalence bordered on indifference."[2] Still, they connected in Paris, and she shared a dismal afternoon and evening with him and an ex-girlfriend of his.

Green and Newman got together for dinner after this with *Bells Are Ringing* star Sydney Chaplin, and during the course of the meal Chaplin invited her to join them all in Switzerland at his father's house. She agreed, and it was after this that her relationship with Green went to a new level, at least for him. She continued travels on her own for a while, and then Green joined her—and some of her friends and later more of his—in Italy. He proposed in Rome. Newman, however, was not ready to accept. She had grown tired of his antics with his friends and felt that he had been callously oblivious to what she wanted to do during her first big European trip. She couldn't say "yes" to the proposal, and they parted company and returned to their individual travels.

Once home, while Green and Comden were offering *A Party With* at the Westport Country Playhouse, Newman and a friend attended one performance. That night "something struck me about Adolph," Newman writes in her memoir, *Just in Time*, adding, "I suddenly fell hard."[3] During the fall their dating became more serious, even as Green moved into a new seven-room apartment in the Beresford on Central Park West. Columnist Burt Boyar announced the move in a *Philadelphia Inquirer* column on September 11, noting, "He's a bachelor!"

Green's life as a single man, however, would last only another five months. Newman and he decided to tie the knot, and on January 29, 1960, they obtained their marriage license. The following day they were married in a ceremony at what had been his "bachelor pad" at the Beresford, with Jule Styne himself playing "Here Comes the Bride" to start the ceremony. At the reception afterward at the Sheraton East, the newlyweds took to the floor, sharing their first dance as husband and wife to the tune of "Lucky to Be Me" from *On the Town*.

MORE BELLS ARE RINGING

Sydney Chaplin was there for Green in January 1960 when he and Phyllis Newman were married, and on March 6, 1960, Green was there for Chaplin when he married dancer Noelle Adam. Green served as Chaplin's best man, and Lauren Bacall, who was co-starring with Chaplin in *Goodbye, Charlie* on

Broadway, served as Adam's attendant in a tiny ceremony held on Long Island. Chaplin was romantically linked for a time to Judy Holliday during *Bells Are Ringing*, and, according to Walter Winchell, Holliday refused to attend Green's wedding because her ex-beau was to be there with his new fiancée.

While the Green-Newman romance gathered momentum, Comden and Green capitalized on the upswing their lives had taken as writer-performers thanks to *A Party With*. Because of the show's success, both found themselves being offered acting roles. Comden, for instance, was approached about starring in *Goodbye, Charlie*, by George Axelrod, author of the hits *The Seven Year Itch* and *Will Success Spoil Rock Hunter?*, which had been produced by Styne.

Comden and Green, however, were a team through and through, and despite such offers they preferred to perform together, whether on the West Coast for one night only as a benefit for one of Hedda Hopper's pet charities, in Connecticut where their *Party* played to record-breaking crowds for the Westport Country Playhouse, or even on television. Before the end of the year, they were slated to offer it as an early pay-per-view program, but issues about syndication rights ultimately tanked a deal that would have brought the show (which earned a *Village Voice* Obie Award for best musical) to a wider audience. For those who were unable to see the production off or on Broadway, however, there was a Grammy-nominated album from Capitol Records that preserved their performances.

Regardless of the setback for the TV deal for this show, Comden and Green found that there were other ways to ramp up their work on the small screen, and soon they were involved with two major network specials. The first came in November 1959, when they joined Andy Williams for *Music from Shubert Alley*. The hour-long special toasted Broadway songwriting from the beginning of the century through the present day, and Williams's other guests included Alfred Drake, Lisa Kirk, Doretta Morrow, and Ray Walston, who performed both songs they had originated in shows such as *Oklahoma!* and *Kiss Me, Kate* and numbers from some of Broadway's best-loved musicals.

For Comden and Green it was a chance to offer up a song they had brought to Broadway as performers and two others they had penned. In the former category was "Good Morning," their opening for *A Party With*. In the latter was "Just in Time," which they performed with Williams, and "New York, New York," which was used as the lightweight finale for the variety program.

More substantial was the special that Comden and Green contributed to in January 1960: *The Fabulous Fifties*. Produced by Leland Hayward for

CBS, the show was a two-hour retrospective of the events of the decade that had just ended. Humor and more-serious topics combined as the program chronicled the decade, and Comden and Green were on hand as both writers and performers, appearing in one sequence that examined changes to the movie industry and another that lampooned the way in which women were portrayed in advertisements.

Both offerings harkened back to the sort of writing and performing they did when they started out as part of the Revuers. The difference was that they were no longer working in the tiny Village Vanguard space or on the shoestring budget they had to contend with in the late 1930s and early 1940s. In the movie sequence they gibe at Cinemascope, demonstrating its so-called intimacy with electronically generated echoes as they shout at one another from the confines of a thin extended band of space that stretches across viewers' TV screens. In the advertising sequence Green and a beautiful woman, revealed in evening dress amid a barren Dali-esque landscape, come to life and toast the joys of a fictitious brand of vodka.

Comden and Green's sequences brim with the sort of pop-cultural satire that had become, at least partially, their trademark. What's interesting about the program is that it also featured performances from Mike Nichols and Elaine May, whose improvised sketch routines were growing in popularity and acclaim nationally. Many saw this team's wry topical comedy as a natural extension of Comden and Green's work, and by the end of the year Nichols and May would even follow in Comden and Green's footsteps, offering their own *Evening With* at Broadway's John Golden Theatre, where *A Party With* had played.

In some respects the parallels between the two duos are almost uncanny. During the program Nichols and May perform one of the ads for the show's sponsor, General Electric, while dressed in formal attire and with "Someday I'll Find You"—by Comden-and-Green favorite Noël Coward—playing in the background. Their dialogue, delivered in crisp British accents, parodies a standard-issue breakup between a high society couple even as it includes the pitch for the many features of a new refrigerator. During this it's not hard to imagine Comden and Green penning a sketch called "What If Coward Had to Write Radio Commercials?" when they were beginning their careers together.

But Nichols and May were not simply echoing Comden and Green's work. They were expanding on it, making it edgier. In a scene that imagines two office workers taking a water-cooler break to bemoan the Charles Van Doren quiz show scandal, they also discuss topics ranging from warfare to integration to political speechwriting. Their work—and that of others—would become something with which Comden and Green would have to contend as the 1960s moved forward.

The pair got a sense of the changing tastes six months later, when MGM released the movie version of *Bells Are Ringing*. In an early June 6 *Variety* review, critic "Tube." noted that "cinemusiccomedies have become scarce commodities of late," and while praising Holliday's and Martin's performances and Minnelli's direction, the critic also noted that the screenplay "is not by any means the sturdiest facet of the picture, but it's a pleasant yarn." General press reviews were less forgiving of the screenplay. In Bosley Crowther's June 24 *New York Times* review, he lauded Holliday and her talents and then damned the writers who "shoved her forth and left her on her own" in "a jangled romance…made up of one slight gimmick and a lot of surrounding gags." Other reviews in New York and beyond were more forgiving of the screenplay, but audiences were not convinced, and the film did only respectable business, although it did show a modest profit.

Comden and Green, however, never allowed critical brickbats to faze them for long, and even as *Bells* was opening and they were preparing for the television specials, they were at work on two new musicals with composer Styne, both of which looked as if they might be fast-tracked to Broadway during the 1960–1961 season by David Merrick. And in between their work on the two television shows, Comden and Green flew to Las Vegas for a preliminary meeting with the man who had agreed to star in one of these: Phil Silvers. The comedian was planning to make his return to Broadway in a musical version of a novelette by Garson Kanin, *Do Re Mi*, for which Comden and Green were writing lyrics.

Kanin, of course, had written *Born Yesterday*, the play that catapulted Judy Holliday to stardom in 1946. He was also the author of many other Broadway shows and the screenplays for the Katharine Hepburn–Spencer Tracy classic *Adam's Rib* and the Ronald Colman classic *A Double Life*. Further, Kanin had extensive credits as a director on Broadway, including the stage adaptation of *The Diary of Anne Frank*. Silvers came to *Do Re Mi* with several Main Stem credits, including *High Button Shoes*, Styne's first stage musical, but he was best known, then as well as now, for his portrayal of Sergeant Bilko on his eponymous television show. On paper the combination of Silvers with such a respected creative team made it look as if *Do Re Mi* would be a box-office bonanza.

Kanin's tale originally appeared in *Atlantic Monthly* in May 1955 and then was published in book form, with illustrations by theatrical caricaturist extraordinaire Al Hirschfeld, in November of that year. In it Kanin imagined a two-bit con, Hubie, who finds himself doing "six to ten (months)" and, at the suggestion of the prison chaplain, writes about the events that led to him being arrested and convicted (again). It turns out that Hubie had come up with a way to earn a quick and semi-legitimate buck by gathering some old con cronies to enter the jukebox business. They muscled out competition by promising the owners of places where they put their machines 10 percent of the take.

When they learn that part of the jukebox business is also having exclusive rights to hot performers, they decide to create a star themselves. It almost looks like they find it with a kazoo group, but they ultimately hit the jackpot with Nan, a woman they meet running an elevator in a midtown Manhattan building. Originally from Tennessee, she's got a sound that proves to be a hit as she sings southern-fried tunes that she learned as a girl and accompanies herself on the zither.

Although some of their business practices might be considered a little aggressive, the guys actually do run a legitimate business up until a rival jukebox exec starts romancing Nan. When Hubie and his pals discover this guy's boss is a former enemy of theirs from the old days, things get messy, and after a nasty showdown in Atlantic City, Hubie is left holding the bag (along with a quartet of guns).

It's a clever Damon Runyon–like tale, and its comic appeal was enhanced by the amusing Hirschfeld illustrations. The book's actual layout also adds to the merriment of the novelette. It's typeset as if it is a verbatim reproduction of Hubie's handwritten tale, with misspellings and ungrammatical and sometimes odd syntax intact.

Film rights for *Do Re Mi* went to 20th Century Fox just as it was being published in *Atlantic Monthly* in May 1955. Over the course of the next 18 months the studio would heavily revise Kanin's story, turning the project into a vehicle for Tom Ewell, who had recently played a sweet, befuddled businessman with an overactive imagination opposite screen sexpot Marilyn Monroe in *The Seven Year Itch*. In the process, the movie, which had another blond bombshell, Jayne Mansfield, as Ewell's co-star, became known as *The Girl Can't Help It*.

The picture, released in December 1956, ultimately bore scant resemblance to the novelette. Beyond one gangster whose nickname is "Fats" and who has the same sort of personality as Kanin's Fatso and a recording industry exec who has the same name as one character in the novel, the movie has little to do with Kanin's work. It's only toward the end of the picture, when Fats undertakes to run an old crony out of the jukebox business in order to promote a single that his girlfriend (Mansfield) recorded, that a glimmer of Kanin's original plot appears.

The genesis for the stage version began almost concurrently with the idea of a movie adaptation. Styne read the novelette and approached Kanin about adapting it for the stage. However, the writer told the composer-producer that the property wasn't available, so Styne abandoned the idea. Then, sometime later, after the release of the movie, Styne happened to run into Kanin's stepson, Jones Harris. Styne knew the young man and felt that

Harris, the son of Kanin's then-wife Ruth Gordon and producer Jed Harris, had both an excellent knowledge of the theater and genuine potential.

During this meeting Styne suggested that the younger Harris consider producing, as his father had. Harris sloughed the idea off, but a few months later he returned to Styne. He thought that his stepfather's book would be a great stage venture and that Kanin might be interested in working on it. Obviously, Styne agreed, and Harris set about securing a release from 20th Century Fox and assembling the creative team. David Merrick signed on as lead producer, and Styne committed to writing the score. Kanin agreed to adapt and direct, with Comden and Green on board as lyricists.

Once the team and, later, star Silvers were in place, Merrick put the show on a fast track for the 1960–1961 season, meaning that everyone involved would have less than a year to write, refine, and rehearse the new production.

Meetings—among the collaborators and sometimes with the star— took place during the winter and spring of 1960. Kanin, who was working on a musical for the first time, began drafting a book, and his expertise with dramatic works shows in his early conceits for this musical. For instance, he envisioned an overture that would be played entirely by jukeboxes featuring segments of cover versions of songs from the show. Kanin also created sequences in which entire scenes were played out as phone conversations. For these sections of the script he imagined that actors would not be on different areas of the stage but rather heard through speakers that would be placed throughout the theater.

As for the story line, Kanin wrote something that remained staunchly faithful to his novelette with only minor tweaks to its original plot, which on the page had a pleasant, comically ambling quality. On stage, however, this sort of storytelling could prove unsatisfying. To help address the problem, Styne, Comden, and Green began to craft songs that would inform the book, character details, and story line.

One of the first songs they wrote was "Take a Job," which creates the underpinnings for one of the major dramatic conflicts in the show. In this number, Hubie's long-suffering wife, Kay, urges him to settle down into a normal life and to start working for her father's dry cleaning business. Hubie, however, believes that he will use his jukebox scheme to both make them wealthy and achieve his goal of becoming someone important, a man with whom the world will have to contend.

Styne, Comden, and Green penned other such numbers to define character, such as "I Know about Love," which paints a picture of a record executive named Wheeler who, although he might flood the market with tunes about romance, never gets to experience it himself. Other songs propel dramatic action, such as "Ambition," in which Hubie convinces Tilda, now a waitress at a Greenwich Village diner rather than an elevator operator, to embark on a recording career with him and his pals, and "Fireworks," which establishes what becomes the show's central romantic story, that between Wheeler and Tilda. These characters also delivered the show's classic "Make Someone Happy."

Not all of the musical contributions were meant to drive the story, and with some of these Styne, Comden, and Green seem to be enjoying poking fun at the pop music industry as they did with "Chief of Love" in *Say, Darling*. They wrote a trio of tunes meant to echo the banality of much of what was hitting the charts during the mid-1950s: "Love in Outer Space" (laughingly heard—at least in part—before "I Know about Love,"), "All You Need Is a Quarter" (a perky number that establishes the jukebox craze), and "What's New at the Zoo?," a goofy novelty song that Tilda delivers after becoming a star vocalist.

THE BROADWAY RECORDING BUSINESS

Styne wanted to ensure that "Make Someone Happy" was on the airwaves in advance of *Do Re Mi*'s opening, and as bidding intensified for the show's cast album he used RCA's keen interest to accomplish his goal. He stipulated that the company could record the score but only if it also released a Perry Como single. Execs agreed, and so did Como. After the singer heard a demo of the tune, Theodore Taylor reports in the biography *Jule* that Como said, "That's it," and cut the single. Thus, five days before *Do Re Mi* played its first tryout engagement, Como's recording—deemed a "bright rhythmic ballad" headed straight to the "spinning top" in a November 2 *Variety* review—was in stores.

Beyond adapting the basic story of *Do Re Mi* for the stage, Kanin also had to factor in current events and changing times as they developed the musical. Since the publication of the novelette there had been investigations into racketeering in the jukebox business on both local and national levels. Ultimately, such inquiries come into play in the show as Hubie's partners lose sight of the fact that they are supposed to be operating as "legitimate" businessmen. They bring in another old crony and hire him to start damaging Wheeler's machines. This attracts the attention of the Senate, and hearings are held to discover who the big man is behind the operation. All of Hubie's "pals" point their fingers at him, and he's delighted. He suddenly has become the celebrity he's always wanted to be.

Kanin cast the show with both Broadway vets and newcomers. Several in the former category had previously delivered Comden-and-Green material. Nancy Walker, the original Hildy in *On the Town*, snagged the role of Hubie's wife, Kay, and David Burns, whose relationship dated back to being their castmate in the ill-fated *My Dear Public* and who was later the lead gangster Dapper Welch in *Billion Dollar Baby*, played Brains, one of Hubie's old cronies. At his side were George Matthews as Fatso, whose extensive credits included the original production of Tennessee Williams's *A Streetcar Named Desire*, and George Givot, whose career as a musical theater performer began in 1929 with one of Earl Carroll's revues.

The show's newcomers played its central youthful romantic couple. Nancy Dussault, a recent graduate of Northwestern, got her first Broadway role as Tilda, and John Reardon, a tenor who segued between Broadway and opera with ease, snagged the role of jukebox exec Wheeler.

Rehearsals for the show began in October, and by the second week in November the company settled into hotel rooms in Philadelphia, where *Do Re Mi* was to play its first tryout engagement, opening on November 7. The next morning Henry T. Murdock offered a mixed review in the *Philadelphia Inquirer*, noting that Kanin was "a full length playwright rather than a librettist" and that the production was overlong. Further, he complained that it wasn't until the middle of the first act that "misgivings [about the musical] disappear when Jule Styne provides three show-stopping songs in a row." In the *Philadelphia Daily News* that day, Jerry Gaghan deemed *Do Re Mi* "a passable Broadway musical." A couple of days later *Variety* critic "Waters." derided the show, noting in particular that "for the most part Styne's score is more vociferous than melodious." While he did say that overall the show had "plenty of possibilities," he predicted, "The rebuilding is not going to be a short or simple process."

Indeed, retooling the show would be a hefty undertaking, particularly with regard to Kanin's conceit of having phone conversations interspersed throughout the proceedings. Gaghan's review was one of the few to mention them, and after writing that Boris Aronson's sets were "delightfully distracting," he added, "not so the telephone voices which come on for every scene change." After the Philadelphia opening, the sequences, which ran between 30 seconds and two minutes, remained in the show for a few more performances but then were summarily cut. Unfortunately, these excisions meant that Kanin had to struggle with how set changes would be accomplished in the absence of the voice-over scenes that had masked them.

When the show moved to Boston's Colonial Theatre, critics greeted it with both caution and enthusiasm. Cyrus Duggin's November 30 mixed review in the *Boston Globe* concluded by calling it "coarse rather than clever" and "loud rather than witty," before telling readers, "Each to his taste in a free theatrical country."

Unlike Comden and Green's previous experiences out of town, *Do Re Mi* did not require any hasty songwriting as it moved through its tryout engagements to its Broadway berth at the St. James. Kanin, however, did continue to tweak the book before the show's official December 26 opening.

As was the case with *Bells Are Ringing* and *Wonderful Town*, the reviews for *Do Re Mi* praised the stars—in this case, Silvers and Walker—while also heralding a terrific new talent, here Dussault. More important, the show itself proved a hit with New York's critics. Richard Watts Jr. in the *New York Post* described it as being "fast, professional, tuneful, funny, and delightful." In the *New York Times* Howard Taubman wrote, "In a tough season for musicals let us be grateful for one that has not entirely abandoned the amusement standard." And in the *New York Journal-American* John McClain enthused that the show was "a brassy and bountiful blockbuster."

The positive reviews established *Do Re Mi* as a bona fide hit, so much so that President-elect John F. Kennedy decided that he wanted to take it in during his last visit to Manhattan before taking the oath of office. Just before arriving in the city, his press secretary, Pierre Salinger, called the theater's box office requesting tickets for Kennedy, his guests, and members of his Secret Service detail. Salinger was gruffly rebuked by staff, who assumed that the call was some sort of practical joke.

Calls to Styne and others involved with the show established the validity of Salinger's request, but there was still a problem with accommodating the soon-to-be president. The performance was sold out; it was being used as a benefit for a synagogue. As the house filled up, ushers spoke to seated patrons to explain the situation. Eventually, through the good graces of ticketholders who shifted to folding chairs at the back of the orchestra, Kennedy was accommodated. Whitney Bolton, in a syndicated column at the end of March 1960, quoted Silvers as saying that what happened at the performance "proved one thing: Americans are good sports. There wasn't a squawk or refusal."

LIFE IMITATES ART?

Not only were illegal activities in the jukebox business on government officials' minds, but authorities were also concerned about an ever-growing trend of counterfeit LPs. In May 1961, members of one ring trading in bogus records were apprehended. A *Variety* story on May 10 described the arrests as stemming from "a cloak-and-dagger operation involving police agents posing as collaborators of the racketeers." The *Variety* story went on to report that the gang was planning on pressing 20,000 copies of the original cast recording of *Do Re Mi*.

As winter 1961 turned into spring, theatrical awards season arrived in New York, and with it came recognition for *Do Re Mi*, which received five Tony Award nominations, including one for best musical. In a season that also included *Camelot* and *Bye Bye Birdie*, the show failed to win in any category, although at the dinner in which the awards were presented, Richard Burton, who won best actor in a musical for his portrayal of King Arthur, walked over to Silvers and said, "I'm bringing the award here, where it rightfully belongs."[4]

Do Re Mi would continue on Broadway into the early part of 1962, but when it ended its 400-performance run, it was no longer playing at its original home, the St. James Theater. The production had moved to the 54th Street Theatre to make way for another show, Comden and Green's 10th Broadway offering.

CHAPTER 13

Writing a Darker Musical
Fairy Tale

In order to work on *Do Re Mi*, Comden and Green set aside a show that had been on their minds and in process for nearly three years: a musical version of Edmund G. Love's *Subways Are for Sleeping*. The book was a series of portraits of people who navigated through life in New York without the benefit of a permanent address or full-time job. He wrote it after finding himself in the same position, after a series of events left him in "a whirlwind of my own. When it all ended I found myself walking the streets. I needed more than a job. I needed to reassess life."[1]

Subways was not an anthropological study. Love did not enter into the world of these people to study it but rather because he "couldn't escape it." During this period he learned to admire the people he came to know who were living on the fringes of society: "They are people of ingenuity who do not conform to the patterns of life which 'sound' people prescribe." More important, he discovered that the distinction between himself and the people he spent time with during this period and someone who might be considered "a down-and-out bum" was a "matter of hope."[2]

Readers first encountered *Subways* when one section of what became the book was published in *Harper's Magazine* in March 1956. The following August, the CBS Radio Workshop broadcast a dramatization of what had been printed, and in late 1957 this tale, along with another nine, was published as the book *Subways Are for Sleeping*. In an October 6 *New York Times* review, Meyer Berger praised it for causing readers "[to] marvel that you have lived in Manhattan all your life, yet never been aware of these shadowy characters." Six weeks later a *New York Herald Tribune* review said that it was "a fascinating book about a remarkable group of people."

As national recognition *Subways* and the people Love profiled continued to grow, Jule Styne acquired the stage rights in February 1958, even as he, Comden, and Green were watching *Say, Darling* head into its first out-of-town performances.

By August 1958, a musical version of Love's book looked as if it might become a reality during the 1959–1960 season. Comden and Green agreed to write the lyrics, and Abe Burrows, coming off of *Say, Darling* and *First Impressions* with composer-producer Styne, committed to both adapting the stories and staging the production. Styne shared additional details about plans for the show the following May, just days after the opening of *Gypsy*. He and Comden and Green were planning to begin work on the songs for the *Subways* musical "right away."[3] Further, the musical, which had been pushed to the spring of 1960, would be one that would be a vehicle for Comden and Green as performers.

Within a month a new name, playwright Ketti Frings, became attached to the project. She, rather, than Burrows or Comden and Green, would write the book for *Subways*. Frings's history with them dated back to their days starting out as the Revuers; her husband, Kurt, had served as their agent. At that time she was best known for having written the story "Memo to a Movie Producer," which inspired the film *Hold Back the Dawn* and later her own novel of the same title. In the years that followed she had written screenplays for movies such as *Come Back, Little Sheba* and *The Shrike* and most recently was responsible for the stage adaptation of Thomas Wolfe's *Look Homeward, Angel*, for which she won the Pulitzer Prize for drama.

Frings wasn't the only new name attached to the aborning tuner. It also acquired a producer during the summer of 1959: David Merrick, who, believing that the writing team was off to a promising start on *Subways*, began accepting résumés in August 1959 from performers wanting to appear in the show.

During the last months of 1959, as Kanin developed the book for *Do Re Mi*, Comden and Green continued to collaborate with Styne on the score for that show while they also moved forward on *Subways* with him and Frings. But in late January 1960, Frings withdrew from the project, and Comden and Green stepped in to write the book as well as the lyrics for the musical. This change in the *Subways* creative team did not deter Merrick, and in the February 24, 1959, edition of the *New York Times*, Sam Zolotow reported: "It looks as if 'Subways Are for Sleeping' should be ready for a mid-September opening at the St. James."

ALWAYS MULTITASKING AND LOOKING AHEAD

Even as they were writing lyrics for *Do Re Mi* and book and lyrics for *Subways*, Comden and Green were able to play nearly 40 roles in the July 1960 issue of *Esquire* magazine courtesy of photographer Dan Wynn. He captured them as all of the characters they described as being part of the opening for the fictional musical *Ziggy!* Dressed and wigged ludicrously, Comden and Green portrayed everyone from the society types who attended to the ushers, actors, and back-stage technicians. It was a four-page spread that delivered a simultaneous comic punch and loving valentine to the theater, and for a brief moment they even considered adapting the pictorial scenario as a musical for themselves.

The potential September 1960 opening for *Subways* shifted to January 1961 when Merrick announced that Tyrone Guthrie was considering the script and might direct it. Having Guthrie helm the piece would have been a coup for both Merrick and Comden and Green. The British-born director had distinguished himself staging plays, both on Broadway and at the Stratford Shakespeare Festival, which he helped found, as well as at the theater that bears his name in Minneapolis. As for musicals, he had staged only one: the original production of the epic and picaresque *Candide*, which had music by Comden and Green's old friend and collaborator Leonard Bernstein. With both its subject and the style and vision that an artist such as Guthrie would bring to the production, *Subways* was going to be an unusual musical for the team.

Over the summer the writers enthused about their work on *Subways* and Guthrie's involvement. Comden told the Associated Press's Jack Gaver for a July feature: "Although we are working from the book, it has no story, being simply an account of certain backgrounds and characters, so we really had to start from scratch." And Green added, "We showed our first draft to Tyrone Guthrie, the famous British director, and he is as anxious to do the show as we are to have him. You know, many regard him as the world's finest stage director. We hope everything will jell so we can get it on next spring, but if it doesn't we'll wait for Guthrie to be free to do it."[4] The admiration was mutual. Leonard Lyons reported in one of his early July columns that Guthrie had told him: "I'm willing to pay to do this musical and be the world's oldest apprentice."

Even as director and writers were touting each other, Merrick was deal-ing with the schedules for his myriad projects. In May he announced that his production of Jean Anouilh's *Becket* would play the St. James as an in-terim booking so that he could hold the musical-friendly house for *Do Re Mi*. It was an indication that *Subways* would not be part of the 1960–1961 season, and that became official within a few weeks when Merrick announced that he would present *Subways* in the 1961–1962 season. Unfortunately, the delay meant that Guthrie had to withdraw from the production due to other directing commitments.

Comden and Green, of course, had to tend to the rehearsal and out-of-town tryouts for *Do Re Mi* and its December 1960 opening, and as 1961 dawned they took time away from their lives as writers to enjoy some time as performers. It started with their being able to celebrate the fact that, after 17 years, their first musical had finally received an original cast recording, or as good a facsimile of one as was possible. Columbia Records took Comden and Green, along with original cast members Nancy Walker and Cris Alexander, into the studio to record their numbers. Original company member John Battles did not take part in the sessions. In his place the role of Gabey was sung by John Reardon, who was working with Comden, Green, and Walker on *Do Re Mi*, during the Leonard Bernstein–conducted recording.

Comden and Green dialed back the clock in a similar fashion in February when they made their first appearance in a New York City nightclub in more than 15 years, accepting an engagement in the Empire Room at the Waldorf Hotel. As had been the case when they appeared downtown at the Cherry Lane several years before, the run was both quickly sold out and acclaimed. In a February 4 review for the *New York Times*, Arthur Gelb extolled their "artless, witty" performances, making special note of a new bit about international relations that fused the words of Joyce Kilmer's "Trees" with the music of "Brazil." "Try singing it—it works fine," Gelb advised readers, even as he also noted that they "sneakily conceal portable microphones on their persons."

After their four weeks at the Waldorf, Comden and Green flew to Florida to offer a one-night-only performance of *A Party With* at the Four Arts Theatre in Palm Beach, and then it was back to work on *Subways*. What astonishes is that even with all of the activity in their lives, Comden and Green finished a nearly complete draft of the *Subways* script, with indications of 15 numbers (more than eight of which would become reality) before they departed for their Palm Beach *A Party With* dates.

MRS. GREEN PERFORMS TOO

Green was playing a new role in early 1961, that of being a dad. On January 16, he and Newman welcomed their first child into the world, a son, Adam. Much like her always-busy husband, Newman worked during her pregnancy, taking a lead role in a new television whodunit series, *Diagnosis Unknown*, opposite stage and television star Patrick O'Neal. Newman learned of her pregnancy just after being cast, and the producers were supportive. As she explained to Harry Harris for a July 24, 1960, *Philadelphia Inquirer* feature: "I can play all of my scenes in a roomy lab coat. And they can bring the camera in closer and closer."

Comden and Green crafted characters for the *Subways* musical by drawing on Love's original in two distinct ways. With the lead male character, Tom, they fashioned a composite drawn from several men whom the author profiles. For the show's secondary romantic couple, Charlie and Martha, they drew more specifically from two sections of the *Subways* book, "No Fixed Address," about a man who survives by being a permanent guest at friends' homes, and "The Girl Who Wore No Clothes," which centers on a woman who staves off eviction from her hotel room by wearing only a towel and feigning illness.

To bring the lives of these three characters together, Comden and Green invented one central character: Angie McKay, a secretary to a soda business exec, Stewart Gates. As the musical begins, Angie is about to marry her boss and embark on a transcontinental honeymoon cum business trip designed to serve as a goodwill junket for the cola. After an unfortunate combination of nerves, alcohol, and pills (taken in advance of her world tour) causes her to bolt into the streets, she finds herself relying on Tom's street smarts to survive a night living outside.

By morning they've fallen for one another, and although there are some obstacles, ranging from his reticence toward being pulled out of his loner's existence to her fiancé's attempts to force her back into his life, Tom and Angie reach a happy ending. Ironically, Comden and Green have it come with a booming business success for Tom, which leads to the couple living a "normal" life.

Charlie and Martha meet and fall for each other concurrently with Tom and Angie's adventures. Martha initially thinks that Charlie might be a guy she can milk for a few dollars, but when she discovers that he's as penniless as she is, they form an odd bond. And when Charlie finds out that Martha needs to fork over $1,100 for back rent, he promises to help her, not knowing exactly how.

Coincidentally, he runs into Angie and recognizes her as the woman who's jilted his old prep-school pal Stewart. Charlie realizes that he might be able to get Stewart to pay some sort of reward—maybe $1,100 or so—to learn Angie's whereabouts. He sets the plan in motion, but when he learns that Tom loves her, Charlie, being a good egg, can't go through with his plan. Eventually, the four devise a scheme that will get Martha out of her predicament, which she embellishes with some blackmail of the hotel manager, and Charlie and she, too, can look forward to a life together as the musical ends.

Comden and Green's *Subways Are for Sleeping* at this juncture was a unique combination of the sort of New York–centric fairy tales they wrote for *On the Town* and *Bells Are Ringing* and something darker and more adult, in keeping with how musicals had begun to embrace more serious topics in the late 1950s. Beyond this, the work was prescient in anticipating what the mood would be at the end of the 1960s, when an era of free-spiritedness enveloped much of the country.

As the book took shape, Styne, Comden, and Green were able to begin working on songs that were carefully woven into the story. Styne's music, always melodic, continued to be so for this new project, but inspired by the subject, many of the tunes took on an edge. This quality is particularly apparent in "Ride through the Night," a song devised for an overnight subway journey that Angie takes with Tom. There's an ethereal quality to the tune as notes slide from one to another, making it almost seem akin to an adult "Never Never Land." Similarly, with "Strange Quartet," a number later abbreviated to "Strange Duet," Styne devised a way to musically bring four (or two) disparate voices together with bouncy tunefulness.

In other numbers, Comden and Green were providing bite with their as always colloquial and seemingly effortless lyrics. In "Be a Santa," performed by a group of sidewalk Kris Kringles, they have the guys extol their part in the season to "Help sell the spell of old Noël Noël," and with this one line the writers jab at the rampant consumerism of Christmastime, even in charity.

Likewise, in "Getting Married," an exuberant tune that sounds as if it might have served as the theme song for an early 1960s screwy newlywed sitcom, Comden and Green outfit Styne's melody with some rather ominous signs of the expectations Angie's fiancé has for the marriage. He's eagerly anticipating the tax deduction the union will offer him, having a wife and secretary rolled into one, and, worst of all to her, gaining someone to mother him.

Not all of the music and lyrics were designed to underscore the drama of the show. A prime example of charm in both music and lyric is "Comes Once in a Lifetime," a duet for Tom and Angie. Styne outfits this number with a jaunty and utterly carefree melody, making it sound as if it had been written for Frank or Dean or Tony or Sammy, and with a line like "Each day that comes comes once in a lifetime" Comden and Green deliver a punch of simple, saccharine-free sentiment. Interestingly, pieces of two numbers that Styne wrote for *Subways* that went unused later surfaced in his hit *Funny Girl*. An untitled song for Tom about his life as a businessman carried the melody of "Don't Rain on My Parade," while another song, "A Man with a Plan," contained the rousing melodic section in "Parade," where the Bob Merrill lyric includes lines such as "Who is all ginger and jazz..."

Early casting for the show also came into focus during the first half of 1961 when Sydney Chaplin was cast as Tom. This decision was made even though the show still had no director. It wasn't until June that Michael Kidd, who created the dances for the Comden and Green–penned movie

The Band Wagon and was a co-star in their *It's Always Fair Weather*, would direct and choreograph. Then over the summer there was additional casting news. Carol Lawrence, who originated the role of Maria in *West Side Story*, would return to Broadway to play Angie.

But news of Lawrence's casting was overshadowed in short order by word that Frank Sinatra had paid $1 million for the film rights to the show. The deal, widely reported in both industry and general interest publications, not only included his film company, Essex Productions, bringing the musical to the screen with him as the star, but it also reportedly included the rights to the original cast recording, which would be released by Sinatra's Reprise Records. Further, the deal was said to stipulate that he and other artists from the label would record singles of the show in advance of its December opening.

In a move that anticipated other events in *Subways'* difficult journey to Broadway, the Sinatra deal fell through within days of its announcement because producer Merrick had agreed to allow Columbia Records to release the cast album of the show. In the absence of having the rights to the show's music, Sinatra and his company withdrew from the film deal.

With the approach of rehearsals, Kidd finalized casting. For the role of Charlie he turned to comedian Orson Bean, who after years on the night-club circuit had come to Broadway in both the revue *John Murray Anderson's Almanac* and the comedy *Will Success Spoil Rock Hunter?* And although names such as Julie Newmar and Edie Adams circulated as possibilities for Charlie's towel-clad love interest, it was Phyllis Newman who snagged the role of Martha. Newman's path to the show was anything but smooth. The writers, of course, all knew her and thought she would be perfect for the part. Merrick, however, was reticent about the nepotism of casting Green's wife in the production. Auditions followed auditions, and it wasn't until she agreed to show up and perform in character—and wearing Martha's signature draped and tied terrycloth costume—that she won her spot in the cast.

Among the others whom Kidd cast was a young man getting his Broadway debut, Michael Bennett. He would, of course, go on to change the face of musical theater as a director-choreographer in the 1970s with his work with Harold Prince on musicals such as *Company* and *Follies* and later on his own, with *A Chorus Line*.

Subways rehearsals began on October 5, three-and-a-half years after Styne bought the rights to Love's book, and less than a month after that the company headed to Philadelphia for two days of preparation at the Shubert Theater before opening there on November 6.

The following morning the Philadelphia critics were reservedly supportive of the show, which had run two hours and forty-five minutes the night before. In the *Daily News*, critic Jerry Gaghan noted that the musical began with an "offbeat idea" and contained many "ingratiating" elements but suffered from "much repetition and some labored dialogue and situations." His biggest complaint was the romance that develops between Tom and Angie. After this came into play, he wrote: "The plot gets weaker as it devolves along a pretty predictable course." In the *Inquirer*, Barbara L. Wilson gushed about Styne's score, assuring readers that the show contained at least a half-dozen tunes that would be "'musts' for inclusions on everybody's top 10." Further, she wrote that Comden and Green's "topical and humorous lyrics put tasty frosting on his melodies." Wilson's major problem with the show was with the book and the way it seesawed between the Tom-Angie romance and the Charlie-Martha one.

Both critics agreed on two things. First, Newman was a stunner with a showstopper, "I Was a Shoo-In," a wildly comic number in which Martha, still clad just in a towel, describes the disappointments and injustices of the beauty-pageant circuit and states her resolve to never give in. Second, they fell for Will Steven Armstrong's scenic design, and each made specific mention of his set for the show's opening scene: a re-creation of the Metropolitan Museum of Art's Egyptian Wing.

Ironically—and before the reviews appeared—Merrick had corralled the writers and creative team, and chief among his complaints about what he had just witnessed was this set. "The scene is deadly," Merrick biographer Howard Kissel quotes the producer as saying. "The set and the scene are gone. The public can go to the Metropolitan Museum any day—for free!"[5]

Following this meeting and during the course of the next two months, Comden, Green, Styne, and Kidd would work nonstop revising the show. Before the production left Philadelphia, the character of Angie was entirely reconceived. She was no longer a bride fleeing a potentially unhappy marriage. Instead, she was a reporter for a fashion magazine who is sent to surreptitiously observe Tom and his world for a story. In the process she becomes smitten with both him and his worldview. In fact, as Love's book wound down he described how a newspaper woman came to be in the exact same position.

Green described their activity just after the out-of-town premiere to the *New York Times*'s Maurice Zolotow for a December 17 feature: "I'll never forget one ghastly week-end in Philadelphia when Betty and I wrote fifty pages of new dialogue on Friday and Saturday, and Mike Kidd put it into rehearsal Sunday."

As they rewrote the primary story line, two numbers were eliminated from the show, including "Getting Married," which was no longer pertinent to Angie's story, and "Got to Think of Her," a climactic number for Tom as he realizes he has new responsibilities because of his feelings for Angie.

As Comden and Green reworked the show's opening to obey Merrick's edict about the scene at the Met, they realized they needed to devise a new way to introduce audiences to Tom and his compatriots' world. In the process they, with Styne, found a way to write a title song for the show, an ersatz classical piece that introduces both the characters' worldview and the loopy tone of the musical. As they explain their lives, "The Sleepers" sing humorously about the age of "social security" and "unemployment insurance" letting them down, and these syllabically intricate phrases sit on rapidly cascading notes to delightful comic effect.

Just before the show opened in New York, Comden described how they took what were monologues for Tom and integrated the information in them into the number: "It was more dramatic to sum up the show musically this way."[6]

With the new opening, the excisions, and the new plot line for Angie, the show traveled to Boston for a November 28 opening, which was filled with its own off-stage drama between Merrick and one of the town's chief critics, Cyrus Durgin at the *Boston Globe*. Durgin was opting not to cover the musical and instead planned to see a one-night-only performance by the Netherlands Chamber Orchestra. In his place he was sending the paper's second-string critic, a man who would go on to have a reputation as both critic and biographer, Kevin Kelly. Merrick threatened to bar Kelly from the performance, and indeed on opening night he kept the reviewer out of the theater.

Kelly, however, had traveled to Philadelphia to see one of the musical's final performances there and used that for his evaluation in the *Globe* on November 29. Merrick needn't have worried about Kelly. While not raving about the show, the critic was supportive, calling the musical "a large, tuneful entertainment for the masses." He did have concerns, notably "lack of focus on Miss Lawrence in Act 1," but he still was able to offer praise while swiping at the producer in his conclusion, saying that theatergoers should start writing Merrick "at the North Pole or Transylvania, or wherever he lives," to request a similar holiday treat for the following season.

There was still work to be done, and in the next month several new numbers were inserted into the show, such as "Girls Like Me," an opening number for Lawrence that helped to ground her revised character more soundly, and a short dance number for Angie and a pair of teenagers that opened Act Two, which had originally been just a book scene between Lawrence's and Bean's characters on a subway platform. Kidd conspired to have her enter solo and engage in a stylized version of "The Twist" with a pair of teenagers (one of them played by Michael Bennett) who were waiting for a train.

The show also gained a new final number before it left Boston. It had not come easy. When he heard of the request, Styne protested. "He thought the old finale was good. He didn't want to write another one. He lost his temper and for almost two hours raged against Comden and Green."[7] Eventually tempers cooled, and Styne relented, writing the necessary music.

Finally, *Subways Are for Sleeping* opened on December 27, and as the house filled, Comden and Green might have been thinking about one of their recent descriptions of a first-night audience: "One large collective Nero about to say 'Thumbs up or down!'"[8] The following morning they found the reviewers had given them both. In some instances, the critics were, as they had been on the road, supportive, if not overly enthusiastic. A prime example came from Richard Watts Jr. in the *New York Post*, who called it "a likable entertainment" while also noting "the suggestion of being unfinished does cling to it."

Other critics were unable to get past the subject matter. In his *Journal-American* review, John McClain wrote: "There is nothing highly hilarious or entertaining or remotely believable in this hoked-up kingdom of vagrants who infest the city." And in the influential *New York Times*, Howard Taubman described the musical as one that "stumbles as if it is suffering from somnambulism. Its book is dull and vapid, and its characters barely breathe."

At this juncture producer Merrick again took center stage, along with the show itself. He had been as newsworthy as the musical he was presenting throughout its journey to Broadway. Beyond the Sinatra snafu and the Kelly flap in Boston, he sparked headlines when he went head to head with New York's Metropolitan Transportation Authority (MTA) after being told he needed to change or remove his below-ground advertising for the production because it seemed to be promoting subway vagrancy, carrying only the words "subways are for sleeping." The producer took this spat further when he agreed to pay legal expenses for a man who was arrested for having slept on the trains.

In the wake of the reviews, he concocted a scheme that he hoped would uniquely and memorably put his production in front of the public. It became one of the theater's most infamous advertising stunts. After having members of his staff troll the phonebooks for men who bore the same name as the first-string critics for all of New York's daily newspapers, Merrick invited each of them with a guest to dinner and offered free tickets to the show. In return he asked that they each lend their name to a supportive quote (written by his publicist) about the production.

The men agreed. Howard Taubman announced that the show "lends luster to this or any other Broadway season," and John McClain proclaimed it was "a fabulous musical." Merrick took these and the others' quotes and created a full-page display ad that was sent for placement in newspapers, and before editors caught on to the scheme the ad ran in some editions.

Ultimately, though, it was pulled. The effect, however, was felt for weeks to follow as both arts journalists and editorial writers discussed the stunt.

It wasn't, however, enough to ensure *Subways'* longevity. The show barely made it to summer, concluding a 205-performance run on June 23. It would be remembered by fans thanks to a handsome cast recording released during the run, by theater buffs fond of scandal thanks to Merrick's she-nanigans, and by Newman herself, who picked up a Tony Award for her performance as Martha. As for Comden and Green, they would look back on it some 30 years later, when the show was featured as one of the Christmas windows at Saks Fifth Avenue. Comden described the show as being "about people in New York finding their way back into society and normal life." And Green added, "It was a romantic show...a beautiful fable of New York."[9]

WHO RIDES THE *SUBWAY*?

Controversy spilled over onto *Subways Are for Sleeping* during its run because of how the show had been cast. In April 1962, protestors picketed in front of the St. James to decry the lack of diversity in the show's company, and among the placards they carried was one that read, according to a story in the April 4 edition of *Variety*, "Merrick Operates an All-White Subway." The sad irony with this situation at the dawn of the civil rights era is that Comden and Green's work from the outset had included African Americans. The integration of *On the Town* had, of course, sent Louis B. Mayer into a rage.

Comden and Green had brought two musicals to Broadway in the space of 18 months, and as 1962 got under way they took an uncharacteristic break professionally. They had no specific project to work on, and yet, as was their practice, they met every day at Comden's to discuss ideas. During that time one project that they might have been mulling was a musical about the life of comedienne Fanny Brice.

Film producer Ray Stark announced his intention to bring the show to Broadway just weeks before *Subways* opened, and when he did Styne was named as the aborning show's composer. Eventually, the book- and lyric-writing responsibilities for the show that became *Funny Girl* fell to Isobel Lennart and Bob Merrill, respectively, but for a while Comden and Green were reading through a nearly 200-page transcript of an interview with Brice about her life and marking ideas for character and musical numbers in it.

They were also attempting to spark interest in a musical version of the classic movie *Sunset Boulevard*. They approached a potential star, Rosalind Russell, and director-producers Harold Prince and George Abbott about it, but to no avail. Neither she nor Abbott felt that it contained the appropriate elements to make a successful musical. Prince, however, was intrigued and made some attempts to interest Jerome Robbins in the idea, again with no luck. Eventually, though, a musical version of the Billy Wilder classic had to wait until 1993 when one with music by Andrew Lloyd Webber premiered.

During this period, too, Comden and Green began conceptualizing a television series based on *Bells Are Ringing*, but it would have to wait, because as they hit the mid-point of 1962, three new projects started to loom. Two of the pieces would take them into the familiar territory of light-hearted satire. One, like *Subways*, would require them to stretch artistically while also reuniting them with an old collaborator.

CHAPTER 14

Stage and Screen
Confections...and Something
a Little Deeper

A s was the case with the films they wrote for MGM, Comden and Green did not initiate their next project. Instead, they found themselves working with material that originated with another writer, novelist Gwen Davis, who was at the start of her career in 1962, with two books to her credit. Her first, *Naked in Babylon*, was a pulp paperback featuring a cover which promised "a perceptive novel of the young successful, or hungry in a new and very different Hollywood." Davis's second novel, *Someone's in the Kitchen with Dinah*, centers on a newlywed couple who move to the suburbs to discover that their neighbors are all swingers.

Written before both of these books was a story called "The Richest Girl in the World," and in it Davis inverts the trope of a standard-issue gold digger (such as the one Comden and Green created for *Billion Dollar Baby*), painting a portrait of a title character who can't imagine a life of wealth and luxury. Rather, she wants to live simply in a small cottage with a man whom she loves. Unfortunately, fate intervenes after she marries the man she believes will allow her to fulfill her dreams. He unexpectedly becomes a successful business man who works himself to death, leaving her a wealthy widow. Other marriages, husbands' deaths, and additional sizable bequests follow.

The tale had attracted the attention of Gene Kelly, who for a period held the option to turn it into a movie, but eventually he sold the rights to publicist Arthur P. Jacobs, who also saw big-screen potential in Davis's tale. In particular, Jacobs, who transitioned to the role of producer with this project, believed that "Girl" could become a terrific vehicle for Marilyn Monroe, who was indeed interested in the project. Unfortunately, her untimely death in August 1962 forced Jacobs, as well as director J. Lee Thompson (*Cape Fear* and *The Guns of Navarone*), who had joined Jacobs on "Girl," to rethink who might be their leading lady. By the end of November they had tentatively secured screen legend Elizabeth Taylor, then at the height of her long film career, to star in their film version of Davis's story.

Along with this news, Jacobs and Thompson announced that they had signed Comden and Green to adapt the short story for the screen. The team had actually been at work on the film for a while, having already penned the first draft of a treatment with the title *I Love Louisa*.

Jacobs and Thompson were going to spare no expense on the film and reportedly had agreed to pay Taylor $1 million to star. They were also seeking actors such as Frank Sinatra and Cary Grant to play Louisa's various husbands. As *I Love Louisa* moved from preproduction to filming, the extravagance of its producer and director was widely reported, particularly with regard to costumes. One Edith Head creation was a white chiffon gown, hand-embroidered with nearly 100,000 crystal beads. The film also featured jewelry from Harry Winston valued at more than $2.5 million.

Eventually, Taylor opted not to do the film, and in her stead the producers turned to Shirley MacLaine, riding high on the success of *The Apartment* and *Two for the Seesaw*, to play the often-married, often-widowed, always-enriched Louisa. Playing opposite her in the film, which eventually became known as *What a Way to Go!*, were Kelly, Robert Mitchum, Dean Martin, Paul Newman, and Dick Van Dyke.

It was this last actor who was cast as Louisa's first unlucky husband, Edgar Hopper, a childhood friend who quotes Thoreau and only vaguely attends to the business of the small store he owns in the town where they grew up. Martin, playing Leonard Crawley, who also grew up with Louisa and Edgar, comes from the family that runs the town with an iron fist, and when he insults Edgar's ability to care for a wife, Edgar decides it's time to beat Leonard and the Crawley control. He turns his tiny store into a huge discount shopping mecca and succeeds in putting the Crawleys out of business. At the same time, he puts himself into his grave.

Louisa, walking away with a $2 million inheritance, heads to Paris, where she meets American expatriate Larry Flint (Newman), a painter who uses Rube Goldberg–like contraptions set in motion by sounds from jackhammers and explosions to create his art. In him, Louisa thinks she's found a man with whom she can live happily ever after in penury, but after she casually suggests he use symphonic music to set his machines working, he becomes the toast of Paris and also an absent husband, who meets his death in a freak accident in his studio.

Similar fates await Louisa with husband three, Rod Anderson (Mitchum), a maple syrup tycoon who longs for a simple life, and husband four, Pinky

Benson (Kelly), a small-time song-and-dance man from Jersey City who becomes a screen idol thanks to Louisa.

The movie contains some of Comden and Green's goofiest plotting for the screen, some of their gently barbed wit, and also variations on gags and scenarios that had served them well before. In the latter category the most obvious is the psychoanalyst's couch from which Louisa tells her life story. Like the furniture in the climactic scene in *Auntie Mame*, it's on hydraulics and it can rise, fall, and rotate at the touch of a button. As in the earlier picture, the comedic possibilities that arise when its occupant finds herself higher than expected are exploited to their fullest.

Comden and Green, in a similar vein, also insert four parodies of cinematic genres into the screenplay. As Louisa describes each of her marriages, she relives her earliest days with each husband as if they were some sort of movie, and her visions come to life in the film. With Edgar it's a cutesy silent film. She sees her early days with Larry as "one of those wickedly romantic French movies," and this sequence is filled with quick cuts between scenes of Louisa and Larry making love, often in awkward positions that are made more awkward by "artistic" camera angles. Comden and Green also take a jab at subtitles in this portion of the film. Characters speak for extended periods in French, each of which is followed by a short phrase such as "She's pretty."

Lush Budgett (LB) Productions is behind the third Tinseltown parody, in which MacLaine, clad in Edith Head's expensive over-the-top finery, parades across the screen from one society party to another as the spouses perpetually remind each other to say "I love you." In the process there are also visual digs at some of the screen's top pictures of the time, including *My Fair Lady* and *Cleopatra*.

Finally, with Pinky it's a big, brash Hollywood movie musical, and here Comden and Green take aim at Jeanette MacDonald–Nelson Eddy operettas, the cinematography of Busby Berkeley, and even their own MGM canon. The sequence also includes two original songs by Comden, Green, and Jule Styne, the instantly forgettable "Love on a House Boat" and the charming ballad "I Think That You and I Should Get Acquainted," which helps to launch Pinky's career.

When Comden and Green's writing is matched with the sensibilities of director Thompson and his designers, each of these sections of the movie amuses, but unfortunately they also serve to enhance the disjointed nature of the film and its plot. As Louisa careens from one husband to the next, it's difficult not to feel as if each of the movie's four sections is somehow a stand-alone sketch rather than part of a cohesive narrative whole, despite Comden and Green's attempt to create two through-lines in the script. The first concerns Louisa's confession to a psychoanalyst (played by Bob Cumming), to whom she tells her tale of woe after being thwarted in giving her entire fortune to the IRS. The second concerns Leonard Crawley, the wealthy man from her hometown whom she refuses to marry when she's a young woman. He shows up late in the picture, and the film's coda concerns the happy ending that Louisa ironically finds with him.

Still, despite the fractured nature of the screenplay it brims with some of Comden and Green's zestful humor. When Edgar learns that Louisa loves him, he promises, "I'll make you happy. I'll never work hard. I'll never make good. I swear it." The inversion of typical pre-wedding oaths combined with Van Dyke's earnestly dry delivery makes the moment priceless. Similarly, a society dowager proclaiming about a piece of Larry's art, "If only Beethoven were alive he could hear this painting," drips with silliness on its surface and cuts deeper if one remembers that at his death the composer was deaf.

Comden and Green were, interestingly, never shy about not being particularly proud of the movie despite such assets. As it was preparing to open, Comden observed, "I think the picture could have been produced as well on a lesser budget and with some, ah, judicious cutting. But we wouldn't want to bite the hand that's feeding us."[1]

Critics were less politic than Comden when the reviews started appearing. In the April 1 issue of *Variety*, "Anby." announced that *What a Way to Go!* was "a big, gaudy, gimmicky comedy which continually promises more than it delivers by way of wit and/or belly-laffs." In the *New York Times* on May 15, Bosley Crowther echoed this sentiment, deriding the film's "disjointed social satire, slapstick farce and sheer unadulterated nonsense carried to the nth degree."

Critics from outside the New York area weighed in similarly. Richard L. Coe's May 21 review in the *Washington Post* opened with "'What a Way to Go!' has everything except wit, taste, and style." And the next day Philip K. Scheuer in the *Los Angeles Times* described it as a movie "filled with surprise gags and some not so surprising, and its satire often labors past the point." Yet this critic also knew that it was "a guaranteed audience-pleaser."

As the summer progressed Scheuer's prediction proved correct, and *What a Way to Go!* clicked with audiences. During its first week in New York, *Variety* noted its success in a May 20 headline for a story about box-office grosses: "'What a Way!' to Spite Critics, Going for Wow $73,000 N.Y." The story that followed noted that "in the face of many crix barbs," the film was "soaring." The story also mentioned that the film's success was even more surprising when the normal downturn in business because of warmer temperatures was factored in. Once the movie moved beyond Manhattan, it joined *The Pink Panther*, *Becket*, and *From Russia with Love* as one of the top 10 grossing movies in the country, according to *Variety's* weekly "National Boxoffice Survey." And even though critics warned moviegoers away from the picture, *What a Way to Go!* remained in the top 10 of the list for 10 weeks and in the top 20 for an additional five.

AN OVERSIZE OPENING FOR AN OVERSIZE FILM

For its New York premiere, Jacobs and Thompson conceived of a way in which the title *What a Way to Go!* could become literal. They scheduled the film's first showing at the Better Living Pavilion at the World's Fair in Flushing. Subway cars were specially outfitted for the event, and audience members, including the film's stars, were shuttled to the gala event from Times Square on a day that had been dubbed "Subway Day at the Fair." Beyond providing reporters and columnists with ample opportunity to discuss the plans for the premiere, it also offered an opportunity for the movie's title to become the night's catchphrase, as everyone attending could announce "What a way to go" as they got on and off the trains.

The *What a Way to Go!* premiere came just five weeks after Comden and Green celebrated the Broadway opening of their newest musical, *Fade Out– Fade In.* The show was devised as a vehicle for a comedienne seemingly traveling on a meteoric arc toward fame: Carol Burnett. She burst onto the scene as a star when *Once Upon a Mattress*, a musical version of *The Princess and the Pea*, debuted off-Broadway in 1959. Burnett played the title character in this zany interpretation of the fairy tale, and her performance won raves and helped propel it to a Broadway run.

Before this, Burnett had worked steadily in nightclubs, such as the Blue Angel (where Comden and Green once appeared with the Revuers), and had made television appearances, primarily on *The Garry Moore Show*, quickly becoming a face and name both familiar and popular in homes across America. Comden, Green, and Styne penned their new show specifically for her, and in November 1962, after another Broadway venture she was considering fell through, Burnett firmly committed to the project, then known as *A Girl to Remember*.

The story Comden and Green devised centers on Hope Springfield, who's plucked from the chorus of a Broadway revue and whisked to Hollywood by Lionel Governor, the head of F.F.F. Studios. His plan? To make her a star. Unfortunately, she's the wrong girl. Governor, who runs the studio with an iron fist, has six nephews who serve as his lackeys. He refers to each by number rather than name, and because he's wary of one, Ralph (#4), Governor has developed a mental block about the number four and is unable to say it. Thus, when he tells an underling which girl to take from the chorus, he indicates the wrong one. Although he wants to say four he says five, and that girl is none other than Hope.

Governor, however, isn't on hand to discover the mistake when girl-next-door-type Hope arrives. He's in Vienna being treated for his phobias about his nephews and business, which have resulted in chronic nightmares.

In his absence, Ralph takes it upon himself to put Hope into her first film, pairing her with the studio's biggest male star, Byron Prong, and the film *The Fiddler and the Fighter* goes into production.

Hope can't believe her good luck, and neither can another of Governor's nephews, Rudolf, a good guy who knows that there has to have been some mistake about Hope. She simply isn't his uncle's type, which, as he says "has up till now been more of the floozie type." Rudolf, who prides himself on not making waves at the studio and has the sad, silly job of taking care of the studio's trained seal mascot, doesn't act on his misgivings about what might have led to Hope's presence at the studio and finds himself falling for Hope. The feeling's mutual.

When Governor finally returns from Hollywood, he does two things. First, he gives Hope (whom he still hasn't met) a new name, Lila Tremaine, and then, upon meeting her, fires her, demanding that the chorus girl he originally intended, a statuesque beauty named Gloria Curie, be brought to California immediately. Governor also makes sure to follow through on his promise that Hope will never work in Hollywood again, getting her fired from a succession of jobs, including waitressing at the Brown Derby and working as a manicurist.

Gloria, though looking marvelous, faces trouble on and off the set, and eventually Governor comes to realize that his no-talent discovery, who cannot remember the simplest of lines, has only been using him, and while in filming, she has been romancing Byron. With a premiere just scant hours away he's in a terrible bind about the picture, but ultimately Rudolf comes through for his uncle, Hope, and himself. Even though Governor ordered all of the film of Hope destroyed, Rudolf kept it, and it's that version of the film that premieres at Grauman's. The evening proves, naturally, to be a smashing success, and the musical ends with Hope becoming the star she always dreamed of being, Governor having a success, and, yes, a marriage for Hope and Rudolf.

To accompany this tale, Styne composed a host of melodies that sound as if they might have come from the 1930s and, at the same time, have an early 1960s Broadway zest to them. Comden and Green brought their signature slyness to the songs, which run the gamut from an anthem for Governor's nephews expressing what propels them in their work, "Fear," to a purposefully cutesy tune for out-of-work Hope and an African American actor, who's also been released from F.F.F. Studios. A Shirley Temple–Bill "Bojangles" Robinson parody called "You Mustn't Be Discouraged" has them singing brightly about how you can't be fazed by hardships because "there's always one step further down you can go."

The team's lyrics burst with their combined encyclopedic knowledge of 1930s filmmaking, and nowhere is that more apparent than in Hope's Act

One finale, in which she revels in the new name that the studio has given her. It's a tune that Comden and Green pack, to often hilarious effect, with the names that screen greats from Cary Grant (Archibald Leach) to Boris Karloff (William Pratt) cast aside as they started their careers.

With Styne they were also able to craft numbers that catered to their star's particular strengths, especially her gift for impressions and vocal prowess in making unusual sounds. "Discouraged," for instance, gives Burnett a chance to riff on Shirley Temple's sweet, slightly lisping voice. In the love song "Forbidden Fruit," the actress is called on to mimic Jimmy Durante's signature sound, and in Hope's big opening number, "It's Good to Be Back Home," Burnett approximates the sounds associated with a number of Hollywood studios' iconic trademarks, from MGM's lion's roar to RKO's radio tower beeps. The number further asks her to imitate the sound associated with F.F.F.'s signature opener, a seal's bark, which indicates that the film has gotten "the seal of approval."

Comden and Green completed a draft of the script, including lyrics for many of the songs, by the spring of 1963, and at that juncture 75-year-old George Abbott, who staged their first musical nearly 20 years before (and guided Burnett in *Mattress*), came on board to direct their newest. In addition to the announcement of Abbott as director, the producers (composer Styne and partner Lester Osterman) scheduled a Boston tryout in late October and set a provisional Broadway opening date for November. In addition, *A Girl to Remember* got an unusual producing partner: American Broadcasting Company–Paramount Theatres, which was making its first foray into the world of Broadway. The deal was to back three musicals, all of which would have scores by Styne. The agreement also gave the company the right to release the original cast recording of the shows.

Abbott continued planning and casting during late spring 1963, and then, in June, the production, which already "had an advance sale close to $1,000,000,"[2] suddenly had to postpone its opening until May 12, 1964. The reason was that Burnett, who had just married television producer Joe Hamilton, was pregnant, and the delivery date would come sometime before the end of the year. Quite obviously she would not be up to the rigors of opening a new musical while in her second and third trimester. It was the first of what would become an increasingly complicated series of health-related issues that would affect the production, and in a June 26 column for the *Christian Science Monitor*, Melvin Maddocks would humorously—and presciently—quip: "Nothing of recent memory can rival the drama Miss Burnett has given [theater fans]."

During the last half of 1963 Abbott used the time to finalize casting for some principals. Lou Jacobi, who had appeared in such Broadway plays as *The Diary of Anne Frank* and *The Tenth Man*, was cast as Governor. Tina

STAGE AND SCREEN CONFECTIONS (167)

Louise, who had appeared in several Broadway revues and also the musical *Li'l Abner* and would eventually play the iconic role of Ginger on *Gilligan's Island*, snagged the role of Gloria, the chorine whom Governor intended to bring to Hollywood. Other casting included Dick Patterson, who had among his credits *Bye Bye Birdie* in which he replaced Dick Van Dyke, as Governor's nephew Rudolf; Mitchell Jason, an actor at the beginning of a Broadway career that would reach into the late 1980s, as Ralph; and Tiger Haynes, after stints in *New Faces of 1956* and a revival of *Finian's Rainbow*, playing Lou Williams, the black actor who finds himself in painfully stereotypical subservient roles at F.F.F.

The last piece of major casting for the show came just before the start of rehearsals. Jack Cassidy, the dashing leading man who was just coming off the musical *She Loves Me*, signed to play Byron Prong, the arrogant star who reluctantly finds himself sharing the screen with Hope.

ANOTHER MIGHT HAVE BEEN

Comden and Green might have had a chance to have a working relationship with one of the *Fade Out* principals, Lou Jacobi, before the musical began rehearsals. In early 1960 they, along with Jule Styne, took an option on the play *One Shoe Off*. The script was by a young writer who had been steadily making a name for himself in television: Neil Simon. Because of other commitments the team ultimately ended up passing on the opportunity to bring the show, which became Simon's breakthrough hit *Come Blow Your Horn* and featured Jacobi as one of its principals, to Broadway.

As Abbott completed the casting process, the musical got its final title. No longer *A Girl to Remember*, the show, which was briefly retitled *The Idol of Millions*, was now known as *Fade Out–Fade In*, which referenced a central number in the tuner, based on one of Hope's catchphrases. Whenever she was surprised by a turn of events, she would utter "fade out, fade in," referencing how quickly things can change in life, as on screen. The writers expanded on it to create a romantic ballad for Hope and Rudolf as they begin to realize their feelings for one another.

In late April 1964 the show and company moved from New York to New Haven, and on April 21 *Fade Out–Fade In* opened its first tryout engagement. The following day the *Hartford Courant*'s theater critic, T.H.P., summed up the show as "big, busy and bright." More so than with Comden and Green's previous two musicals, the reviewer was taken with *Fade Out–Fade In*, although there were concerns about the show's arc: "More comic skits spread more evenly over the show would be the best medicine."

In *Variety* that same day critic "Bone." was less charitable, noting that the show had an "antiquated book" and that Burnett "does well, except when they hand her pedestrian material." Still "Bone." recognized that Comden and Green's lyrics were "better than average" and that director Abbott could most likely handle "the considerable polishing yet to be accomplished."

Abbott and the writers set about working on the show, and by the time *Fade Out–Fade In* reached Boston two numbers had been cut and a new one written, "Take the Time to Fall in Love." This latter song replaced a pair of reprises during the show's final moments as Hope and Rudolf are nearing their happy ending.

Opening on April 29 in Boston, the show received some distinctly diverging reviews from the Beantown critics. In the April 30 edition of the *Boston Globe* Kevin Kelly wrote that the musical, though loaded with "a good deal of satiric humor," was "like its title: out, in, off, on, up, down." Two days later, in the *Christian Science Monitor*, however, Harold Rogers raved about book, lyrics, and score, noting particularly that "Miss Comden and Mr. Green have restored our pre-atomic security. They have given us back our Hollywood when men were men, girls were girls, and often the twain did meet."

The *Fade Out–Fade In* Boston run lasted several weeks, and it was during this period that the show underwent some of its most substantial changes. Most notably, and as they had with so many of their musicals, Comden and Green heavily revised the opening. Originally, the musical began with a professor offering a lecture on the history of 1930s movies and, in particular, Hope's unusual career. The framing device provided Comden and Green with the opportunity to satirize academic over-analysis of the period's featherweight entertainments, but the scene didn't set the proper tone for the paean they were about to offer to both the style of pictures at the time and Hope's adoration for Hollywood. To replace the sequence they devised an equally barbed one, featuring a washed-up Bryon Prong leading a group of tourists on a tour of Hollywood. As he does, he offers an ode, "The Thirties," to the days when he was a star. Comden and Green also cut the show's second scene and number ("They're at the Post"), which allowed audiences to encounter Hope and Gloria in the Broadway revue in which Governor first sees them.

Also notable among the Boston changes was Comden and Green's decision to move the title song from the first act to the second, where it became the musical's final number, replacing the hastily written "Take the Time to Fall in Love." To replace "Fade Out–Fade In" in Act One, Comden, Green, and Styne created a new number for Burnett that showed her goofier side as she falls for Rudolf, "Call Me Savage." This new tune resembled another one called "Forbidden Fruit," which was in the second act. It was cut, and in its place they slotted one more freshly written song, "Close Harmony," a zesty, Latin-infused number that musically gives life to the world at F.F.F. after Gloria arrives.

With these changes the show moved into the Mark Hellinger Theater and officially opened on May 26, and in response the following day critics were unanimous in their praise of Burnett. As for the show itself, the reviewers were more reserved. Some, like John Chapman in the New York Daily News, gushed: "I never stopped enjoying it while it was on." Others, though, including Howard Taubman in the New York Times and Walter Kerr in the New York Herald Tribune, deemed the material to be, as Taubman put it, "old hat." Both of these critics even chose the same point of comparison: Moss Hart and George S. Kaufman's Once in a Lifetime, a spoof of Hollywood that premiered in 1930.

But even Taubman admitted that thanks to Abbott's direction and Burnett's performance the musical "spreads enough good cheer to suggest that it will be around for quite a while." Ticket sales reflected this prediction, and the show was immediately playing to standing-room-only crowds eight times a week. Unfortunately, and right out of some Hollywood soap opera from the era being spoofed, events began to transpire against Fade Out–Fade In. On June 16 Burnett, who just seven months before had given birth to daughter Carrie Hamilton, suffered an abdominal ailment that forced her to miss a performance. Then in July a taxi in which the star was riding braked suddenly and "her head was thrust forward, producing an effect described as whiplash."[3] Burnett found herself unable to move several days later and as a result missed an additional two performances. Shortly afterward it was announced that she needed a week off for what was described as "minor surgery."[4]

Producers Styne and Osterman scrambled to find a suitable replacement for the week when Burnett would be hospitalized and soon announced that Betty Hutton, who began her career on Broadway in the early 1940s before moving to Hollywood, would go on for Burnett. Hutton's presence in the production had a certain novelty factor to it, but it was not sufficient to sustain the sort of ticket sales that Burnett had been generating. However, once its original star resumed performances at the top of August, Fade Out–Fade In was again doing capacity business.

As fall approached, CBS announced a new series in which Burnett would appear as well as a Christmas special that the actress would headline. Not long after, Burnett had to miss several Fade Out–Fade In performances due to muscle spasms, and by the middle of October she announced that she would require another hospital stay. Her doctors said that she needed to be placed in traction "for an indefinite period"[5] to treat injuries to several cervical vertebrae.

Burnett's departure from the show for an indeterminate time meant that Osterman and Styne had to either find a replacement of equal caliber or temporarily close the show. Unable to find a suitable substitute, they eventually posted a closing notice, but before they did they filed two separate actions. One was in New York Supreme Court, where they asked that an injunction be made against CBS from using Burnett for any television work. The other filing was with Actors' Equity, where they hoped to have the union compel Burnett to honor her contract.

Following the closure of *Fade Out–Fade In* on November 14, the battle between the producers and Burnett unfolded in the papers, often with vitriol. Burnett also filed charges against her bosses with Equity. She stated that they were "trying to destroy me as a performer."[6] She also held a press conference on November 24, where she said, "I believe everything the producers have done has been for the sole purpose of extracting money from me—they want me to buy my way out of the show."[7]

The battle and hearings continued into 1965, even as Burnett would occasionally report to work for taping at CBS. Finally, on January 26, all parties involved reached a settlement, and although its terms were not made public, the producers and star could announce that *Fade Out–Fade In* would resume performances on February 15.

When the musical started back up it was hardly the same show that audiences had seen the previous year. Comden and Green had made substantial changes to the book, eliminating the opening and rewriting Hope's backstory. She was no longer a former chorus girl but rather an usherette, which as *Variety* critic "Kenn." pointed out in a February 24 re-review, "seems more likely."

The score also had been revised, with perhaps the most notable change being made to Burnett's Act One closer. "Lila Tremaine" was dropped in favor of the title song they had written when the musical was known as "A Girl to Remember." The change allowed Burnett to end the first half of the show on a more exuberant and less comic note. Comden, Green, and Styne also wrote "Notice Me," a gently plaintive ballad for Rudolf as he begins to realize his feelings for Hope, and "Everybody Loves a Winner," which was inserted at the top of Act Two, replacing Hope's bluesy "Go Home Train." But this latter song wasn't always offered. In the *Variety* review "Kenn." noted that it "was not done at the performance caught."

It wasn't just the material that changed. There were also differences in the company. Jack Cassidy had departed, and Dick Shawn had replaced him as Byron. Additionally, although she had been with the company for a while, Judy Cassmore was now Gloria—this following Tina Louise's departure the previous June to start her work on *Gilligan's Island*.

Unfortunately, whatever momentum the show had in late 1964 did not carry over into 1965, and as *Fade Out–Fade In* resumed performances it played to half-full houses. Further, during the first three weeks of the show's reopening Burnett missed several performances, which necessitated refunds. Ultimately, Osterman and Styne posted a closing notice, and the musical ended its run on April 17, having cumulatively played 271 performances.

As the strife over *Fade Out–Fade In* unfolded, Comden and Green could take refuge in another musical project, one quite different from either of the lighter-than-air confections they had been working on in their recent past. The new one had been on their minds well before *What a Way to Go!* and *Fade Out–Fade In*: a musical adaptation of Thornton Wilder's *The Skin of Our Teeth*.

This project reunited them with their first collaborators on Broadway, Leonard Bernstein and Jerome Robbins, and was announced just weeks before their involvement with *What a Way to Go!* was made public in 1962. At that time the creators told the press they anticipated that this new venture would be ready for a premiere during the 1963–1964 season. Comden commented on why they were looking at such an extended development process for the show, saying, "We haven't started work on it yet." She did note, though, that they had "been meeting on and off whenever we can."[8]

The quartet had continued to be busy since then. Comden and Green wrote both a movie and a musical. Robbins's schedule included a production of Bertolt Brecht's *Mother Courage and Her Children* and Styne's *Funny Girl*. Bernstein had a grueling schedule with the New York Philharmonic. Eventually, Robbins's slate grew to include *Fiddler on the Roof*, which opened September 22, 1964.

As Robbins was shepherding this last musical to Broadway, Bernstein announced that he would be taking a sabbatical from the Philharmonic to ensure that he would be able to dedicate himself to the new musical. And as soon as *Fiddler* opened, he, Comden, Green, and Robbins could concentrate on *Skin of Our Teeth*, which the creators now envisioned as being part of Broadway's 1965–1966 season.

The delay did not, however, deter the show from gaining an important investor. Just before the *Fiddler* opening, CBS announced that it would be the sole investor in the new musical. The deal included a commitment of "$400,000 plus a 20 percent overcall if more funds" were needed.[9] It was only the third time that the company had backed a Broadway musical. CBS's previous investments were in two by Alan Jay Lerner and Frederick Loewe: *My Fair Lady* and *Camelot*.

Wilder's play was an unusual choice for musicalization. The 1942 Pulitzer Prize winner takes audiences on a surreal journey with Mr. and Mrs. Antrobus; their two children, Henry and Gladys; and the family maid, Sabina, as they endure everything from a modern-day ice age to a world-devastating flood to a colossal war. Biblical and classical allusions collide in the play, which is set in suburban New Jersey in the then–present day, and the result is a simultaneously absurd and cutting drama about humankind's seemingly indomitable spirit.

When the play premiered on Broadway, and in many subsequent productions, the Antrobuses were portrayed as pillars of the community, good, upstanding exemplars of Yankee wholesomeness and stoicism. As he began work on the project in 1963, Robbins asked his partners if they would consider a "comic approach and get Zero Mostel and Ethel Merman to play the Antrobuses."[10] Comden and Green slowly gravitated toward—and ultimately embraced—Robbins's idea, and even while they and their partners were working on other projects, the concept was one that informed their earliest ideas about what the new musical might be and also fueled their meetings with Bernstein, which began in earnest over the summer of 1964.

As soon as *Fiddler* opened, Robbins joined the meetings and work sessions that were taking place at Bernstein's Upper West Side home. Eventually, they opted to leave the city and have a retreat in Martha's Vineyard, where they could devote themselves to writing and shaping the piece, which came to have the working title of *Help! Help! Hooray!*

A draft of a full book, with lyrics to nearly half the 17 numbers conceived for the show, was completed by early December. Robbins's approach to Wilder's work inspired Comden and Green, who took what had already been a loopy theatrical ride and made it zanier. Their playfulness begins with the show's title and a song of the same name, a simple yet sly revision to the familiar "Hip! Hip! Hooray!" Both were meant to indicate a simultaneous plea for assistance and an exuberant cry of joy.

As they maintained the basic arc of Wilder's play, they streamlined it and also expanded upon its meta-theatrical qualities. In the original, a stage manager is on hand to help steer the action. For *Help! Help! Hooray!* this character's presence is more keenly felt, as is the antagonism between him and the actress playing Sabina as she attempts to make the tale more palatable for theatergoers, much to the stage manager's chagrin.

Comden and Green's unique ability to reference pop culture also comes into play repeatedly in their draft script. They have Sabina break into a phrase of Rodgers and Hammerstein's "Getting to Know You," from *The King and I*, because it's a chipper tune. And when the Antrobuses show a home movie of the plague of locusts, Comden and Green indicate that it should be accompanied by a portion of Herbert Stothart's score for *The Good Earth*. In their drafts they even go so far as to jeer at one of their own shows, *Peter Pan*, as Sabina asks the audience to clap if they believe in survival.

While Comden and Green were energized by the seemingly boundless possibilities this adaptation offered them, Bernstein was battling with finding a musical sound for the show. "Skin is stalled," he wrote in a November 29 letter to Jack Gottlieb. "Life, this agonizing November, is a tooth with its skin stripped off. I don't know what I'm writing. I don't even know what I'm *not* writing."[11] Nevertheless, during their working sessions Bernstein did develop melodies for at least six of the show's songs.

Just over a month after Bernstein wrote this, and only three weeks after the date on Comden and Green's draft script, a press release arrived on journalists' desks announcing that the team was abandoning the project. There were too many other commitments each had to honor, "particularly Mr. Bernstein's return to the Philharmonic in mid-summer." As a result they felt there was "too little time in which to fulfill this difficult process." When questioned about what happened, Comden insisted that she, Green, Bernstein, and Robbins parted amicably and that their decision stemmed merely from their "having problems solving the adaptation, which had created production difficulties."[12]

Bernstein, however, may have been less politic. In Sam Zolotow's report about the dissolution of the partnership in the January 5 edition of the *New York Times*, he told readers that Bernstein told an unnamed friend that he felt that six months' worth of work "had gone into the wastebasket" because of "a dispute with colleagues." Bernstein's output from this period was not totally wasted, as he eventually used portions of songs written for *Hooray!* for his *Chichester Psalms*, which premiered in July 1965.

Speculation about what happened to *Help! Help! Hooray!* continued as 1965 progressed, and when Bernstein wrote a poem about his year's sabbatical for the *New York Times*, readers gained some additional clues as to what happened. Bernstein describes their "bleak reward." They found themselves "uneasy" with their work, and so "we gave it up and went our several ways/Still loving friends."[13]

Indeed, Bernstein and Comden and Green would continue to be close friends and would work together in the future, which confirms both his and Comden's insistence that acrimony was not a factor in their decision. Intriguingly, Bernstein's November letter, which references his despondency over the sudden, violent deaths of President Kennedy and Marc Blitzstein, gives credence to Robbins biographer Amanda Vaill's theory about why the creators abandoned the work. "All four collaborators apparently had second thoughts about where their vision would take them. 'We did not want to think of a world after nuclear war,' said Jerry."[14]

Regardless of why the project was abandoned, there was one certainty for Comden and Green. They were starting 1965 with a clean slate professionally. This, however, did not mean they were idle, and as had increasingly become their habit during the past few years, they threw themselves into their social lives and myriad smaller projects even as they worked to develop new stage and film properties.

THORNTON WILDER ON A MUSICAL *SKIN*

A July 20, 1975, letter in Nigel Simeone's *The Leonard Bernstein Letters* finds Thornton Wilder saying, "While I'm alive no one will write or compose an opera based on [*The Skin of Our Teeth*]." The impetus seems to have been a renewed interest Bernstein had in some of the songs he had written with Comden and Green 10 years before. Wilder's wishes were not adhered to after his death, and a musical based on his play by Joseph Stein (book), John Kander (music), and Fred Ebb (lyrics) appeared at regional theaters between 1999 and 2007. The work never reached New York, however, and ultimately the rights reverted to the Wilder estate.

CHAPTER 15

Part of the Times, Personally
and Professionally

In just four years Comden and Green had opened three musicals on Broadway and scripted one feature film. They had also, during this period, managed to continue their active social lives and attend to family matters.

In an era when a working mother was still not the norm, profiles of and interviews with Comden would often turn to her life at home with her husband, Steven Kyle, and her two children, making her appear to be a woman who, as the phrase would go 10 or 20 years hence, "had it all," a career and a terrifically stable family life. She even described, just after *Fade Out–Fade In* had opened, how she believed that being a working mom was beneficial to her family: "I think [Steven and I] both feel we have a better family situation. I don't see myself as keeper of hearth alone."[1]

Similarly, and during the middle of preparing for *Subways Are for Sleeping* rehearsals, her prowess as an "exotically beautiful hostess" for the parties she threw for her children and their friends was touted by women's columnist Florence Pritchett Smith in the *Philadelphia Inquirer*'s "Weekend Food Guide" on July 13, 1961. "I like my children to have what we call adventures in eating," Comden said. This extended to the young people's friends, and Smith's column described a fete Comden threw for the kids that featured a Chinese meal she had cooked. It also included Comden's recipe for sweet and sour spare ribs and outlined her decorating tips for women who wanted to entertain similarly.

From 1964 forward Comden, as well as Green, began to shift priorities to life outside the theater and film. It wasn't that they stopped having their daily meetings to discuss and develop new ideas and work on projects; they simply began trying to achieve more of a balance between their work and their private lives.

This had begun with Comden even as the fate of *Fade Out–Fade In* was being decided by attorneys and arbitrators, and it resulted in a family trip to Europe that was scheduled to coincide with Susanna and Alan's Easter break from school in spring 1965. She later described the reaction that greeted the news in a self-penned travelogue for the December 1965 issue of *Vogue*: "The children, cool characters both, reacted with spontaneous, uncontrolled emotion, and actually wept with joy." She reported that after this they ecstatically cried, "At last we can go to Liverpool!"

Neither Comden nor Kyle was enthusiastic about dedicating one of the few days in England (they had allotted five) to a side trip to the city that gave birth to the Beatles, and yet they couldn't deny their kids' request. They set aside a day for a pilgrimage to a rock 'n' roll mecca, but before this they were in London, enjoying traditional sights along with two visits to the famed Ad Lib Club, which were arranged by Comden and Green's friend photographer Richard Avedon. There the children met members of the Rolling Stones and Herman's Hermits. The experience made them, as Comden quipped in her *Vogue* story, "the most hated kids on the block."

The family, also through connections, visited the set of the Beatles' movie *Help!*, where they all were able to meet and chat with the Fab Four. As they did, the guys convinced the young people there was no need to travel to Liverpool, and for this Comden wrote in her *Vogue* story, "In the U.S.A. there is one mother who is eternally in their debt." Susanna and Alan were able to return home with a souvenir of the city they never visited: A friend of Comden's sent them a plank from the floor of the club where the Beatles started out. It was autographed by owner Ray McFall, guaranteeing its authenticity, and the wood was, Comden told her *Vogue* readers, "reverently and lovingly" carried by hand, alternatively Susanna's and Alan's, back to New York.

PRESERVING THE MUSICAL THEATER HERITAGE

In 1964 Comden and Green joined forces with pianist Richard Lewine for an ambitious but never fully realized project for Fred Astaire's Ava label. The trio was to curate a series of eight LPs that would become an anthology of American musical theater. The first album, *Remember These*, was one cut by Comden alone, featuring songs from two obscure musicals: George and Ira Gershwin's *Treasure Girl* and Richard Rodgers and Lorenz Hart's *Chee-Chee*. Sadly, the LP received only mild critical praise, and in response, the series was abandoned. Not to be outdone, Green went into the studio himself around this time, though not for this project. He sang the Danny Kaye role in a studio recording of *Lady in the Dark* that was headlined by opera great Risë Stevens.

In Green and wife Phyllis Newman's household there were also now two children. Newman gave birth to a daughter, Amanda, on December 29, 1963. As she had while carrying her now four-year-old son Adam, she worked during her pregnancy, primarily appearing on the game show *To Tell the Truth*. "I stayed on the show until a couple of days before she was born," Newman told AP reporter Cynthia Lowry for a January 1965 wire service feature, adding, "All it took was a couple of mornings a week, a few changes of blouses or tops—all that showed was the tops."

Adam would watch his mom when the shows were broadcast, and it led to an amusing moment at his nursery school. When he was asked what his mother did, he quipped, "She gets up and she sits down."[2] After Amanda's birth, and while Green contended with the maelstrom over *Fade Out–Fade In*, Newman continued to appear on the game show and also became a regular on NBC's *That Was the Week That Was* (or "TW3"), which could be considered an early precursor of *Saturday Night Live* and, on some levels, an extension of the work that Comden and Green had done with the Revuers.

Because the Greens' children were so much younger than Comden and Kyle's, there weren't European vacations for them, but Adam still was a "boldface name" because of his parents' celebrity. On December 18, 1964, columnist Radie Harris in *Newsday* reported that the boy, along with Kate Burton (daughter of Richard Burton and Sybil Christopher), would be co-hosting a Christmas party for "all the 'in' children in town," such as Angelica Page Torn, daughter of Geraldine Page and Rip Torn.

Comden and Green's ascension as members of New York's high society was escalating during this time as they and their working spouses strove to also concentrate on their home lives. They lent their names to an increasingly varied array of charitable groups, from arts organizations to Jewish causes. In addition, they also found time to support political candidates whose views coincided with their own. In late 1964, for instance, they attended a benefit for Robert Kennedy's senatorial bid at diplomat William vanden Heuvel's home in the famed Dakota apartment building at 72nd Street and Central Park West. Along with artistic friends and collaborators such as Leonard Bernstein and Abe Burrows, the guest list included a who's who of the upper echelons of New York society, from Jackie Kennedy to Gloria and Wendy Vanderbilt. One guest commented that hostess Jean vanden Heuvel had "accomplished the impossible: She made the West Side look like the East Side."[3]

The Greens' acquaintance grew with former First Lady Jacqueline Kennedy, and by late 1965 they were deemed part of "the nucleus of the Jacqueline Kennedy Group," which comprised "stage personalities, writers, painters, and beautiful girls. Anything but old line society."[4] Comden was also part of this group, but she was not as heavily identified with it or any of the other cliques that were becoming the mainstays of the societal whirl in Manhattan at the time. Still, when Truman Capote hosted his famed "Black and White Ball" in November 1966, both the Greens and the Kyles were among the carefully chosen guests. Green reportedly was in "high spirits" that night after another partygoer told him, "You dance just like Fred Astaire."[5] The comment came from the dancing legend's sister, a whiz on the floor in her own right, Adele Astaire Douglass.

Beyond such festive events there were more somber affairs on the Comden and Green schedule during this time. In particular they had to contend with the death of and memorial service for their old friend Judy Holliday, who passed away from cancer in June 1965. Similarly, the assassination of President Kennedy that so haunted composer Bernstein as they worked on the musical version of *The Skin of Our Teeth* continued to be a part of the team's consciousness and life, as they were frequently called on to lend their names to the events raising money for building the library bearing his name in Boston.

The team didn't curtail their busy social schedule as new projects became part of their lives during the final months of 1965, and in fact pieces of their private lives became woven into their next project: a screenplay that MGM producer Arthur Freed requested.

The film that Freed brought them on board for was one that he had been trying to get in front of cameras for a couple of years: a major motion picture using the Irving Berlin songbook. Freed began preparations for it after he had MGM purchase rights to the Berlin tunes, turning to Arthur Laurents to write a screenplay in mid-1963. Given Laurents's acclaimed work on the books for *Gyspy* and *West Side Story*, Freed's long track record at the studio, and Berlin's unparalleled canon of music, hopes were high for the project, but by August 1964 there were rumors that there were troubles with the film's development and that Freed had brought in Leonard Gershe, who had written the screenplays for *Silk Stockings* (for MGM) and *Funny Face* (for Paramount Pictures), to do a revision. As columnists wondered in print if the film would get made, Freed assured them that the project was still on schedule and that talk of the film's shooting being delayed into 1965 were not to be believed.

Freed, however, was just putting on a brave face, and a year later he announced that he had brought Comden and Green to the project. At this juncture Freed also indicated that Julie Andrews, cresting on the releases of *Mary Poppins* and *The Americanization of Emily* in 1964 and then *The Sound of Music*, was interested in starring in this movie, titled *Say It with Music*.

RESPECTFUL YET SARDONIC

Agent Irving "Swifty" Lazar brokered both Arthur Laurents's and Comden and Green's deals for *Say It with Music*. Lazar didn't represent composer Berlin, but he knew and respected him. "He was one of the smartest business-men and traders in the business," Lazar recalls in his memoir, *Swifty*. The agent also describes how Berlin would always attempt to spread his earnings out over many years and how a quip from Green best "pegged" the composer. Lazar reports that Green asked Berlin: "Why don't you take a dollar a year for a million years?"

By the beginning of 1966 Comden and Green had completed several drafts of their screenplay and solved the issue of how to incorporate approxi-mately 25 of the composer's existing tunes along with seven new ones. They borrowed a page from their development process for *Singin' in the Rain* and realized that they needed to reference the variety of periods in which Berlin, whose songwriting career began in 1907, had written. Thus, their film cen-tered on a trio of tales: one set in the 1910s, one set in the 1920s, and one set in present-day New York. The uniting thread for the parts was that they told girl-meets-boy stories, with the central female character in each considered to be, at least for the time in which she lived, "a modern woman."

In the film's earliest time setting, this character was Jane, an Upper East Side heiress to a banking and publishing fortune who, thanks to the guid-ance of a left-leaning editorial cartoonist, becomes aware of the plight of the women employed by her father, as well as other working women in the city. Jane soon becomes involved both in labor issues and the women's suffrage movement and with the cartoonist himself.

Jane's counterpart a decade later is Jill, a chorine in a Broadway revue, set, naturally, at the Broadway venue Berlin owned, the Music Box Theatre. One night there she meets her childhood screen idol, Larry Wallace, a man who bears distinct similarities to Green's own idol of the time, Charlie Chaplin. Larry, preparing to open a film that will discard the persona that has become his onscreen trademark, develops an almost immediate roman-tic interest in Jill, but before sparks can fly between them a producer offers her the chance to star in a Broadway show, which means that she will not be able to travel with Larry to California or beyond, his destination being entirely dependent on the reception his new project receives.

For the third story in *Say It with Music*, Comden and Green imagine Jenny, a young woman living in New York in the mid-1960s at work on her PhD in sociology. When a publisher approaches her about adapting her master's thesis into a self-help or do-it-yourself paperback, she initially bristles at the idea. Then she decides that she can accomplish the hypothesis she set forward in her paper: that any woman can establish herself as the city's most-photographed, sought-after, and intriguing personality if she goes about it with cunning and determination. Jenny succeeds and in short order becomes the toast of New York, so much so that she ditches the editor who first came to her (and also has a romantic interest in her).

It's in Jenny's tale that Comden and Green filter in facets of their own lives, going so far as to give Kenneth—a.k.a. Kenneth Battelle, who styled the hair of, among others, Mrs. Kennedy, Comden, and Newman—a cameo in the movie. References to Sybil Christopher bring in their nights at Arthur, the discotheque opened by the former Mrs. Richard Burton, in which Green had invested; also, intriguingly, Jenny's guise for her first society outing, an opening at a museum, presages the ensembles that would be worn by women such as Comden and Newman at Capote's "Black and White Ball," which was still months away.

As unrelated as Jane's, Jill's, and Jenny's stories might seem, they all carry one unifying theme: romance. With each of these characters it blossoms and then becomes compromised by the women's ideals and drive, although it's not surprising that in this triptych of movie musicals they, and their respective beaux, arrive at happy endings.

Comden and Green's early 1966 draft pleased both Freed and Berlin. Green recalled: "Berlin was crazy about the script....He jumped on the phone and told us so, and we thought that was all we needed. He was so excited we thought we'd surely get it done."[6]

Berlin's enthusiasm, however, was not enough to get *Say It with Music* in front of cameras, even though the movie was to be directed by Vincente Minnelli. *Say It with Music* continued to be on Freed's and Minnelli's dockets until early in 1967, at which point it appeared as though the project might turn into a vehicle for Frank Sinatra and Shirley MacLaine. For the balance of that year the film went into a sort of limbo, and it wasn't until Berlin's 80th birthday was approaching that the title and its prospects resurfaced. When it did, it came with a new director, Julie Andrews's husband, Blake Edwards. As for the screenplay, it would be based on Comden and Green's with a "final polish" by a "'name' scripter."[7]

Eventually, the studio shelved the project, which began with a $1 million outlay for the rights to the Berlin songs and was now expected to cost in excess of $15 million. Comden later illuminated the situation: "But it was just too much money.... They absolutely had to have Julie Andrews, and that was expensive. We mentioned a girl named Barbra Streisand but they said no, she wasn't big enough. Too unknown."[8]

Comden and Green's interest in using their work to examine the world in which they were living was not just limited to Jenny's frivolous tale and her exploits among the glitterati of the mid-1960s. For a brief period they, along with Jule Styne, held the rights to musicalizing Billy Wilder's movie *The Apartment*. Unfortunately, the agreement stipulated that their musical had to be produced by June 1968, and when this proved to be unfeasible the rights reverted to the film's writer, director, and studio, paving the way for Burt Bacharach, Hal David, and Neil Simon to transform *The Apartment* into the musical *Promises, Promises*.

The announcement that Comden, Green, and Styne would not be adapting Wilder's film came less than two months after the premiere of another musical they wrote about romance in then present-day New York, *I'm Getting Married*. It wasn't a tuner for the stage but was written for television, specifically ABC's *Stage '67* series. In this one-hour mini-musical they chronicled a woman's fears about her impending nuptials after her fiancé, Paul, announces that he's received a huge promotion. What follows is a scenario reminiscent of the plot discarded from *Subways Are for Sleeping*: Paul tells his intended, Virginia, that because of his new responsibilities their honeymoon has become a business trip. They will visit hotels around the globe that are owned by his employer. They fight, and he storms out.

After he does, Virginia frets. If Paul's willing to do this, what other things might she not know about the man she believed was her soulmate? She thought he was a guy who shared her passion for simplicity and Victorian romance but now worries that his actions prove her wrong. He might be a lothario, or worse still he might be a sadist or philanderer. As she frets, her fearful imaginings unfold in fantasy sequences, not unlike the scenarios that the husband and wife envision about their infant in the "Baby" sketch in *Two on the Aisle*. In a twist worthy of O. Henry, Paul returns to her and announces he turned down the promotion, but she won't hear of it. If their love can't weather such changes, she reasons, they shouldn't be getting married at all.

Along with the teleplay, Comden and Green penned the lyrics for five songs, and, as with the script, a sense of recycling pervades. The title song, of course, echoes a discarded number from *Subways*, and another song in the show, "Forbidden Fruit," is a minor revision to a number cut from *Fade Out–Fade In*.

Starring Anne Bancroft (Oscar winner for *The Miracle Worker* and just about to be immortalized as *The Graduate*'s Mrs. Robinson) and character actor Dick Shawn, a television favorite, *I'm Getting Married* aired on March 16, and the following day George Gent's review in the *New York Times* lambasted the writers. He called them "one of Broadway's most sophisticated teams" and condemned them for creating something that was "a witless pastiche that committed the unpardonable sin in show business: it was incredibly dull." Other reviews were equally dire, and *I'm Getting Married* faded into the annals of television arcana.

The wan comedy that Comden and Green developed for this television musical was a sharp contrast with other work they wrote both before and after it, especially two songs that addressed significant contemporary issues of the period. The first came in 1963 when they and Styne transformed the traditional Israeli folk song "Hava Nagila" into "Now!," an anthem for the civil rights movement. Lena Horne introduced it during a benefit concert she and Frank Sinatra offered at Carnegie Hall on October 6, and by the end of the month Dorothy Killgallen reported in her syndicated column that an hour after it had been played on a radio show on New York's WNEW "orders came in from three cities for 50,000 copies." Five years later Comden and Green—this time to music by Bernstein—provided words for an anthem for the antiwar movement: "So Pretty." This one was also introduced at a benefit concert, Broadway for Peace, where it was delivered by Barbra Streisand.

But before they wrote this latter song, they wrote lyrics for a new Broadway show, one that featured a book by Laurents and music by Styne. It also happened to be a project that echoed many of the issues that were central to the tune they wrote for Horne.

The creative team for and title of the musical, *Hallelujah, Baby!*, were announced in July 1966. At that time it was intended to be a potential vehicle for, as Radie Harris put it in a July 1, 1966, *Newsday* column, "a top Negro star." In point of fact, Laurents wrote the musical expressly for Horne, but as he recalled, "This was at the period when civil rights was just taking hold, and someone got to her." Laurents said that Horne never read the script nor heard the music before turning the project down. He recalled that her decision was simply because "she should not do any musical written by whites."[9]

Horne biographer James Gavin contradicts Laurents's recollection, reporting that she had heard the score, growing "livid"[10] as she listened to a demo tape Styne sent her. Horne had expected some of the dynamic qualities that informed "Now!," and they just were not there. A feature on Horne in the *New York Times* on July 28, 1968, supports the notion she had heard the score and read the book. In the *Times* story, Joan Barthel writes that "by 1945 [Horne] was turning down 'St. Louis Woman' on Broadway because she thought it was 'old-fashioned, full of clichés.'" Barthel also reports that Horne declined to star in *Hallelujah, Baby!* "according to her friend and manager Ralph Harris, for much the same reason."

Regardless of whether Horne rejected the project because of its Caucasian authors or because she had actually read and heard it, the book that Laurents wrote was unusual and innovative for its time. The script tells the story of an African American woman, Georgina, who traverses the first five decades of the 20th century but never ages. In each era this 25-year-old character has the chance to step out of the only role her mother believes she can play—a maid—thanks to opportunities afforded her by working as a performer. Interestingly, less than a year before the show was officially announced, Horne herself wrote that while looking back on her life and career she realized that she couldn't have known as a child that "most of my successes were to be the result of being exhibited."[11]

As Georgina moves from the 1910s to the 1920s to the 1930s and beyond, there are three constants in her life: her mother; her African American boyfriend/fiancé, Clem; and a white man, Harvey. Laurents creates an awkward romantic triangle for Georgina and these men and examines how all three characters evolve with the times in different and sometimes diametrically opposed ways. For instance, Clem becomes increasingly politically involved and militant, and by the time the musical reaches the 1960s his activism seems as if it might destroy any chance that he and Georgina have for a life together.

An early draft of the script, along with the belief that Laurents would convince his friend Horne to star in *Hallelujah, Baby!*, was enough to attract producer David Merrick to the project, but his involvement was short-lived. After it became clear that Horne would not do the show and after Laurents and Merrick disagreed about necessary changes to the book, the producer withdrew. As he did, Merrick said, "Every producer along the line has turned down something that eventually becomes a big hit," and while he had not yet made that mistake, he said, "'Hallelujah, Baby!' very well might be my first one."[12]

The following four months were tumultuous ones for the creators as another set of producers came and went. It wasn't until the end of 1967 that *Hallelujah, Baby!* had a producing team, director, and choreographer. The show would be brought to Broadway by Albert W. Selden and Hal James (who had backed *Man of La Mancha*), along with Jane C. Nussbaum in her second and final outing in this capacity, and Harry Rigby, who in less than four years would be inspiring a nostalgia craze with revivals of musicals such as *No, No, Nanette* and *Irene*.

As for the director, Burt Shevelove, who with Larry Gelbart wrote the book for *A Funny Thing Happened on the Way to the Forum*, was engaged to stage this piece of presentational and self-aware musical theater. It was only Shevelove's second outing as a director on Broadway, but at his side as choreographer was Peter Gennaro, who had a long list of Broadway credits and had worked with all of the writers. He had performed in Comden, Green, and Styne's *Bells Are Ringing* and co-choreographed Bernstein, Stephen Sondheim, and Laurents's *West Side Story*.

The show's star, Leslie Uggams, was announced even as there were questions about who would be producing and staging the musical. *Hallelujah, Baby!* would mark Uggams's Broadway bow, but it was not her first professional credit; she came to the production having achieved considerable success on television and in club appearances.

Nearly 40 years after the show opened, Laurents looked back on her casting and the decisions he and Comden and Green made about the material with respect to their new star and said, "What we should have done was abandon the show.... Instead it was rewritten for a woman who is one of the nicest women I have ever met in the theater." As a result, he said, "The show lost its edge."[13]

Early drafts of both the book and songs do indeed indicate that the writers were attempting to imbue *Hallelujah, Baby!* with an anger about the injustices that African Americans faced. One proposed song for Georgina was "I've Got the Answer." In this number, which appears to have been intended for the 1930s section of the show based on a reference to people not having money for maids, Georgina would have turned into a huckster in order to con women into hiring her as their psychic adviser. What makes this unused number particularly interesting is how it portrays Georgina, specifically her disdain for the white people who might use her services.

Another number drafted during the August 1966 period was "When?" Like "Answer," the song was never used. Unlike the other song, where Horne's name is penciled in at the top of a lead sheet, however, there's no indication as to which character would deliver this biting piece of writing. The title truncates the central idea of the song, "when are you going to change?," and it could have been a meant as a number that Clem would sing to Georgina or vice versa.

As Laurents, Comden, Green, and Styne continued to reshape the book and score, Shevelove completed the casting process. The two men in Georgina's life would be Robert Hooks, who had appeared on Broadway in a trio of dramas and would go on to found, with Douglas Turner Ward, the acclaimed Negro Ensemble Company, and Allen Case, who played Sir Harry in *Once Upon a Mattress* and after *Baby!* segued into the business world. Shevelove cast Lillian Hayman as Momma, and following the musical she snagged a role she ended up playing for nearly 20 years, Sadie Gray on the soap opera *One Life to Live*.

As the cast began rehearsals at the end of February, they found that *Hallelujah, Baby!* was filled with music. The show boasted nearly 20 numbers, and while none may have had the intensity of the two that went unused, Styne, Comden, and Green had stretched to fit both the show's ambitious time frame and the important issues it explored. The most lightweight were songs such as "Feet Do Your Stuff," a zesty nightclub number for the 1920s sequence; "Witches Brew," used as Georgina rehearses an experimental production of *Macbeth* during the 1930s (which recycled the melody of Carol Burnett's big number from *Fade Out—Fade In*, "Call Me

Savage"); and the title song, which was part of Georgina's act as she became a successful crossover singer in the 1950s.

Beyond this diegetic material were book songs, such as the first act closer, "Being Good," in which Comden and Green's ability to use a simple, direct phrase to dramatic effect beautifully stands out. As the 1940s section winds down, Georgina announces, "Being good just won't be good enough/ I'll be the best, or nothing at all." The songwriters also outfitted the show with numbers that commented on the action and on the obstacles and prejudices that African Americans faced during the first half of the 20th century. In these, Comden and Green provided some of the show's edgiest moments. In "The Slice," for instance, they reference the threat of the Ku Klux Klan even as Clem tries to humorously recount how his winnings from a card game disappeared, and in "Smile, Smile," Georgina, Clem, and Momma all laughingly sing about the way they feel white people believe they should behave. Comden and Green even deploy some of the funny-sad lyrics they wrote for the title song for the abandoned musical *Help! Help! Hooray!* in one *Hallelujah, Baby!* song, "Another Day."

As rehearsals progressed, creative differences sparked between choreographer Gennaro and the writers, and as a result he departed the production. Kevin Carlisle, who had appeared on Broadway in such musicals as *Oh Captain!* and *Redhead* and had created dances for television shows such as *The Garry Moore Show* and TW3, was brought on to stage the *Hallelujah, Baby!* musical numbers. Shortly after his arrival, *Sunday Telegraph* reporter Alan Brien, who was working on a feature about the production, overheard one of the lyricists quip: "This show is further behind than any show I've ever worked on."[14]

PAYING TRIBUTE TO MARC BLITZSTEIN
AND *THE CRADLE WILL ROCK*

In the 1930s section of *Hallelujah, Baby!* Georgina works as an actress in a WPA production of a Haitian-themed *Macbeth* that gets shut down by the government. Given that all of the writers knew of the closeness their colleague and friend Leonard Bernstein felt to composer Marc Blitzstein and given that Comden and Green performed in the memorial concert that Bernstein conducted to honor Blitzstein in 1964, this detail (and obstacle for the heroine) was most likely intended as a tribute to Blitzstein and his seminal *The Cradle Will Rock*, which faced similar government intrusion when it premiered in 1937.

The change in choreographers did not delay the show's scheduled March 21 opening at Boston's Colonial Theatre, and the following morning the musical received what could be called, at best, mixed reviews. In the *Boston Globe*, Kevin Kelly deemed it to be "a mindless piece of showbusiness [*sic*] that pretends to have something on its mind." As for the music and lyrics, Kelly called them "ordinary in the extreme." The next day in a *Variety* review, "Padu." noted that *Baby!* offered "a sugary and overoptimistic view of Civil Rights problems," making Laurents's book the show's "weakest link." The writer did offer some kind words about Comden and Green's lyrics, calling them "singable, direct and often imaginative."

The creators and director quickly began to reshape *Hallelujah, Baby!* as it played its two-week engagement in Boston and then three weeks of previews in New York. By the time the critics arrived at the Martin Beck Theatre, Laurents had streamlined the book and cut five songs. There was also a new finale, "Now's the Time," expressing Georgina's recognition that she needs to become part of something greater than just a career for herself.

Two of the cut songs directly related to Georgina's relationships with Clem and Harvey. "Ugly, Ugly Gal" was an anti-romantic tune that Clem sang in the second act, while "Hey" was a first-act song for Georgina in which she attempts to express her gratitude for Harvey's kindness. Also excised was the song that originally opened and closed the show, "When the Weather's Better." Although the number was one of the finest in the score, it delivered a confusing, dichotomous message. The lyric attempted to establish through the metaphor of rain that there needed to be a day when racial equality was a reality in the United States and also to assert the primacy of Georgina and Clem's romance in the musical. All these revisions appear to have been made to address the Boston critics' concerns that the show was too delicate in addressing the issues of the civil rights movement, unwisely subordinating them to the Georgina-Clem romance.

On April 27, the day after *Hallelujah, Baby!* opened, the New York critics responded in ways similar to their Boston counterparts. They admired the show's ambition but were not convinced—entirely—that the creators had succeeded in their goals. The *New York Times*'s Walter Kerr summed up many of the reviews when he wrote that the writers "have put together with the best intentions in the world a course in Civics One when everyone in the world has already got to Civics Six." One of the exceptions to the generally qualified praise the show got (although it was unanimously unqualified for Uggams's turn) came from John Chapman in the *Daily News*, who called the production a "stunning piece of show business." Comden and Green's work divided the critics. Some, like Chapman, found their lyrics to be "splendidly polished," while others, such as Martin Gottfried in *Women's Wear Daily*, described them as "competent at best, strained and clichéd at worst."

The reviewers' complaints weren't enough to keep the show from enjoying healthy, if not entirely robust, business. In the weeks following its opening,

Hallelujah, Baby! took in approximately 75 percent of potential box-office revenue. As happened with Comden and Green's previous musical, *Hallelujah, Baby!* arrived after the Tony Award cutoff for 1967, and so it wasn't until nearly a year after its Broadway bow that Comden, Green, Styne, Laurents, and their collaborators could celebrate the show's nine Tony Award nominations. When the prizes were handed out, the production ended up picking up five of them, including the ones for best musical and best composer and lyricist. The recognition certainly was gratifying to all concerned, but it was also bittersweet. *Hallelujah, Baby!* had closed in January, having played 293 performances. The musical became the last original one that Comden and Green would write for more than a decade, but this didn't mean that they would not be contributing to New York's theatrical landscape as the 1960s ended and the 1970s dawned.

COMDEN AND GREEN ON THEIR PARTNERSHIP

As they were prepping *Hallelujah, Baby!*, Comden and Green sat down with John Gruen, who profiled them in his book *Close-Up*. Comden told him that at this point "you might say we have radar communication. As writers we are the same. As people we are different." Green echoed this with, "That's so true. She turns into Craig's Wife, and I turn into Sloppy Joe. I lounge around, she paces and fumes. The only thing that keeps us together is twenty-five years of total stardom and success." Comden did offer another similarity: "We're both pessimists—it's why we're married to optimists."

CHAPTER 16

Going Backstage, Then Getting Nostalgic

J ust before *Hallelujah, Baby!* opened, Green and Phyllis Newman hosted a party at their Central Park West apartment to celebrate the 25th wedding anniversary of Comden and her husband, Steven Kyle. The Central Park West home was decorated entirely in silver for the soiree, and the guests were asked to dress similarly: silver gowns for the ladies and black tie with silver accessories for the men. Among those present were Comden and Green collaborators such as Leonard Bernstein, Arthur Laurents, and Jule Styne and stage stars such as George Segal and Patrick O'Neal. Lauren Bacall was also at the party, which was so glamorous that it got a two-page photo spread in *Vogue,* and in a moment that anticipated a collaboration two years down the road, Bacall "sang dozens of songs in a husky, sexy, bittersweet voice."[1]

Some of the guests would continue to be at Comden and Green's side as 1968 moved forward, and they all did their utmost to raise funds for Eugene McCarthy's presidential bid. Almost exactly a year later Comden and Green took part in a political cabaret that was simultaneously a memorial for Dr. Martin Luther King Jr. and a McCarthy fundraiser. A few months after this, the team raised campaign money for the senator from Minnesota by offering a private performance in a Long Island home. The contribution to see them perform in this intimate setting was supposed to be $100 per couple, but any size donation was accepted. As Dick Zander reported in *Newsday* on June 1, one man had been able to offer only $5, saying, "If I had a $100 I'd be a Republican!"

Green's keen interest in what was happening politically during this historic period compelled him to attend the infamous Democratic National Convention in Chicago that August. He never became embroiled in the tumult surrounding the event, at which Hubert Humphrey rather than McCarthy secured the nomination.

JEWELRY FIT FOR A KENNEDY

In late 1968, designer Kenneth Jay Lane launched a line of paste jewelry that became all the rage among New York society women. He ironically nicknamed the pieces "George Raft Gems," after the actor who primarily portrayed tough guys on the screen. One of the first women to receive one of Lane's creations was former First Lady Jacqueline Kennedy. Not long after, Green's wife, Phyllis Newman, became a proud owner. She received the piece from someone who had not been able to attend a dinner she gave for Stephen and Jean Kennedy Smith. Comden, too, owned this jewelry, and even modeled it for a photo feature on the line in a September edition of the *Saturday Evening Post*.

As Comden and Green participated in the fundraising for McCarthy's campaign, a new musical inspired by the movie *All About Eve* took shape in the background. The concept belonged to composer Charles Strouse, who with lyricist Lee Adams had written the scores for *Bye Bye Birdie* and the Sammy Davis Jr. vehicle *Golden Boy*. It was in the early 1960s that Strouse first latched onto the idea of musicalizing the classic Bette Davis film about a great actress who finds herself betrayed by a younger aspiring thespian, but it wasn't until 1967 that he was able to start working in earnest on turning his concept into a reality.

The process started when he mentioned the project to playwright Sidney Michaels, who had written, among other things, the Tony Award–nominated play *Dylan*, which starred Alec Guinness as the titular Irish poet. Michaels, who thought the film was "magnificent,"[2] was instantly excited about the idea and suggested that their first step would be to acquire the rights to the Joseph L. Mankiewicz screenplay. Unfortunately, 20th Century Fox refused to release them. This didn't deter the men, including lyricist Adams, and by early 1968, when the three had interested two producers in their plans, a solution presented itself.

The producers were Joseph Kipness and Lawrence Kasha, men who had worked steadily on Broadway for many years but never together. Kipness, who was also a restaurateur, had been producing since the early 1940s, and among the shows he brought to the stage were Jule Styne's first musical, *High Button Shoes*, and the popular French revue *La Plume de Ma Tante*. Kasha, who had worked as a stage manager since the mid-1950s and directed the musical *Bajour*, was breaking into "above the title" credit producing with this musical based on *Eve*.

It was Kipness and Kasha who secured the rights, not to the screenplay but rather to "The Wisdom of Eve," the Mary Orr short story from the May 1946 issue of *Cosmopolitan* that had inspired Mankiewicz. Orr still had the stage rights to the tale, and Michaels, along with Strouse and Adams, could build their tuner from it.

As the writers proceeded, what emerged was a story more in line with the film than Orr's original, which is a slight tale of betrayal as Eve Harrington dupes Broadway star Margola Cranston and her producer-director husband, Clement, into believing she is someone that she is not. When Eve garners raves at an open-call audition, having been coached by the couple, she reveals her ruse to the press, believing it will solidify her status as a great performer. After all, if she can fool two insiders, she must have talent. Unfortunately, her plan backfires, and soon Eve is unable to find any sort of acting work until she receives a helping hand from a friend of Cranston, who is married to a prominent playwright. This woman recommends Eve to her husband, who casts her in one of his shows. Eve proves her mettle once again in the production and finally achieves the success that she ached for.

Michaels's script obviously kept the arc of Eve's deception that Orr originally conceived, inspired by a tale about a duplicitous secretary who worked for the Viennese actress Elisabeth Bergner. But otherwise the book for the new musical essentially resembled the film. Michaels even retained the new name that Mankiewicz gave the younger woman's patroness-patsy: Margo Channing. The one stark contrast between *All About Eve* and Michaels's script is that the latter did not include the character of critic Addison DeWitt, indelibly played on screen by George Sanders, who picked up an Oscar for his performance.

Michaels couldn't include this venomous scribe because he was an invention for the movie. Yet Addison serves an important role in the plot. He's simultaneously an ally and foe to the conniving Eve. Michaels, recognizing that such an opponent would be needed on stage, devised a similar part for the new musical, that of a producer, Robinson DeWitt, who both admired and lusted for her and was quite aware that she was not at all as sweet as she appeared to be. Michaels also used Robinson as a guide for the audience throughout the show, having him directly address theatergoers with lengthy monologues.

Strouse and Adams outfitted Michaels's book with more than a dozen songs, including one that gave the show a working title, *Welcome to the Theater*, and by late 1968 there were reports that the musical might reach Broadway sometime in the current 1968–1969 season. However, that timeline proved overly optimistic. Nevertheless, by March 1969 the musical appeared to be a reality when Earl Wilson reported in one of his syndicated columns that the producers had found a star to play the part of Margo Channing. "Lauren Bacall's agreed tentatively to star on Broadway in the musical version of 'All About Eve' (retitled 'Make Believe')."

Wilson was on the money about Bacall's interest in making her musical theater debut in the show, but as spring turned to summer her participation came into question as she began to have concerns about Michaels's book. As Strouse puts it in his memoir, *Put on a Happy Face,* "She didn't feel that he wrote the way she spoke," adding, "What she wanted was to bring in Comden and Green to write a new book."

Given Bacall's closeness with them (they made a special trip to Hollywood just after her husband, Humphrey Bogart, died, to comfort her) and their successes on stage and screen, her choice for new book writers was understandable to the songwriters and the producers. Further, Bacall was, as Strouse remarks in his book, "the one who was making the show happen." So, he says, "We had to listen to what she wanted."

Bacall, in her autobiography, *By Myself,* remembers the change in book writers differently. "A decision had been made to replace [Michaels]. The producers asked how I would feel about Betty Comden and Adolph Green taking over." And although she was worried about working with close friends, she felt that "it was a good idea nonetheless—they were so smart and funny and talented."[3]

Strouse's account of how Comden and Green came to the project appears to be the more likely of the scenarios for several reasons. First, Michaels's draft draws a good deal of the attention away from Margo and Eve and onto the producer. Second, Michaels embellished his script with theatrical abstractions, which, for the period, might have been more suited to a play. In one instance he envisioned Robinson DeWitt above the action maneuvering characters attached to strings, like marionettes. For a star such as Bacall, who would be taking a professional risk by tackling a musical, Michaels's script probably appeared to be too much of a gamble.

By July, Kipness and Kasha reached an agreement with Michaels and another with Comden and Green, who would be working for the first time just as book writers on a musical. As the producers made this change public, they also were able to announce that Bacall had officially signed her contract. There was one more important development: The producers had continued negotiations 20th Century Fox, and the new musical would be able to include "a limited amount"[4] of the Mankiewicz screenplay in its script. Further, Kipness and Kasha revealed that the show would be staged and choreographed by Ron Field, who most recently had devised the dances for the musical *Zorba,* earned a Tony Award for his work on *Cabaret,* and was here making his debut as a director.

"Betty and Adolph worked quickly," Bacall reports in her autobiography, adding, "As new scenes were written, they were read to Charlie and Lee so that all the collaborators could decide on changes or adjustments." This included new songs, and after just over two months working on the project, Comden and Green completed the first draft of a substantially rewritten book for a musical that was now known as *Applause, Applause.*

In their new draft, the arc of Eve's methodical clawing her way to a pinnacle remained the same as it had been in both the movie and Michaels's draft. Also remaining was Margo's insecurity about the difference in age between herself and her director-lover, Bill Sampson. Where they diverged significantly from the film and the first book was in the character of Margo's confidante and maid, Birdie. The character was no longer a woman. Further, the role was no longer that of a maid, but rather of Margo's hairstylist, Duane. In the process the writers were helping to break ground, creating the second openly gay supporting character in a Broadway musical (the first was dress designer Sebastian Baye in Alan Jay Lerner and André Previn's *Coco*, about Coco Chanel, which ended up battling with *Applause* for best musical at the 1970 Tony Awards). Comden and Green also heavily curtailed the part of the producer that Michaels created. In their version the role, which they renamed Howard Benedict, still exists, but as with Addison in the movie, he remains primarily on the sidelines as the Margo-Eve drama unfolds.

Comden and Green's new book also sparked with contemporary energy thanks to small details throughout. For instance, they often referred to characters either by type, such "Chic Young Man," or by what they are wearing, including "Middle-Aged Mini-Skirt" and "Girl in Pajamas." These latter character descriptions helped to firmly ground the show in styles of the day, while the former gently satirized women who were attempting to be au courant in clothing that was not age appropriate. For Eve's backstory they included details about her political activism and disillusionment after the assassinations of Robert Kennedy and Dr. Martin Luther King Jr. In many ways the details they infused into their writing were the same sort that had brought them fame 30 years before, when they were just starting out. Their adaptation of *All About Eve* markedly demonstrated their affection for New York City, its denizens, and the theatrical profession itself.

The revisions meant that new songs were needed, and as Comden and Green worked during July and August, Strouse and Lee developed new numbers, including "Fasten Your Seatbelts," an ensemble number that took its title directly from the classic line in the film, "Fasten your seatbelts; it's going to be a bumpy night." Another new number, "Who's That Girl?," reflected a major change that Comden and Green made to the story. In this new version Margo's career started in Hollywood, and, much like Bacall herself, she has transitioned to the stage. Finally, a third new tune, "Applause, Applause," served to give the show a new title.

A FIRE CAN'T STOP WORK

For years Green had kept a home in East Hampton as both a refuge and a workspace, and in June 1968 Comden bought a place not far from him. Their proximity to one another in the summer of 1969 should have been a boon as they started working on *Applause*, but, unfortunately, Green needed to contend with a disaster at his beach getaway home. In August, a four-alarm fire, inadvertently started by caterers' sterno as the Greens hosted a wedding, destroyed their house and much of what it contained. Impressively, Green persevered with writing the musical, and the following year the Greens made headlines as they erected a temporary prefab house as work began on rebuilding.

Although it was originally slated for a December opening on Broadway, *Applause*, as it came to be known, eventually acquired a winter-spring schedule, which provided Comden and Green with time to continue honing their book. During this period Strouse and Adams refined their score as well, and director-choreographer Field worked individually with Bacall and completed the casting process.

When rehearsals for the show began in late November, Field's cast included an unknown in the central role of Eve. Although actresses such as Bernadette Peters and Sandy Duncan were rumored to be contenders for the part before Bacall officially signed her contract, Field selected Diane McAfee to play it, even though her résumé included only two minor Broadway credits. Len Cariou, cast as Bill Sampson, Margo's director and lover, came to the production with a host of classical credits, including a *Henry V* that had just concluded its Broadway run, but he had never starred in a musical.

Many of the show's featured players were also relatively fresh faces on Broadway. Garrett Lewis, originally cast as Duane, had a pair of minor stage credits but came with one major film role to his name: He played Jack Buchanan (the British actor who starred in *The Band Wagon*) opposite Julie Andrews's Gertrude Lawrence in *Star!*. During rehearsals of *Applause* Lewis departed the production and was replaced by Lee Roy Reams, who started out in the ensemble of *Sweet Charity* and had just finished playing Will Parker in *Oklahoma!* at Lincoln Center. Brandon Maggart, with a pair of Broadway credits, and Ann Williams, with a single Broadway role under her belt, were cast as playwright Buzz Richards and his wife, Karen, and Robert Mandan, who would play the wily producer Howard Benedict, had originated two roles on Broadway and understudied in a third production. The company also boasted a future television star, Bonnie Franklin, who would go on to play Ann Romano in television's *One Day at a Time*. She was making her Broadway debut, playing the unofficial leader of the gang that hangs out at Joe Allen's and fronting the ensemble in two of the show's biggest production numbers, including the title song.

The first out-of-town stop for *Applause* was Baltimore's Mechanic Theatre, where a newspaper strike meant the city's dailies would not cover the show. Nevertheless, after it opened on January 27 there were reviews for the team to consider. In the trade publication *Variety* the next day, "Luce." wrote: "Work is what 'Applause' needs." A day later in the *Washington Post*, Richard L. Coe's assessment clearly defined the show's strengths, which included Bacall, Franklin, and some of the songs, and its weaknesses, such as the sets and what he deemed was a book that moved in "fits and starts." Worse was his assessment of McAfee's performance: "This Eve is no threat to her star." Coe closed by noting that the show's "two-month tune-up can lead to a glittering smash or a ho-hum fizzle." Perhaps most damning was William Collins's February 1 *Philadelphia Inquirer* review, which bluntly stated: "The production fails to rise above a level of dismal mediocrity."

Kipness and Kasha had slated eight weeks of tryouts for the show, including three in Baltimore (as compared with the one-week break-in runs Comden and Green had experienced in so many New Haven engagements). During the tuner's Maryland stint, Comden and Green and their colleagues set out to carefully revamp a show that had clocked in at three hours when it opened.

Comden and Green began to shrewdly trim and fine-tune the book. Strouse and Adams removed a trio of songs, including one of the earliest ones they wrote for the show, "Smashing New York Times," a number that ironically commented on what theater artists crave most in life: not necessities or love but rather good notices. Also excised was "It's a Hit," which coincidentally was a stepchild to material Comden and Green had written both for the Revuers and for the lyric they penned for "The Intermission's Great" for *On the Town*. In lieu of a number that expressed explicitly the diverging opinions of first-nighters, Adams crafted a lyric for a song that gave a more general sense of buzz after the performance: "Backstage Babble."

But the changes to the material did not address one central issue facing director Field and the producers: the 21-year-old McAfee's suitability for the role of Eve. As Bacall remembers in her memoir, Field admitted to being wrong about casting her: "She doesn't come across as all the things Eve should be," and, he continued, "It's my mistake, but until I saw her in the show I couldn't be sure."[5] Strouse expresses similar feelings in his book, remembering that they told McAfee why they needed to replace her: "'You're too young and rosy to scare Margo Channing,' we assured Diane. 'Especially Lauren Bacall's Margo.'"

A call went out to a performer who had auditioned for the show, Penny Fuller, whose credits included replacing on Broadway as Corie Bratter in

Barefoot in the Park and Sally Bowles in *Cabaret*. Fuller joined the production in Baltimore and opened it in Detroit. Her experience and age (she was 30) meant that, as Strouse put it, "She was able to be a real threat as Eve to Bacall's strong Margo. The show began to work."[6]

When *Applause* opened at Detroit's Fisher Theater on February 19, the reviews were much better. In his *Detroit Free Press* write-up the next day, Lawrence DeVine posited a question: "Is 'Applause' worthy of Lauren Bacall?" His answer: "It is." His praise extended to Comden and Green's book: "Wisely they gerrymandered the screen version and made 'Applause' all about Bacall." But he did express concerns about the show's length and even went so far as to suggest where the production could be trimmed.

Comden and Green set about cutting, and at the same time they, along with Strouse and Adams, honed the details of the love story for Margo and Bill. They had already changed the end of the show from their original concept. "[We] had Margo actually dumping Bill in favor of her career in the theater," Strouse recalls in *Put on a Happy Face*. He adds, "[It] was very true to life and very true to Bacall herself." Ultimately, however, they went with a sentimental ending, and Margo chose Bill. They could feel that it worked for audiences—but not fully. So Strouse and Adams developed two new songs to replace Bill's first, "It Was Always You," and Margo's last, "Love Comes First," both numbers that expressed the characters' feelings bluntly. To replace these, they inserted midway through the Detroit run "Think How It's Gonna Be," for the former, a number that expresses Bill's love for Margo in charming, playful terms, and "Something Greater," which echoes a line from the film and outlines Margo's reasons for marrying in less saccharine terms than those in "Love Comes First."

Finally, *Applause* arrived at Broadway's historic Palace Theatre on March 26, just eight months after Comden and Green had come aboard. After three previews it opened to critics, who raved about Bacall and generally loved the production, with special nods to Comden and Green's reworking of the familiar story. Richard Watts in his *New York Post* review informed readers: "'Applause' is emphatically not a sentimental tale of the dear old theater," and in the *New York Times* Clive Barnes applauded the book's "welcome, lovely cynicism about show business" that made it "a musical play that is bright, witty, direct and nicely punchy."

The musical settled in for a comfortable run at the Palace, and when the Tony Awards were presented in April the show picked up four, including the all-important best musical prize. In addition, Bacall beat out another screen legend making her debut in a tuner, Katharine Hepburn in *Coco*, and Field won for both his direction and choreography. The show's staying power extended to national tours, a London production, and in 1973 a filmed version for television.

THE LION'S FINAL ROAR

On May 3, 1970, a massive auction took place in Culver City as props and costumes that had been used in MGM pictures for four decades were sold to bidders. A UPI wire service report from May 4 noted that the sale represented an "end of an era." The sense of a collective cultural loss that this event represented might have been one of the factors behind a nostalgia craze found both on Broadway and in Hollywood for the first part of the 1970s. Comden and Green were present at the auction, as was *Singin' in the Rain*'s Debbie Reynolds, who purchased many items with an eye toward creating a "Hollywood hall of fame" to glorify the studio's legacy.

Applause may have felt, sounded, and looked contemporary, but one month later another musical—Stephen Sondheim and George Furth's *Company*, which explored marriage in America in 1970—opened, and it carried an even greater sense of being of the moment in tone and subject matter. Despite these shows and others, Broadway in 1970 was also in the nascent stages of a nostalgia craze that would continue for several seasons. The trend began with a revival of Sandy Wilson's valentine to 1920s musicals, *The Boy Friend*, which opened between *Applause* and *Company*. The retro craze on Broadway firmly took hold when a revival of Vincent Youmans, Irving Caesar, and Otto Harbach's 1925 confection *No, No Nanette* swept onto Broadway in January 1971, entrancing critics and audiences alike.

Less than three months later, Comden and Green were brought into Broadway's collective backward glance as producer Jerry Schlossberg announced he would be backing a revival of *On the Town*, which would be directed and choreographed by Field and open in early fall. According to the *New York Times*'s Louis Calta, in a story on April 14 that announced the production, Field "had been thinking about it for more than a year." And, after a program from the show fell off a bookshelf while he was visiting Comden at her home, Field related to Calta, "I read it, and I exclaimed to Betty, 'I've found the forties musical I've been looking for!' "

The revival, which featured slight revisions by Comden and Green, proceeded to Broadway as Schlossberg had planned. Its cast featured, among others, Phyllis Newman as man-obsessed anthropologist Claire (the role originated by Comden) and Bernadette Peters, whose credits included her breakout turn in *Dames at Sea* off-Broadway and then *George M!* on Broadway, as man-hunting cabbie Hildy. Donna McKechnie, who had a host of Broadway credits and was just a few years away from her acclaimed turn as Cassie in *A Chorus Line*, played Ivy Smith, the subway's Miss Turnstiles for June. As for the three sailors, Field cast a trio of men who were just at the start of their careers, each boasting just a couple of minor credits: Kurt Peterson (Gabey), Bill Gerber (Ozzie), and Jess Richards (Chip).

The show had a single tryout engagement in Boston that opened on October 5. The next morning Kevin Kelly in the *Boston Globe* reported, "The current, misguided production makes a feeble pass at the kind of nostalgic warmth that ran through the recent production of 'No, No Nanette.'" Kinder words came a week later in *Variety* when critic "Ster." wrote: "Not another 'No, No Nanette,' perhaps, but a flashy evening of memory-mongering."

Rebounding from reviews that had been more supportive of the female leads than the males, Field recast two of the sailors. Ron Husmann, who played featured roles in shows such as *All-American* and *Tenderloin*, came on board to play Gabey, and Remak Ramsay, not much more seasoned than his predecessor Gerber, joined the company as Ozzie.

When the production opened at Broadway's Imperial Theater on October 31, the critical response was warmer than it had been in Boston, but no one reviewer was overly enthusiastic. In addition, many expressed concerns about whether the innocence of the show suited the energy or mood of New York in 1971. For instance, Clive Barnes, in his November 1 *New York Times* review, wrote that the show "may serve to remind people of wartime innocence—when New York was a visitor's paradise."

In the wake of the reviews, the production ran a mere 73 performances, and a few years later Comden attempted to assess what had gone wrong, saying, "'On the Town' wasn't at all typical of show of the '40s. It was atypical in its use of the symphonic sound of Bernstein's music, its modern ballets, its feeling of improvisation. So it wasn't the show to make you nostalgic for the '40s. It just wasn't the World War II equivalent of 'No, No Nanette.'"[7]

Nostalgia, for themselves and their work, was also on Comden and Green's docket as the *On the Town* revival wended its way to Broadway. Specifically, they were looking back on the creation of *Singin' in the Rain* as Viking Press prepared a published version of the screenplay, for which they wrote a comprehensive overview of the history of the movie and their work on it.

But the duo was also attempting to initiate new projects during this period. For a brief time they contemplated an adaptation of Jean Anouilh's *The Waltz of the Toreadors* as a vehicle for Zero Mostel. Sadly, they had to abandon this intriguing project when they were unable to reach an agreement with the playwright regarding royalties from the musical version of the piece.

Another new work that Comden and Green turned to during 1972 and 1973 was a musical version of *The Ghost Goes West*, a frothy 1935 film that centers on what happens when a wealthy American transports an entire Scottish castle to the United States. When the structure is moved, it comes with the ghost that haunts it. An exploration of the clash between modern American flash and old-world elegance, the project was Jule Styne's brainchild and had been on his mind since the late 1950s, when there were reports that he might write it as a vehicle for Cyril Ritchard. At this juncture, Styne anticipated that Comden and Green would write the book and that his son, Stanley, would collaborate with them on the lyrics. Styne also hoped that the show would tempt Comden and Green to try their hand at directing.

The project faded from his docket for a few years and then resurfaced as one of the trio of musicals that were to be backed by ABC-Paramount as it entered the world of Broadway producing with *Fade Out–Fade In*. Once again, the show disappeared from mentions of musicals that were actively on Styne's theatrical agenda. He, along with Comden and Green, returned to the idea in 1972, and by September the team had completed a draft script as well as at least seven songs. And though a report in *Variety* on February 23, 1973, announced that the show might become a vehicle for Alan Bates, nothing more came of it, perhaps because all three artists found themselves dedicating their energies that year to one more nostalgic Broadway tuner.

The show that consumed them was a new version of *Gentlemen Prefer Blondes*, which had made a star of Carol Channing. With music by Styne, lyrics by Leo Robin, and a book by Joseph Fields and Anita Loos, the 1949 musical ran nearly two years on Broadway and then was turned into a movie in 1953 starring Marilyn Monroe and Jane Russell. In 1972, Channing, who had been back on Broadway only once since her triumph in *Hello, Dolly!* in 1964, wanted to revisit the role of Lorelei Lee. However, to do so meant that the show would need to be rethought to account for the 23 years that had elapsed since she first played it.

The idea of a new version of *Blondes* first surfaced in June 1972, when *Variety* obliquely announced that Styne was writing new songs for a staging that would star Channing and "run in music tents"[8] for summer stock. Two months later plans had changed. The new production, *Lorelei*, would not be developed for summer stock but rather for a full-scale national tour that would culminate in a Broadway engagement during the 1973–1974 season. Channing herself had demanded this unusual arrangement: "I always enjoyed touring and the road is where it's happening. I wouldn't think of playing New York before Oklahoma, California, and the wide open spaces,"[9] she told reporters as the musical was announced.

As producers Lee Guber and Shelly Gross made this plan public, they also shared the names of the creative team for *Lorelei*. The musical would boast a book by Gail Parent and Kenny Solms, whose work together included, among other things, scripting for the *Carol Burnett Show* and an episode of the *Mary Tyler Moore Show*. Comden and Green signed on to provide lyrics for the "six or seven"[10] new songs that Styne was writing, and to direct and choreograph the producers turned to Joe Layton, who began his Broadway career as a dancer in *Wonderful Town* and had subsequently gone on to a career directing and choreographing musicals. Among his credits in this capacity were Richard Rodgers's *No Strings* and the biotuner *George M!*.

Theoretically, Comden and Green's involvement with the production, which revisited the events of *Blondes* as a flashback after Lorelei attends the funeral of the man she married, would have ended as soon as they completed their work on the new lyrics. But when the show played its inaugural tour engagement at the Civic Center Music Hall in Oklahoma City in February 1973, it ran for three hours and critics noted that something was amiss. On February 27, Bill Crawford in the *Lawton Constitution* tactfully complained, "The musical has some belt tightening to do and the usual doctoring of stage ailments, which plague major productions in their infancy." Less politic was a quote from Bill Donaldson's review in the *Tulsa Tribune* that was included in the Associated Press wire service story "State Critics Praise 'Lorelei.'" "There isn't an important tune in the new score." And while *Variety* critic "Jon," like the local critics in Oklahoma, lauded Channing, the strongest sentiment this reviewer could muster in a February 28 write-up was "'Lorelei' comes off sweet."

In the wake of these reviews, Layton set about revising and reworking the production, which moved on to stints in Houston and then Indianapolis, where Charles Staff in the March 14 edition of the *Indianapolis Star* was less forgiving of the production's flaws. He took aim at the show's length and also Layton's work on the production numbers, describing one, "Bye, Bye Baby," as "static," and writing "'Coquette,' though sumptuously costumed with Miss Channing as a table of desserts, doesn't cut it." By Detroit, reports were that Layton had left the production for a scheduled vacation in Mexico and that Styne had flown to the Midwest to rehearse the orchestra. Also on hand were Comden and Green, ostensibly just to celebrate the opening at the Fisher Theater.

The morning after *Lorelei*'s March 21 opening, Lawrence DeVine, in the *Detroit Free Press*, wrote that "Joe Layton is a whiz," but he also gingerly swiped at how the writers had revised the original: "The 'new' show has a spate of contestable 'new' credits." As with the critics who preceded him in reviewing the production, DeVine was, however, rapturous about Channing's performance.

Another writer at the paper, columnist Shirley Eder, was also touting the production while simultaneously chronicling its backstage woes. On March 25 she noted that the show was in need of its director, who was on a "prolonged Mexican vacation" and who, as a choreographer, had "done better in the past than he has with 'Lorelei.'" Two days later she told readers that Comden and Green were "the new book doctors" for the musical, and by the beginning of April they stepped in as directors, working with Ernie Flatt, who was brought in as choreographer.

The changes in the creative team in Detroit prompted *Variety* to assign a critic to re-assess the show, and, in its April 25 edition, a review from "Thur." lauded the new staging: "[It's] done much to brighten up the formerly dull stretches of the show." By this point Styne, Comden, and Green had provided Channing with a new song to close the first act, the jazzy musical diatribe "Men," which deftly gave the show's heroine a smart feminist edge.

Comden and Green continued to guide the musical as it crisscrossed the country until December. At that juncture Robert Moore, who had directed the musical *Promises, Promises*, stepped in to fine-tune the staging before the show reached its Broadway berth at the Palace Theatre, where it opened on January 27, 1974. There *Lorelei* still boasted four of the five new Styne-Comden-Green songs that had been performed when the show opened a year before in Oklahoma, along with "Men" and a tune the writers had slipped in after Detroit, "Miss Lorelei Lee." Numbers that had gone to the wayside during the year-long tour included "A Girl Like I" and the standard-issue title song that brings to mind other odes to musical heroines, particularly Jerry Herman's "Mame."

The reviews on January 28 echoed much of what had been written while *Lorelei* was on the road. The critics, like audiences, loved seeing Channing, but as Douglas Watt pointed out in his *Daily News* review, she was in "a creaky vehicle, at best." Clive Barnes in the *New York Times* did mention that "Comden and Green offer a few nifty lyrics," but like his colleagues he was underwhelmed, closing with "Carol Channing is 'Lorelei's' best friend." Audiences were not deterred by the critical response, however, and unlike the ill-fated *On the Town* revival that preceded it, *Lorelei* ran for most of 1974, playing 320 performances.

Lorelei didn't completely end Comden and Green's return to entertainments that evoked earlier decades of the 20th century. However, as the 1920s-set show was winding down on Broadway, they started to collaborate with a new partner, one who would reinvigorate them, propelling them in new directions as the 1970s continued.

CHANGING TASTES

Not everything was nostalgic on Broadway during the first half of the 1970s. One of the new musicals that opened during this time was Richard O'Brien's *The Rocky Horror Show*. It played at Broadway's Belasco Theatre, named for the producer who was known as the "Bishop of Broadway" because of the white collar that he regularly sported. Comden, along with celebs such as John Lennon, Elton John, and Dustin Hoffman, was among the glitterati who attended the March 7, 1975, opening, and in his syndicated column that ran immediately after, Earl Wilson reported her as quipping that the raucous show meant that "David Belasco is probably spinning in his clerical collar."

CHAPTER 17

Returning (Artistically)
to the 1930s

Following the year-long saga of the *Lorelei* tour on the road, Comden and Green took some time to regroup in New York. Throughout the first half of 1974 they were frequent guests at fundraising events, often entertaining with some of their old material and sometimes delivering new specialty routines they had developed for a particular charity.

Green, during this period, also worked as a stay-at-home dad for a brief time while Phyllis Newman took to the road with a cabaret act. Newman had not performed since her turn in the 1971 revival of *On the Town*, and with a break in Green's schedule she took the opportunity to branch out as a solo performer. Later that year she took on another assignment, as director, when she accepted an offer from Wynn Handman to stage a new revue at the American Place Theater, which he founded.

The show was to be both a comedic and dramatic examination of what life might be in the future. Among the diverse group of writers contributing to the piece were novelist Donald Barthelme; playwright Marshall Brickman, who in two years would win an Oscar for *Annie Hall* and later go on to co-write *Jersey Boys*; and Peter Stone, book writer for musicals such as *1776* and *Two by Two*. The songwriters involved were an equally varied group, and numbers came from Stephen Schwartz, who had burst onto the theater scene in 1971 with *Godspell* and followed that with *Pippin*, and Galt MacDermott, who had written, among other things, *Hair*.

Newman, not surprisingly, wanted to have Comden and Green involved in the show, and when she approached them about contributing she suggested that they consider working with Cy Coleman, a composer who had been a friend for a while. Coleman, whose career included classical and jazz performances during his childhood and teen years, had, in adulthood, written the music for shows such as *Sweet Charity* and *Seesaw* and was also responsible for such pop hits as "Witchcraft" and "The Best Is Yet to Come." He, along with Comden and Green, were intrigued by the idea of collaborating and set to work on developing some material for the revue, titled *Straws in the Wind.*

The songwriters eventually wrote three numbers for *Straws,* two of which were used in performance. Their association with Coleman energized Comden and Green, and their lyrics for *Straws* are among the sharpest they had penned in some time. With "The Lost Word" they imagined that there could come a time when people would be unable to express their emotions to one another. The Comden and Green lyric, set to Coleman's melancholy yet driving waltz melody, aches with bittersweet directness as it mourns "a powerful word from a lost world." It many regards, the number echoes the sentiment of impending loss they so eloquently expressed in "Some Other Time."

And while Comden, Green, and Coleman strive for darker tones in this number, they are more comedic in their other song in *Straws,* "Simplified Language," which imagines a future in which gender has been obliterated from language. Siblings are known as "bristers," parents are referred to as "moppas," and they even devised a word for genderless genitalia: "penina." It's their quintessential linguistic silliness set to a lilting Coleman melody.

Straws went into performance in early 1975, playing a limited one-month off-Broadway engagement. With all American Place Theater shows, Handman left the decision to his directors as to whether critics should be invited, and Newman opted not to allow reviewers to attend. This meant that any immediate response to the Comden-Green-Coleman contributions came simply from the subscribers and single ticket buyers who saw the show. Eventually, Comden and Green came to include these numbers in a revised version of *A Party With,* and a few years later critical reaction to one of the numbers came from Howard Kissel, who deemed "Simplified Language" "a marvelous song."[1]

As if they were channeling their earliest days together as revue writers, Comden and Green took on the responsibility of writing the book for another one in 1975, *By Bernstein,* a retrospective of Leonard Bernstein's unused or little-known songs being produced by the Chelsea Theatre Group at the Westside Theater in Midtown. With this show they were able to demonstrate their knack for bringing a disparate group of numbers together in a cohesive fashion; the piece included songs that Comden and Green, as well as Stephen Sondheim and John Latouche, had written with Bernstein. Woven into the show, too, were some of the numbers for which Bernstein had written both music and lyrics, including "The Riobamba" (which a very young Frank Sinatra had once performed) as well as several of the stand-alone songs that he had attempted to insert into *On the Town.*

The conceit that Comden and Green created for the show imagines a bar where cut numbers from shows such as *On the Town, Wonderful Town,* and *West Side Story* are consigned for eternity along with the characters who originally delivered them. During the course of the show, characters ranging from *On the Town*'s Gabey and Claire DeLoone to *Wonderful Town*'s Ruth to Candide and his mentor Dr. Pangloss emerge in a stylized, almost dreamlike setting. Comden and Green conclude the show with a number from the unproduced *The Skin of Our Teeth,* and with it they take the piece to an even more surreal level as the performers say that they don't know which characters were meant to deliver it or even the plot surrounding the tune.

Comden and Green's inventive framework for *By Bernstein* elicited a variety of critical responses. Clive Barnes, in a November 24 *New York Times* review, commented on "[the] too coy a text" that surrounded the Bernstein songs, while John Beaufort in a *Christian Science Monitor* review on November 28 commended the "perky commentary" that Comden and Green had provided for this production "whose pleasures make one forget the rigors of wooden chairs." Allan Wallach's *Newsday* review on November 24 was the most effusive. He informed readers that they would "rejoice" that these lost Bernstein songs had been found and "given a most attractive new home."

Even as Comden and Green revisited the skill sets they developed for the Revuers with these two shows, a new film assignment gave them the chance to revisit the entertainment they were savoring in movie houses at the time. It came to them between *Straws* and *By Bernstein* and represented the first film project they had embarked on in 10 years.

Their subject was the life of Busby Berkeley, whose direction and choreography for 1930s movie musicals such as *42nd Street, Dames,* and the various *Gold Diggers* films had become iconic. The project was the brainchild of producers Irwin Winkler and Robert Chartoff, who were riding high at the time on the James Caan movie *The Gambler,* and who, one year later, would later become the men who brought *Rocky* to the screen.

By the end of the year Comden and Green had written two drafts of the screenplay, which presented not so much a biography of Berkeley as a fictitious slice of his life. Their scripts contained just enough historic and personal details for audiences to learn salient points about Berkeley's life. At the same time Comden and Green offered up a gently satiric tale about Hollywood circa 1935. Specifically, what they imagined was that as Berkeley watches his fourth marriage dissolve and worries that he might be brought up on charges for a car accident that has left one man battling for his life, he also must devise a fantastic finale for a movie. It's not a picture that he's directed, and it's one that appears to be an utter failure unless it ends on such a high note that audiences forgive everything that's come before. In

the Comden and Green screenplay, the stakes for Berkeley on this one production number become even higher, because it's coming at a moment
when the studio will be considering whether or not to renew his contract.

Comden and Green's drafts contain, unsurprisingly, terrific details about
picture making at the time, including sequences that depict how Berkeley
achieved his incredible mirrored shots that made it appear as if his dancers
were stretching to infinity. They also wink, satirically and lovingly, at the
director's excesses. The production number he devises takes its inspiration
from a soda fountain, and throughout the picture Comden and Green include sequences such as one in which dancing girls are turned into the handles on soda fountain mugs and another in which the chorines slide down
straws into sudsy soda glasses. They even have Berkeley demanding a sail-
ing banana-split boat.

Comden and Green's approach to the subject was ultimately not what
the producers had envisioned for the film. Less than a year after *Busby* was
announced, and as Winkler-Chartoff prepared two similar films for production (Martin Scorsese's 1940s-era *New York, New York* and Ken Russell's
1920s-set *Valentino*), they announced that Comden and Green were no
longer attached to the project. Hugh Wheeler was brought in to write the
script, but in the end the producers shelved the venture.

Not working on *Busby* did not mean, however, that Comden and Green
were leaving their return to the 1930s altogether. Just four months after the
announcement that they wouldn't be doing this movie came the news that
they were joining forces with Coleman to write a new Broadway musical. It
would be an adaptation of Ben Hecht and Charles MacArthur's 1932 hit
Twentieth Century.

The comedy unfolds on the famed luxury train that used to whisk passengers between Chicago and New York. At the piece's center are a down-
on-his-luck theatrical producer, Oscar Jaffe, and a glamorous Hollywood
star, Lily Garland, who achieved her first successes on the stage in Oscar's
productions. She also happens to be his former lover. Oscar's goal for the
journey is to convince Lily to star in his next production. If by the time they
arrive in New York he has her signature on a contract, his creditors will be
appeased, and he'll avoid utter destitution.

Set in just three spaces on the train—two adjoining drawing-room suites
and the observation car—the sense of farce in the Hecht-MacArthur
play came from the colorful supporting characters that complicate Oscar
and Lily's lives and serve to both facilitate and thwart his goals. Not only
does Oscar have to contend with Lily's dimwitted hunk of a boyfriend, a
Hollywood agent named George Smith, but also a conniving rival producer
who was once his protégé. Further, there are, as Comden and Green later
called them, "two Oberammergau actors…from a lost company of the

Passion Play"[2] and a physician who's trying to get Oscar to read a script that he's written.

Comden and Green had always thought that the play could serve as a terrific basis for a musical, but Coleman was not convinced when they first raised the idea with him. In particular he was not interested in writing a score that was filled with tunes that were pastiches of the era's musical styles. Coleman later explained, "I didn't mind doing a period piece but it was not a period that I wanted to do."[3]

Comden, Green, and Coleman continued to meet to discuss other ideas for a show that might suit them all, and it was during one of these meetings that they "improvised a musical sequence that was highly flamboyant, verging on the operatic," Comden and Green recalled for a New York Times feature on February 19, 1978, adding, "We laughed, dismissed it as 'too much' and then suddenly realized that that was the way Oscar and Lily should sound." The trio came to realize that the operatic style should extend to the entirety of the musical, and, having found "the key" to the adaptation, they knew they would be able to create a musical based on the comedy.

When the musical Twentieth Century was announced, Coleman was at work on two other projects, including I Love My Wife, and for the balance of 1976 he split his time between the former and the Comden and Green collaboration. By the beginning of 1977 they had completed a draft of the script, and as Coleman dedicated himself to the April opening of Wife, Comden and Green shifted their focus to a new version of the show they had performed on Broadway almost 20 years earlier, A Party with Betty Comden and Adolph Green. Since this retrospective of their work premiered they had offered performances of it variously around the country, generally as one-night-only fundraisers for organizations they supported. In 1976, even as they were working with Coleman, they accepted an offer to do a four-performance engagement at the Loeb Drama Center in Boston. The event quickly sold out and garnered effusive notices for them both as writers and performers. In the Boston Globe Kevin Kelly's September 25 review proclaimed, "[It] is the smash of the season," and he lauded the show as having "spirit, sophistication" and being an "unflagging entertainment."

These kudos were enough to convince Comden and Green, as well as producer Arthur Cantor, that other critics, along with theatergoers, might concur, and so by December 1976 A Party With began a short stint at the New Locust Theatre in Philadelphia, and by the beginning of 1977 the show had been booked as a limited engagement into the now-demolished Morosco Theater on 45th Street, where it opened on February 10. The next morning reviews, much as they had been 19 years before, were glowing. Clive Barnes in the New York Times extolled them as being "fantastic performers" who "sing with grace and zest" and "act out their songs with special fervor." And in the February 21 issue of *Time* magazine, Gerald Clarke wrote: "Rarely has so much wit and fun been packed into two hours."

The reviews didn't result in sell-out crowds, but box office was healthy enough to warrant an extension, which resulted in *A Party With* moving to the Little Theater, because the Morosco was committed to another production (Michael Cristofer's acclaimed drama *The Shadow Box*). The new *A Party With*, preserved in a second, expanded original cast recording that was released before 1977 ended, concluded its Broadway run on April 30, having played 92 performances.

While Comden and Green entertained on Broadway and Coleman opened *I Love My Wife*, they all continued work on *Twentieth Century*. During one interview about *A Party With*, Comden and Green praised the work: "The new score is just glorious. It's given us a new enthusiasm for working in musical theater again."[4] As they worked, they did so with the knowledge that they had producers behind the project, Cy Feuer and Ernest Martin, who had been on board since the trio announced their intention to adapt the Hecht-MacArthur comedy.

Feuer and Martin had an impressive Broadway track record. Among the shows they had backed were *Guys and Dolls*, *Can-Can*, and *How to Succeed in Business Without Really Trying*. They also produced one of Coleman's early musicals, *Little Me*. Unfortunately, they eventually pulled their support of *Twentieth Century* after disagreements over casting with the man who had agreed to direct the show, Harold Prince.

Prince joined the collaboration at the height of his association with songwriter Stephen Sondheim. Together they had brought *Company*, *Follies*, *A Little Night Music*, and *Pacific Overtures* to Broadway. And Prince's work was not limited to this one songwriter. Among his earliest ventures as a producer were groundbreaking shows such as Leonard Bernstein, Arthur Laurents, and Sondheim's *West Side Story* and Joseph Stein, Sheldon Harnick, and Jerry Bock's *Fiddler on the Roof*. When he began directing, he had taken on both the charming *She Loves Me*, with a score by Bock and Harnick, and the audacious *Cabaret*, which boasted music and lyrics by John Kander and Fred Ebb.

With tastes running toward serious musical fare, Prince might have seemed an unusual choice for *Twentieth Century*, but, as he pointed out, his mentor George Abbott directed the original production of the play in 1932. He had also worked with Comden and Green on lighter fare in the early 1950s, when he was stage manager for (and an understudy in) *Wonderful Town*. But Prince's history with Comden and Green dated back even further. As a kid he saw *Billion Dollar Baby*, and in their liner notes for the off-Broadway cast recording of the show, released in 1995, Comden and Green recall, "[He] told us as a growing boy he had been much affected by it and found that it helped change his ideas about what a musical show can be."

With *Twentieth Century* Prince also saw an opportunity for personal artistic expansion: "For me the primary challenge was to see whether I could direct farce—pratfalls, double-takes. Whether I had the capacity to make things outrageously funny and still honest."[5] In addition to finding the idea of this challenge appealing, Prince was enthusiastic about the musical vernacular the team had hit upon for the piece, believing that the score added a new dimension to the comedy.

The casting issues that divided Prince and the producers centered on the sort of leading actors the show needed. Feuer and Martin were advocating performers such as Alfred Drake, who had been the original Curly in *Oklahoma!* and Fred Graham/Petruchio in *Kiss Me, Kate*, and Danny Kaye, whose face was familiar nationwide from his eponymous television show and whose Broadway credits included *Lady in the Dark* and *Two by Two*. Both men would have had unquestionable appeal to ticket buyers. Prince, however, wanted to ensure that the principals could both sing and act the roles, and for a period Alan Bates and Meryl Streep were considered for the roles of Oscar and Lily, respectively.

It didn't take the writers long to find backers to replace Feuer and Martin. Almost as soon as the veteran producers had withdrawn, a newly established consortium working under the umbrella title of the Producer's Circle 2 announced that it would bring the musical to the stage. The Producers Circle was composed of an intriguingly diverse quartet. For instance, one member was Robert Fryer, who was responsible for making *Wonderful Town* a reality. Another was newcomer Martin Richards, who had experience as a singer and in casting at 20th Century Fox. Mary Lea Johnson, heiress to the Johnson & Johnson medical products fortune, was another member of the Producers Circle team, and its fourth member was former actor James Cresson.

A SUPERSTITION IMPACTS A SHOW'S TITLE

Throughout the development process of *On the Twentieth Century*, the musical was known by the title of the play that inspired it: *Twentieth Century*. According to Richard L. Coe in a March 12, 1978, *Washington Post* story about musicals currently on Broadway, "A dominant investor, it is said, was told by a numerologist that for it to be a success, 21 letters in the title were vital." Thus the addition of the five letters in "on the."

With the producers in place in June 1977, Prince finalized casting. The role of Oscar Jaffee (who gained an 'e' on his last name in Comden and Green's book) went to John Cullum, an actor who had distinguished himself in musicals such as *On a Clear Day You Can See Forever* and *Shenandoah*, earning a Tony Award for his work in the latter. Madeline Kahn snagged the plum role of Lily. Kahn came to the show with stage credits ranging from David Rabe's drama *In the Boom Boom Room* to a concert version of *She Loves Me*. She had also been featured in Mel Brooks's movies *Blazing Saddles* and *Young Frankenstein*. As for the relatively small role of Lily's boyfriend, Prince turned to a young actor who was just at the beginning of his career, future Academy Award winner Kevin Kline.

The fourth principal in the company was Imogene Coca, who had made a splash on Broadway in the 1930s in two editions of Leonard Sillman's *New Faces* revues and subsequently gone on to fame on television, notably for her work opposite Sid Caesar in *Your Show of Shows*. Coca was cast as a character that Comden and Green had reworked from the original, a supposedly wealthy religious fanatic named Letitia Primrose. They created this character because, as they streamlined Hecht and MacArthur's play, they eliminated the Passion Play actors. In the process they realized they still needed a character that would inspire Oscar to propose a Mary Magdalene vehicle for Lily. In Letitia, who surreptitiously posts stickers bearing the warning "Repent for the time is at hand" throughout the train, they were able to accomplish this goal and at the same time heighten Oscar's troubles. Mrs. Primrose both inspires him and promises to fully back the show. Unbeknownst to Oscar, though, her financial resources are nil.

COMDEN AND GREEN "FILTHY"?

Coca was, in actuality, not Prince's first choice for the role. Originally, he turned to Mildred Natwick, who had distinguished herself on Broadway in Noël Coward's *Blithe Spirit* in the 1940s and more recently in the Kander and Ebb tuner *70, Girls, 70* and originated the role of the carping mother-in-law in Neil Simon's *Barefoot in the Park*, which she also played on screen. Natwick was prominently billed in early ads for *On the Twentieth Century*, but she withdrew before rehearsals began. As wire service theater reporter Jack O'Brian reported in a November 1977 column: "[She] couldn't stand the filthy 'updated' dialogue by revisionists Comden and Green."

When rehearsals began, Prince and the cast worked with a Comden and Green script that ingeniously opened up the original play to give it the size and a scope of a full-scale musical. The show's first scene allowed audiences to witness a brief glimpse of Oscar's latest flop, an extravaganza about Joan of Arc titled *The French Girl*, as it bombs in Chicago. Further, Comden and Green devised a scene at Union Station in Chicago, where the ensemble could deliver the show's title song, a grandiose paean to the train itself. And then throughout they created sequences when the action flashed back to Lily and Oscar's earliest days, including the moment he discovered her and their life together as lovers while she established herself as a stage star.

Along with their work on the book, Comden and Green also contributed some sparkling lyrics to match Coleman's grandiose melodies. For the production number "Veronique," which presents Lily's first stage success under Oscar's guidance, their lyric includes the amusing lines: "France is saved, and freedom once again can speak/All because of Veronique!" They also found ways to bring period specificity into the show. In a musical duet battle between Oscar and Lily, she brags that her Rolls Royce makes a Cadillac resemble a flivver, using bygone slang for a cheap car or a lemon. In a more emotional vein, they penned the simple romantic ballad for Lily and Oscar, "Our Private World."

They also wrote several more traditional musical comedy numbers for the show, including two that Prince cut during rehearsals. In "Show Biz Is the Lowest Biz There Is," Oscar's press agent and business manager lament the woes of life in the theater to a melody that Coleman later revised; it became "Join the Circus" for his 1980 musical, *Barnum*. And with "Oscar Jaffee," a serenade that a group of chorus girls delivers to the producer, Coleman inserted a jaunty ragtime melody. There was also one jazzy 1920s-style song that remained in the score: "Babbette."

While Comden and Green had a two-month tryout period for *Applause* and endured a year-long one for *Lorelei*, they had only a four-week stint in Boston to hone *On the Twentieth Century*. The production opened at the Colonial Theatre to divided reviews. In the January 12 edition of the *Boston Globe* Kevin Kelly described it as "nothing more than a derivative example of the old Broadway song-and-dancer." In the *Boston Herald* Elliot Norton had an entirely different reaction. He called it a "jubilant musical comedy," noting that the first scene set at Oscar's failed *The French Girl* was "absolute hilarity." Between these two extremes of the daily papers was a January 18 review from *Variety*'s "Snyd." suggesting that "revisions and substantial cuts are in order" and recognizing that there was "sufficient time for the work" while the show was in Boston. "Snyd." also made particular mention of Comden and Green's "literate, amusing lyrics."

Prince and the writers took to retooling the show, and in particular the director concentrated on the central section in the first act, which took audiences back to Lily and Oscar's life together as artistic colleagues and lovers. Comden and Green had already revised this section during rehearsals. Originally, they devised a series of scenes that explored the couple's happiness and loving antagonism at home. These sections of the musical also explored Oscar's philandering, which led to their breakup.

By the time the musical reached Boston, Comden and Green had altered the flashback significantly. Oscar and Lily still were quarrelsome lovers, but instead of Oscar's affairs leading to the demise of their relationship, it was his sabotage of her attempt to appear in a new play by Eugene O'Neill. In the process of revising this section, Comden, Green, and Coleman also wrote a new song, "This Is the Day," an aria that echoes those found in operettas of the 1920s.

After the Boston reviews Prince spent a day rehearsing Cullum and Kahn and honing the flashback scene. The following day, he made a drastic cut and eliminated it altogether. His decision meant that "Our Private World," which was also performed in this section of the show, would have been excised from the score. It was a cut that troubled the writers, so much so that they went to work on creating a new sequence—aboard the train—that allowed the characters to express their feelings for one another. The result was a streamlined first act, with one major scene change eliminated. Further, having Oscar and Lily sing "Our Private World" together aboard the train, though in separate compartments, allowed theatergoers to understand that despite differences they still had romantic feelings for each other.

On the Twentieth Century shifted from the Colonial to Broadway's St. James Theater, where it began previews on February 9 in anticipation of a February 19 opening. In New York, critical reaction was similar to what had been voiced in Boston. Some reviewers were taken with the production, even as they recognized the musical's limitations or flaws. Richard Eder praised it in the *New York Times,* saying, "The musical has an exuberance, a bubbly confidence in its own life," while also warning theatergoers that "it has rough spots, flat spots, and an energy that occasionally ebbs." Others, such as Edwin Wilson in a February 22 *Wall Street Journal* review, were underwhelmed by the show: "The musical's overall lack of purpose takes its toll. Miss Comden and Mr. Green are not writing at the top of their form." Critical consensus centered on one element of the production: Robin Wagner's art deco scenic design that brought the train's interiors and exterior magnificently to life. Despite the reviews, *On the Twentieth Century* performed well at the box office during its first full month on Broadway, and by its sixth week of performances it was playing to 95 percent capacity, an indication that word of mouth for the show and star Kahn was good.

Backstage, however, things were rockier. Throughout rehearsals and the preview period Prince was concerned about Kahn's performance and her ability to sustain it. He recalled, "Some nights her energy level flagged to a degree that she disappeared, and other nights she was so manic that her co-stars couldn't deliver their performances as rehearsed. She seemed unable, or likely unwilling, to give the same performance every night."[6] On the show's opening night, Kahn delivered as Prince hoped, but after this "she rarely gave the same performance again, at least never two nights in a row."[7] Worse still, she started missing performances, and just over two months into the run her understudy, Judy Kaye, assumed the role of Lily Garland.

Three weeks later the Tony Award nominations were announced, and *On the Twentieth Century* snagged nine, including best musical. When the prizes were handed out in June, the production won in five categories, with Comden and Green earning one for their book and sharing one with Coleman for the score.

The duality of performing and writing that was part of Comden and Green's life between 1977 and 1978 continued for the next 10 years as they switched, with seeming ease, between acting jobs and two new musicals. At the same time, as each of them entered their 60s, they discovered that their private lives were requiring more of their attention and energy than ever before.

CHRISTOPHER DURANG SENDS COMDEN AND GREEN TO HELL

In his 1981 play *Sister Mary Ignatius Explains It All for You*, Christopher Durang imagines a list of people "who will go straight to hell" that the title character shares with her pupils. Comden and Green are surprisingly among those consigned to eternal damnation, alongside celebrities such as porn star Linda Lovelace and sexually charged rockers David Bowie and Mick Jagger. Durang explained the reason he included them to Richard Christiansen for a June 20, 1982, *Chicago Tribune* feature, saying that after his musical *A History of the American Film* lost the Tony Award for best book to *On the Twentieth Century*, "I thought 'Damn them to hell,' and so I did."

CHAPTER 18

Ten Years of Performing
and Writing

Almost as soon as *On the Twentieth Century* opened, Comden and Green returned to performing *A Party With,* offering the revue in Florida and later in California, in its first extended West Coast presentation. Audiences around the country also had the chance to see them performing their work in the spring of 1978 when PBS aired an edition of *Previn and the Pittsburgh* that reunited Comden and Green with the group's conductor, André Previn, with whom they'd written the songs for *It's Always Fair Weather.*

Even as they were performing their own work, both Comden and Green discovered that as they entered their 60s, a new range of roles was suddenly available for them, and for the next 10 years or so they eagerly accepted the acting opportunities.

The first chance for performing came for Comden at the beginning of 1979, when Imogene Coca had to miss several performances in *On the Twentieth Century* to shoot a television pilot. It wasn't that Coca didn't have an understudy. She did, ensemble member Peggy Cooper, but the production, nearing its first-year anniversary, had begun to slip at the box office, and Comden's stepping in was a way of potentially boosting ticket sales and generating press. Further, the opportunity for Comden to cavort on Robin Wagner's art deco set must have seemed irresistible.

She was able to show her wacky, modern side four years later when she was offered the role of Tasha Blumberg in Wendy Wasserstein's *Isn't It Romantic?* at off-Broadway's Playwrights Horizons. The comic drama must have had an interesting appeal to Comden when she first read it. Wasserstein's play centers on two women, both just a little younger than Comden's own daughter, as they struggle to balance their careers with romance and family. Comden was cast as one of their mothers, a woman who, like Comden, had taken an untraditional path in her life. Tasha has raised two children, enjoys a marriage that she considers a genuine partnership, and instructs at a dance studio. Similarities between the character and the actress extended to both having fears about their daughters being at sea in their lives: Comden watched her own daughter, Susanna, struggle with a career in the fashion industry. Susanna worked for a time with Donald Brooks, who designed the costumes for *Fade Out–Fade In* and her mom's ensembles for *A Party With*. After this, Susanna was employed at several boutiques before realizing that "she had no interest in the world of fashion."[1] In the end she opted to earn a living as a dog walker.

In a February 1, 1984, *Variety* review "Humm." praised Comden's "delightful characterization" of this Jewish mom who sports tie-dyed workout gear and never cooks breakfast but just orders in. The critic added, "Her comedic timing, needless to say, is flawless."

When Comden accepted the role she joked that it wasn't at all the sort of part she had dreamed about when she was younger and longed to be a performer: "I visualized myself as Amanda Prynne, a great Noël Coward part, in 'Private Lives.'" And by the end of 1983 Comden was indeed playing a grandly elegant part, that of reclusive film legend Greta Garbo in Sidney Lumet's film *Garbo Talks*.

In her memoir, *Off Stage*, Comden describes how uncomfortable she had always been when people suggested that she resembled the Swedish-born screen star: "A shiver of nonrecognition would shake my frame." Similar misgiving arose when the director approached her, but after reading the screenplay she acquiesced to Lumet's request and agreed to appear as the alluring and foreboding star.

Garbo Talks focuses on Gilbert (Ron Silver), whose dying mother, Estelle (Anne Bancroft), has worshipped the title star all her life. Estelle's final wish is to meet her idol, and Gilbert sets out to find her and ask that she visit the ailing woman. During Gilbert's odyssey through New York he gets glimpses of Garbo, but it's not until he's at a flea market that he comes face to face with her and makes his request. For these scenes, as well as an extended scene in Estelle's hospital room, Lumet used another actress, Nina Zoe, to play the statuesque beauty; Comden simply wasn't tall enough. Her screen appearance, with semi-full facial, comes in the movie's final scene as Gilbert and a new girlfriend walk through Central Park and Garbo shows Gilbert a kindness.

A COMMAND PERFORMANCE FOR GRETA

Comden and Green met and performed for Greta Garbo during one of their stints in Hollywood. While they were at dinner at the home of friends, Gene

Kelly was also hosting a party during which he sang Comden and Green's praises. Garbo's interest was piqued, and she asked if Kelly could get them to come over. He managed to track them down, and after apologizing to their hostess, they hurried to Kelly's. Comden recalls in her book, *Off Stage*, that Garbo laughed as they performed. But she remembers little else and quips, "One would think I would remember every syllable, but somehow I remember only a kind of drunken glow."

Green was also in *Garbo Talks*, in a much-written-about party sequence at the Museum of Modern Art that also featured other real-life celebrities, including composer Cy Coleman, columnist Liz Smith, and writer-historian Arthur Schlesinger Jr. In the scene, Green, playing himself, regales them and others with his knowledge about an actress who had, theoretically, appeared alongside Garbo.

This 1984 cameo, however, did not mark his return to the screen. That occurred in 1979, when he accepted a small role in the movie *Simon*. Written and directed by Marshall Brickman, who, like Green, had contributed to *Straws in the Wind*, the movie centers on an eccentric psychology professor, Simon Mendelssohn (played by Alan Arkin), who becomes a guinea pig in a bizarre experiment concocted by five ersatz geniuses at a New England think tank. They plan to brainwash Simon into believing he's an extraterrestrial and then observe how news of an alien that has lived on earth for 40 years affects the American public. What they don't predict are the delusions of grandeur that Simon develops once he believes that he's an alien and the global impact of his growing popularity as he denounces trivial banalities plaguing society, such as Hawaiian Muzak in elevators.

Simon eventually leaves the research facility where he's being kept, and Green plays a man he encounters as soon as he's out: the leader of a commune that worships "the sacred box" (a television), uses a *TV Guide* as a makeshift bible, and intones jingles as its hymns. In his few scenes Green delivers an understated performance that makes the inanity of the character's sermons, "Miltie who begat Lucy who begat Mary who spun-off Rhoda," comically appealing. In a February 20, 1980, *New York Times* review, Vincent Canby wrote that Green's performance "defines for me the meaning of 'laid back,'" adding that he "radiates the lunatic cheerfulness that is the tone of 'Simon' at its best."

Green delivered similarly low-key performances, while also displaying something of his more antic side, in his next two film appearances: as Leo Silver in Richard Benjamin's toast to the early days of television comedy, *My Favorite Year*, in 1982, and as Jerry Silber in the 1984 indie *Lily in Love*, which starred Christopher Plummer and Maggie Smith. Both films cast

Green in the role of an entertainment executive and provided him with more screen time than he had in *Simon*, yet neither drew the sort of critical notice that he enjoyed with the earlier picture.

A few years later Green had the chance to headline a picture with Jules Feiffer's *I Want to Go Home*. The movie centers on a curmudgeonly cartoonist from suburban Cleveland, Joey Wellman (Green), who has to balance his disdain for anything that isn't American and his joy at being included in a retrospective of pop art in Paris. Joey's trip abroad both teaches him some things about himself and allows him to reestablish a relationship with the adult daughter (Laura Benson) from whom he has been estranged for more than two years. The film, directed by Alain Resnais, also starred Linda Lavin, as Joey's girlfriend, and Gerard Depardieu, as a French intellectual with a love for all things American.

I Want to Go Home had its premiere at the Venice Film Festival and later was seen as part of the London Film Festival before receiving a limited American release. Sadly, in the picture that Derek Malcolm labeled "a miscalculation from beginning to end" in a September 14 review for the *Guardian*, Green's turn received only faint praise. The critic "Len." in the September 13 edition of *Variety* for example, described it as "crotchety but basically sweet," and after this picture Green did not return to film work until the mid-1990s.

A MOVIE THAT MIGHT HAVE BEEN

For a brief period in 1980 Comden and Green investigated a return to screenwriting when Francis Ford Coppola, famed for his work on the *Godfather* films and *Apocalypse Now*, began to contemplate directing movie musicals. He partnered with Gene Kelly to create an arm of his film production company similar to the Freed unit at MGM, and one of the first projects was to be a musical about inventor Preston Tucker. The writers, along with composer Leonard Bernstein, spent a week with the director in California discussing ideas, but eventually the project was sidelined because of financial issues facing Coppola's company.

One of the benefits of their lives as performers was that a one-night-only performance of *A Party With* or a few days on set for a film meant that neither Comden nor Green was entirely immersed in the all-consuming process of bringing a new musical to Broadway. For Comden, who had weathered a difficult time as both mother and wife during the past 15 years, this was particularly important.

In 1968 her husband, Steven Kyle, suffered a bout of pancreatic cancer that left him hospitalized for five months. He enjoyed a full recovery and in

1970 retired, closing the decorative accessories store he had opened just after World War II. He and Comden were able to enjoy being together more continuously than they had since they married, because, with the exception of the year-long *Lorelei* tour, she was no longer having to work outside of New York for extended periods. At the same time, they coped with their son Alan's drug addiction, which began just as he entered his teens.

In her memoir, *Off Stage*, Comden recounts with candor the various rehab treatments that Alan attempted. She also details the legal problems he faced—and prison terms he served—overseas because of his addiction. Alan was still away, in Asia, in 1979 when a second bout of pancreatic cancer struck his father. This time the disease took Kyle's life. He died on October 17, 1979.

For the next 10 years Comden, as a widow, would cope with her son's addiction as well as she could while also dealing with her own health issues, notably a much-publicized cornea transplant in 1982. She had been battling "Fuch's Dystrophy," which caused her cornea to swell and fill with water, for 10 years. She gave interviews just two days after the procedure and told reporters that she would be back at work soon; she and Green had written a new show that was just about to go into rehearsal.

Comden and Green had been working on this newest project since just after her husband's death. In it they imagined what happened to Nora, the heroine of Henrik Ibsen's *A Doll's House*, after she leaves her husband and children in Norway circa 1879. Comden and Green would later describe how they came to conceive of the show, which they titled *A Doll's Life*, saying that they were "looking desperately for a story about a strong woman in a male-dominated world."[2] Eventually, they thought of Ibsen's iconic drama, perhaps inspired by having seen a prominent revival of the show starring Liv Ullman that played at Lincoln Center's Vivian Beaumont Theater in 1975.

The story they invented for Nora after she left the security of her home has her traveling to Christiania (now Oslo). She finds, initially, that she must deploy some of the feminine wiles that were her mode of survival both before and during her marriage. Slowly, however, she learns other ways to survive, ones that allow her to speak her mind, even to powerful men, and, although she cannot own property in her own name, she becomes a success as a business woman. At the same time Nora sadly discovers that even in relationships in which she believes she is on an equal footing she must still endure men's condescension.

On its face *A Doll's Life* appears to be a radical departure from the sorts of musicals Comden and Green had previously written, but in some respects for the early 1980s it was a natural extension of their earlier work. They had placed strong, independent women at the center of their musicals starting with *On the Town*. Both the cabbie Hildy and the anthropologist Claire are free-spirited working women, who, in their own ways, champion the concept of "free love" well before it became a rallying cry in the 1960s. Similarly, in *Bells Are Ringing* they brought a female business owner center stage. And even in the unproduced screenplay for *Say It with Music* they explored some of the themes present in *A Doll's Life*, with their early 20th-century heroine becoming aware of the plight of working women in New York and beyond.

As 1980 wound down they took a rough draft, which included some lyrics for songs, to their old friend and the director of *On the Twentieth Century*, Harold Prince. He was immediately enthusiastic and agreed to direct the show as soon as they finished it. He also suggested that Larry Grossman, who wrote the music for Broadway's *Minnie's Boys* and *Goodtime Charley* and off-Broadway's *Snoopy!*, join them as composer.

All four began expanding the initial draft. One of the biggest changes they made during this time involved the framing device that Comden and Green envisioned for the show. In their earliest versions *A Doll's Life* began with the final scene of Ibsen's play being played out by a company of actors in full performance. At the curtain call the actress playing Nora disappeared, immersed in thoughts about what would happen to her character after she slammed the door on her marriage.

This evolved into a rehearsal sequence of the same scene after which the leading actress wanders off consumed by thoughts about her character. The sense of *A Doll's Life* unfolding within the context of an actress in the process of exploring her role was to be enhanced by the physical production, which was to shift from mere indications to fully realistic settings as it progressed. In addition, the book became suffused with short flashbacks to Ibsen's play as Nora encounters situations similar to those that she experienced with her husband, Torvald. Prince, working with a production team that included scenic designers Timothy O'Brien and Tazeena Firth and costume designer Florence Klotz, also found ways in which he could inject visual references to paintings by Edvard Munch, Ibsen's countryman and contemporary.

A sense of fluidity was becoming integral to the book, and Prince's vision for the show also informed Grossman's score. The melodies for *A Doll's Life* evoke both period and contemporary styles, and Grossman's use of underscoring makes the piece feel both dreamlike and through-composed. And yet, even though Grossman's musical voice was unlike any of the other composers with whom Comden and Green had worked, their lyric-writing craft and his style mesh gracefully, particularly in a ballad such as "Stay with Me, Nora" or with the purposefully clichéd and bombastic *Loki and Baldour* opera that plays a significant role in Nora's journey. In many regards this latter piece, heard in significant excerpts during the first act, is a natural extension of the wit of some of their previous work: the Revuers' spoof of operettas, "The Baroness Bazooka," and the overblown "Veronique" from *On the Twentieth Century.*

It took a year for Comden, Green, Grossman, and Prince to ready a full working version of the show, and, as they finished, production plans were announced. *A Doll's Life* would have a 10-week tryout engagement at Los Angeles's Ahmanson Theatre, after which it would open on Broadway.

With this schedule Prince began casting, turning first to Betsy Joslyn, who snagged the part of Nora. Joslyn and Prince had worked together on *Sweeney Todd*, where she began in the ensemble and later assumed the role of Johanna. Prince cast another veteran from *Sweeney*, George Hearn, who took over the title role on Broadway from Len Cariou and played the national tour. He would be both Nora's husband and the attorney, Johan Blecker, who befriends Nora after she has left her home. The other two men central to Nora's new life were to be played by Giorgio Tozzi, who had performed principal bass roles at the Metropolitan Opera and starred on Broadway in a 1979 revival of Frank Loesser's *The Most Happy Fella*, and Peter Gallagher, who appeared in both *Grease* and a revival of *Hair* on Broadway. Tozzi would play Eric Didrickson, a wealthy, chauvinistic industrialist with whom Nora lives for a period and whose beneficence she uses to further her pursuit of financial independence. Gallagher was cast as Otto, a struggling composer whom Nora briefly supports.

A two-month rehearsal period afforded Prince and the writers the time to recraft and rethink the book and score with the company. As work progressed, Prince grew to realize that hiring Tozzi had been a mistake. "He couldn't handle it. He's the nicest man alive, but he couldn't sing it and he couldn't act it,"[3] Prince recalled. To replace Tozzi the director turned to another actor with whom he had worked on *Sweeney Todd*, Edmund Lyndeck, who originated the role of Judge Turpin in the Stephen Sondheim–Hugh Wheeler musical.

During the rehearsal period, Comden, Green, and Grossman were reconsidering the show's ending and developed several different scenarios for Nora as she reaches a pinnacle in her life as a business woman and also returns to her husband and children. Their primary concern was to end her journey so that it satisfied dramatically while mirroring the ambiguous end of Ibsen's play. They wanted theatergoers to question what would happen next in Nora and Torvald's life, given what Nora has learned about herself and the world.

As they considered this, Grossman, Comden, and Green wrote a new song to end the show, "Can You Hear Me Now?," in which Nora simultaneously describes what she has learned and how she has changed and pleads with her husband to understand that they must now continue together the growth process she's experienced. The number, which leads to Torvald's climactic declaration "Nora, we must talk," replaced a simpler and more direct one in which the couple, along with the company, described relationships as being potential miracles, provided partners are willing to work in tandem.

The company traveled to Los Angeles at the beginning of June and after a week of technical rehearsals began a four-performance preview period, which was followed by the June 15 official opening. In his June 17 review for the *Los Angeles Times*, Dan Sullivan wrote, "'A Doll's Life' may be the worst thing that has happened to the play since the Germans demanded a happy ending back in the 1880s" and described the Comden and Green book as "[a] mild-mannered satire in an operetta framework." He complained most bitterly about what he perceived as a disjuncture between it and Prince's frequently "dark and baleful" staging: "The depth of the writing won't support the show's visual superstructure."

Six days later in *Variety* "Edwa." offered a different assessment, stating that *A Doll's Life* "might become one of the great tuners of all time." Further, this critic found that there was no disjuncture between "Prince's brilliant direction" and Comden and Green's book, which he extolled: "The librettist duo are master artisans at musical comedy, and with this one, they're perceptive and intense in their romanticism and fidelity to Ibsen's social commentary."

Other critics from the area were more mixed than Sullivan and "Edwa." A June 25 review from Bruce Fessier in the *Desert Sun* simply labeled the musical as "flawed." It was, the critic wrote, "a tremendous production, a beautifully woven tale," but, sadly, the ending "disappointed."

Prince, Comden and Green, and Grossman had 10 weeks to rework the production, and for the next five they did effect minor changes to the material. After that Prince wanted to give the company time to settle into their roles and the rhythms of the production, and so he left Los Angeles for a month-long vacation at his home in Majorca. Soon after, the *Times*'s Sullivan—along with Sylvie Drake, a second critic from the paper—attended *A Doll's Life*, and on July 18 their two reviews of the revised version ran side by side.

Sullivan, who had spoken with the director, quoted him as saying, "I think you'll see the changes." Sullivan did and wryly commented, "It's a clearer, quicker, lighter show now than it was on opening night, more like its frothy TV commercial," adding "but as a response to Ibsen's 'A Doll's House,' it remains about one inch deep." In her review Drake struggled with what the creators had intended and what they had accomplished. "Sorting out the delicate strands of this muddle is enormously complex," she wrote. Ultimately, the crux of the problem with the show, Drake felt, was that Prince, Comden, and Green "graft a 1980s sensibility onto an 1880s context." Drake attempted to offer a solution, suggesting that each stage of Nora's journey leap forward two decades in order to make Nora an

"Everywoman." What Drake failed to mention was that Arthur Laurents, Comden and Green, and Jule Styne had essentially done just this 15 years earlier with their African American heroine in *Hallelujah, Baby!*

When ticket sales in California were sluggish, Prince, a co-producer, made an unusual decision: He announced that *A Doll's Life* would curtail its Los Angeles engagement by two weeks and proceed to Broadway's Mark Hellinger Theater earlier than had been announced. Rather than opening on October 3, the musical would bow on September 23, after a two-week preview period. As this was announced, Prince described his plans for any further revisions to the piece and its staging: "I'm going to cut a couple of chorus things and re-light using an idea I didn't have before."[4]

On September 24 the morning-after reviews for *A Doll's Life* were dismal. In the *Daily News* Douglas Watt called the show "[a] limpy blend of 'Bitter Sweet' and 'Sweeney Todd,'" and in the *New York Post* Clive Barnes found the show to have a "fascinating concept" but one "gone fairly adrift, an idea gone askew." Frank Rich in the *New York Times* described it as a "perplexing curiosity" in which "confusion reigns once the curtain rises." As for the heroine, "[She] isn't Ibsen's Nora, and she doesn't resemble the fizzy, independent heroines of Comden-Green musicals past." Rich also took aim at how the writers portrayed their feminist message. *A Doll's Life* was, in his opinion, "paradoxically arguing that most men are despicable and that a woman's goal should be to 'act like a man.'"

In tandem with the publication of the reviews came a closing notice, and *A Doll's Life* shuttered on Sunday, September 26, having played just five performances. Three weeks later Jacques le Sourd, who reviewed the show for the *Journal-News* in White Plains, revisited both his reaction to the production and the piece itself, musing about the ephemeral nature of theater. In the end he did not reverse his opinion about the show's strengths or its flaws but did offer this: "'A Doll's Life' was a flop with class, and maybe it deserved to live."

HUMOROUSLY EXAMINING A FLOP

Fifteen years after *A Doll's Life* folded, Comden and Green looked back on the experience with witty clarity. In a December 12, 1998, story for the *New York Times* about musicals that are perceived as "dark," they posited that the success of shows with serious subjects, such as the signing of the Declaration of Independence or a murderous barber, was due only to the whims of three goddesses, maybe named Nora, who convened at Sardi's "got a little tipsy and gave those shows their blessing." As for *A Doll's Life*, they wondered, "Did the Three Noras throw up?"

It was in the months following the sudden demise of *A Doll's Life* that Green and Newman found themselves having to cope with health issues. Before this, they enjoyed being a two-career family, and as the 1970s wound down and the 1980s began there were benefits from the changes in his professional life. In 1979, for instance, he was able to be supportive of a one-woman show she created in collaboration with Arthur Laurents. The piece, semi-autobiographical, began life off-Broadway under the title *My Mother Was a Fortune Teller* and arrived on Broadway in 1979 as *The Madwoman of Central Park West*.

Later that year their son, Adam, enrolled as an English major at Harvard, and before the end of his first year he had contributed to the *Harvard Lampoon*. At the time he joked about his relationship with his dad, "My father and I tend to be irresponsible together."[5] As for their daughter, Amanda, she was finishing up high school and within a couple of years would enroll at Brown University.

There were also challenges facing the Green-Newman household as the decade dawned. In 1983 Newman felt a lump in one breast. A mammogram revealed cancer, and she underwent a mastectomy. Following the procedure Newman learned that while the malignancy had not spread to her lymph nodes, her doctors were recommending chemotherapy, and after consultations with several oncologists she opted to proceed with the treatment. It was at this moment that Green received the offer to film *Lily in Love*, and because it would be filming abroad, "he wanted to turn it down."[6] Newman, however, insisted that he take the part: "I was and am very proud of his having an unsolicited acting career at this time of his life," she writes in her memoir, *Just in Time*.

The following spring Newman's doctors advised a second surgery, and she sought second and third opinions. She remembered one encounter: "Some butcher on the East Side with Adolf Eichmann's charm, said, 'You're sitting on a time bomb, little lady.'"[7] Despite being aghast at this physician's callousness, she had to listen to the doctors' collective wisdom, and in 1984 she underwent a second surgery. By the fall, with treatments completed, Newman returned to the stage, with both her husband and daughter at her side. They appeared in a pair of one-act plays written by Murray Schisgal that opened a new theater at the Upper West Side's Trinity School, which Amanda had attended as a child. Presented under the title *The New Yorkers*, the production received tepidly supportive reviews, but the Greens had had their fun. In addition, Newman and Green had the chance to show off their daughter, "an unusually talented actress and performer."[8]

Just as Newman was enduring her first cancer treatments, a stage version of *Singin' in the Rain* opened in the West End. Comden and Green didn't adapt their screenplay for this venture, and, in fact, no book writer was credited in the program, which gave simply "story and screenplay by" credit to them. Whatever changes had been made were affected by the show's star and director, Tommy Steele, who started out as a rock 'n' roll teen idol in the late 1950s before establishing himself in the theater in musicals such as *Half a Sixpence* and in movies in its film adaptation, *The Happiest Millionaire*, and *Finian's Rainbow*. In bringing *Rain* to the stage, Steele, along with choreographer Peter Gennaro, was not able to use the entirety of the song list from the MGM movie, and so the production was outfitted with songs ranging from the Gershwins' "Fascinating Rhythm" to Jimmy McHugh and Dorothy Fields' "I Can't Give You Anything but Love" to Cole Porter's "Be a Clown."

The production opened at the London Palladium on June 30, 1983, and while critics complained about the show's inability to live up to its cinematic forebear, they were impressed by Steele and the physical production. "Of course, something in us wants to applaud a good imitation; one is awed at the thought of Mr. Steele getting very wet six nights a week," wrote Robert Cushman in July 3 review for London's *Observer*. But critical complaints didn't keep theatergoers away. The show did healthy business and ultimately ran for more than two years.

The success of *Singin' in the Rain* in the West End made a Broadway incarnation seem likely, and, just over a year after the show debuted in the UK, producers Maurice and Lois Rosenfield, who brought *Barnum* to Broadway and were associate producers on the London *Rain*, announced that a new stage adaptation of the classic film would land on the Great White Way. At the helm of the production would be Twyla Tharp, who had been amassing critical and popular acclaim for years with her eponymous dance company. Her style, epitomized in works such as *Nine Sinatra Songs* and *Deuce Coupe*, combined classic dance elements and pop culture, and while her work as a choreographer had been seen on Broadway before, *Singin' in the Rain* would mark her debut as a director-choreographer.

In addition to Tharp's involvement, the Rosenfields announced that they had secured full rights to the MGM property, meaning that the Broadway version would feature the entire song list from the film. Further, Comden and Green were on board to create the stage adaptation of their much-lauded screenplay, and the show was set to open on Broadway in the summer of 1985.

During the first half of that year Tharp assembled her principal performers for the show, including Don Correia, who appeared on Broadway in revues such as *Perfectly Frank* and *Sophisticated Ladies* and was a replacement for central roles in *A Chorus Line* and *My One and Only*; Mary D'Arcy, a relative newcomer whose previous Broadway work was *Sunday in the Park with George*; and Peter Slutsker, who, like D'Arcy, had one other Broadway show to his credit, the 1983 revival of *On Your Toes*. They were playing, respectively, the Gene Kelly, Debbie Reynolds, and Donald O'Connor roles. For the ensemble, Tharp turned to dancers from her company, later admitting that the show was a vehicle for "keeping my dancers employed."[9]

Given the pedigree of the creators and the brand of the property, expectations for a new hit were high, but as rehearsals progressed rumors began to circulate that the show was in trouble. This was confirmed repeatedly in June 1985 when the opening night was delayed three times, performances were cancelled to allow the performers time to integrate new material, and word spread that other directors, including Albert Marre (whose credits included *Kismet* and *Man of La Mancha*), were stepping in to assist Tharp or revise her work in the book scenes.

The production finally opened at the Gershwin on July 2 to reviews that echoed one another as the critics attempted to divine what had inspired the artists and producers to bring such a beloved classic to the stage. Further, the writers strove to explain to their readers and themselves what had gone awry in the adaptation. Frank Rich observed in his *New York Times* review: "'Singin' in the Rain' was a fantasy about the dream factory of the movies. Once transposed to the stage in realistic terms, the fantasy evaporates."

Critics were divided in their response to some of Tharp's additions to the narrative, notably two dance sequences in the second act that starkly departed from the movie. There was an extended choreographic trip through the Warner Bros. studios, where a series of musical numbers were being filmed, followed by an extended number devised for *The Dancing Cavalier*, the movie musical within the stage musical. In his July 10 *Wall Street Journal* review, Edwin Wilson cheered the former sequence, writing, "For the first time in the evening true inventiveness and spontaneity break through." However, Douglas Watt, in his July 3 *Daily News* review, decried it: "The show falls to pieces in the second half with long-winded mishmash song-and-dance routines."

The Rosenfields briefly considered closing the show immediately after opening but decided to allow it to run, sensing it was a crowd pleaser that would override the critical reaction. This led to a cover story for the October 14, 1985, edition of *New York Magazine* titled "Still Kicking." The piece bore the provocative subtitle of "The Amazing Saga of 'Singin' in the Rain,' the $5.7-Million Turkey That Refuses to Lie Down." In it, writer Sharon Churcher chronicled the tumultuous rehearsal process, one in which Comden and Green were at odds with both Tharp and the Rosenfields. Churcher interviewed Green for the story and described him as being "reluctant to talk about his dealings with the couple."[10] The same could not be said of Maurice Rosenfield with regard to Comden and Green. The producer said, "I thought they would know exactly the techniques for adapting the cinema and re-creating it on the stage.... They were driving Twyla crazy." Rosenfield added, "I really didn't think that a book was terribly important."[11] Years later, when asked about the production, Green said simply, "Let's forget about it. Let's talk about the movie."[12]

In the end *Singin' in the Rain* ran nearly a year on Broadway and then spawned a national tour, which used a heavily reworked book that hewed closely to the movie, containing only a few deviations. Directed by Lawrence Kasha, who brought *Applause* to Broadway as a producer, and with some new choreography by Peter Gennaro, this *Singin' in the Rain* launched its tour in Texas as part of the Dallas Summer Musicals series. In a June 25 review, *Variety's* "Togi." proclaimed, "It looks pretty much as if the third time out will be the charm for 'Singin' in the Rain.'" The critic described the new, more faithful stage version as "a very entertaining, spectacularly mounted, and winning version of the nostalgic-flavored show."

After all the drama surrounding the Broadway *Singin' in the Rain* and *A Doll's Life*, having the well-received stage version of the classic film was most welcome for Comden and Green. As the 1980s progressed they continued with their various performing engagements, both on screen and stage, while also looking for that next idea for a new show. But, as they had learned in the past few years, the business of Broadway was changing, and it was taking an increasingly long time for a musical to reach the stage. Nevertheless, before 1990 dawned they were at work on their 17th musical.

WHY THEY KEPT PERFORMING

As they reached their 70s Comden and Green never ceased performing, either their own material or others'. For instance, in 1985 they took part in a starry concert presentation of Stephen Sondheim and James Goldman's *Follies*. A year later Green explained to reporter Alvin Klein, for an April 6, 1986, *New York Times* feature, why evenings like this or ones in which they offered their *A Party With* were such an important aspect of their work: "We love the energy, the fuss and the fun. It's different from sedentary writing and the response gives us reassurance and self-renewal."

CHAPTER 19

A Follies Finish and Farewell

In the years following their work on *Singin' in the Rain* for the stage, Comden and Green continued to pursue their later-life careers as performers. In addition to Green's turn in *I Want to Go Home*, there were cameos for both him and Comden in the indie film *Slaves of New York*. In it Comden plays a zealously chatty woman at an arty Boho party being thrown by her character's daughter who's extolling anyone in earshot about a package tour she and her seemingly mute husband (Green) took to China. As they entered their 70s they were also frequently discussing and performing their work at places such as Lincoln Center and the 92nd Street Y, as well as taking part in tributes, many often taped and televised, to colleagues such as George Abbott, Leonard Bernstein, and Jule Styne.

There were also outings of *A Party With* and variations of it for nonprofit groups, ranging from the New York Public Library and Arena Stage in Washington, DC, to the People with AIDS Coalition and the Gay Men's Health Crisis. As an extension of this philanthropic work, both of them also became actively involved in a nearly year-long battle to save the Regency, a movie theater on Manhattan's Upper West Side that had long been dedicated to reviving classic films. As they planned to join in a celebrity-filled protest at the venerable venue, Green said, "There's no way to get the same impact of these films on TV. This demonstration is to make people realize that there are no revival houses left above 14th Street."[1] (Sadly, their efforts, and those of myriad others, failed to rescue the theater.)

Of course, there were social gatherings for them to attend, from Broadway openings to book-release parties (including ones for Newman's *Just in Time* in 1988). One of the most widely reported of these outings came that same year at a birthday fete for Senator Edward M. Kennedy. The event, held at his McLean, Virginia, estate, was a costume party, and Green arrived dressed as Eleanor Roosevelt's maid. His ensemble was, apparently, a last-minute decision, and he had borrowed it "from the hotel where he was staying."[2]

As for writing projects, Comden and Green kept looking for something new to bring to Broadway. For a while they explored adapting another one of their films, *The Band Wagon*, for the stage, but they had to set this project aside almost as soon as they announced it in 1988. The reason was that another project they had been invited to join was gathering momentum and rapidly becoming a reality.

COMDEN AND GREEN'S . . . *TARZAN?*

Years after *On the Twentieth Century* opened, Cy Coleman mentioned to Robert Viagas for the book *Alchemy of Theatre* that for a while he and Comden and Green "talked about doing a *Tarzan* musical" when they were still struggling with whether or not to adapt the Hecht-MacArthur play. Given Coleman's (and his collaborators') fierce sense of humor, such a statement sounds as if it's a flippant joke. But it wasn't, and as late as 1987 Comden and Green continued to explore the idea of turning Edgar Rice Burroughs's stories about the man who was raised among apes into a tuner.

In the years that followed *On the Twentieth Century*, Comden and Green continued to work with composer Cy Coleman on minor projects. Just after this musical closed they contributed a song for a CBS special that paid homage to the network's 50th anniversary. Six years later they rejoined forces for the 1984 Harold Prince–directed off-Broadway revue *Diamonds*. For this show that examined America's Pastime, baseball, in song, the trio created a number to be used interstitially throughout the production, delivered by a stadium vendor. Beyond this sort of material, the three discussed various ideas for a full-scale musical but nothing clicked. That is, until producer Pierre Cossette approached Coleman about a show that he had been trying to assemble for a number of years.

Cossette started his career as a booking agent and transitioned to television producing in the late 1960s; in 1971 he was the force behind bringing the Grammy Awards to television. About 15 years later he began contemplating a theatrical venture, because he believed "the moment was right to break the British hold on the Broadway musical theater."[3] As he contemplated how he might accomplish this goal, he thought of a one-man show he had seen in the early 1970s, *Will Rogers' USA*.

An American humorist-performer whose work spanned stage, film, radio, and journalism, Rogers was one of the country's first media celebrities. Cossette thought that Rogers's life—which began in 1879 Indian Territory that became part of the newly formed state of Oklahoma in 1907 and ended with a tragic plane crash in 1935—had the breadth and color that would make for a terrific piece of American musical theater. But while Cossette seized on the idea for this show with relative ease, he found that assembling a creative team for the project was more difficult.

Initially, he turned to James Lee Barrett, author of the screenplay for *The Green Berets* and winner of a Tony Award for his book for the musical *Shenandoah*, to write the script, and country music singer-songwriter John Denver for the score. Denver, known for such hits as "Take Me Home, Country Roads," was also an actor with a following, particularly after his performance opposite George Burns in the movie *Oh, God!* in 1977, and he was also set to star as Rogers.

When Barrett's early drafts for the show proved to be unusable, Cossette turned to Peter Stone, who in addition to his credits as book writer for musicals had an Oscar for the screenplay for *Father Goose* to his credit. Unfortunately, Stone was unenthusiastic. To begin with, Stone had an antipathy for putting biographical stories on stage. "If you want to make it interesting you have to lie,"[4] he said. Further, as he told Cossette, "I know Will Rogers' life, and there's nothing in it except his career and the things he said."[5] Stone declined to join the team but then reconsidered as he thought about Rogers's performances as part of various editions of *The Ziegfeld Follies*. Stone wondered, "What if this was not the story of Will Rogers but the story as Ziegfeld presented it?"[6]

After Tommy Tune, with whom Stone had just worked on *My One and Only*, expressed enthusiasm for Stone's concept, Cossette found that he had both a book writer and a director-choreographer for the aborning tuner, along with a composer-headliner. Denver's schedule, however, made collaboration difficult, and there came a point when both Cossette and Stone realized that they would need to look elsewhere for the score. The producer initiated conversations with Coleman, who was interested and suggested that Comden and Green join him as lyricists.

The *New York Times*'s Enid Nemy officially announced the show, which was now called *Ziegfeld Presents Will Rogers*, in a March 13, 1987, column. At that point Stone stated, "There are about half-a-dozen songs written," and Nemy reported, "It probably won't go into rehearsal until early next year." In actuality, because of casting issues, difficulties Cossette had in raising money to back the show, and other projects on Tune's and Coleman's dockets, the musical, which eventually became known as *The Will Rogers Follies*, did not begin official rehearsals until 1990.

In the interim, Denver withdrew from the show, and in his place the team selected Keith Carradine to play the title character. Carradine, most familiar to audiences from movies such as *Nashville* and *The Duellists*, also had Broadway stage experience ranging from the original production of *Hair* to the play *Foxfire*, which also starred theater legends Hume Cronyn and Jessica Tandy. As for the financing, it came together only after Carradine was signed and the team rethought the way in which backers' auditions were held.

Before Carradine's casting, several presentations—featuring Coleman at the piano and Comden and Green as performers—failed to raise capital. Stone came to realize that potential investors were not hearing the show per se but rather watching the acclaimed team in action. He recommended that Carradine perform in lieu of Comden and Green. He recalled, "Betty and Adolph were upset.... They wanted to do their own songs."[7] In the end, however, they understood, and for an event held at Tavern on the Green, Carradine—along with Dee Hoty (who was appearing in Coleman's *City of Angels*) playing Rogers's wife, Betty—delivered the material, with some supporting vocals from the lyricists. Stone's instincts were on target, and after this audition Cossette was able to assemble a consortium of backers that would underwrite the production. Full funding meant, too, that Cossette could book a theater and set an opening date: *The Will Rogers Follies* got the Palace and would bow on May 1, 1991.

LOSING AN OLD FRIEND

On October 14, 1990, Comden and Green's old friend and first Broadway collaborator, Leonard Bernstein, died. Comden recalls in her memoir, *Off Stage,* her reaction to the news: "That was impossible.... We were all sure he would live forever." Green paid tribute to him in a letter to the *New York Times* printed on October 21. In it Green recalled their meeting in 1937 at the Pittsfield, Massachusetts, summer camp: "My life took a lucky turn early on, when Leonard Bernstein and I settled into each other's lives forever." And, as was the case with Comden, Green was incredulous about the death: "Is he gone? I can't quite believe it."

With full funding, Tune completed casting for the production. Along with Carradine and Hoty, who stayed with the show following the Tavern on the Green performance, *Will Rogers* featured Dick Latessa, whose extensive credits included *Follies* and *Rags* on Broadway, as Rogers's dad, Clem, and Cady Huffman, who appeared in the original *La Cage aux Folles* and Bob Fosse's *Big Deal*, as "Ziegfeld's Favorite," a chorine who helps to move the show along, singled out because of an implied affair with the showman.

Before official rehearsals began for *Will Rogers*, Tune slated a brief workshop development period, similar to the one he employed for *Grand Hotel*, which earned top Tony honors in May 1990. During this period he could experiment with dancers and singers on staging ideas and investigate what material from Stone and Coleman, Comden, and Green might need revision.

This preproduction process was particularly important for *Will Rogers* because of Stone's dramatic conceit. The musical included interruptions from Ziegfeld (heard in voice-overs delivered by screen legend Gregory Peck) as he toyed with the biographical narrative to fit a framework that suited him, meaning that Stone did not need to write a linear book. For instance, Ziegfeld could demand that Will and Betty's first meeting take place on the moon. By extension, the show's freewheeling style meant that the songwriters could be called on to create something new for any direction in which the story turned.

In their two years working on the piece, the songwriters had already written and discarded five numbers. Among them were "Mr. Hollywood and Vine," which charted Will's journey through Tinseltown and was to be performed by its starry denizens, and "Filthy Rich," a number that lyrically could have been used in *Billion Dollar Baby*, in which Will and Betty sing about the good times they are enjoying in the heady 1920s. This latter number was used as a lead-in to what Stone had envisioned as a number set in a jewel box, in which the Ziegfeld beauties would be gems.

Interestingly, Stone and the songwriters also had taken the musical into darker realms early on with "Lucky Kid," a number that Will imagined delivering to a child of his who had just died of diphtheria, and "They'll Get Wise to You," which was a warning about the fleeting nature of fame to be performed by Will's father during an extended courtroom sequence. Comden and Green's lyric for this latter number even punned with a legal theme: Will was enduring "an arrested development."

Before rehearsals began, Stone excised the sequences that contained these numbers, so there was no need to replace them. The book writer added a section that expanded on Rogers's run for the White House, and for this, Coleman, Comden, and Green wrote the rousing, John Philip Sousa–like "Favorite Son." The writers also worked to strengthen the romantic through-line of the show. Stone and the songwriting team created a witty stumbling block for Will and Betty's path to the altar with "We're Heading to a Wedding," a number delivered by the Ziegfeld Girls that's halted by the producer because it has come too early in his show; after all, wedding bells shouldn't toll until just before intermission.

Beyond these additions there were three new numbers that were substitutes for cut ones. To extend the tension between Will and Clem, which was central to the comic "They'll Get Wise to You," a more emotionally rich number, "Fathers and Sons," was inserted late in the second act. Similarly, for the whimsical on-the-moon meeting between Will and Betty, the songwriters replaced a specialty number, "Banjo Moon," with the ethereal "My

Unknown Someone." In this song Comden and Green combine wit and genuine feeling as Betty sings "Here I sit mooning/On the moon, mooning/Questioning my existence." A third change involved a rethinking of how to show the birth of the couple's children and Will's vaudeville days. Originally there was a raucous extended musical sequence, "Betty and Me," but this was replaced with "The Big Time," where Comden and Green's zesty lyric perfectly matches Coleman's peppy melody.

Neither the songwriters' nor Tune's work ceased during rehearsals and the show's preview period at the Palace, which was giving Comden and Green their first taste of opening an original musical "cold" (without the benefit of an out-of-town tryout) in New York. Throughout previews, Tune reconfigured the running order of the show, working to calibrate it much in the same way that a director would structure a revue. Coleman, Comden, and Green were available for rewrites and additions as necessary, and later Coleman recalled where they worked: "We rehearsed and rewrote at the Nederlander. Things were changing so quickly that there was no time to leave the theater. The only place left to put a piano was in the ladies room lounge."[8]

THE SHOW MUST GO ON

During rehearsals for *Will Rogers*, Comden tripped over a roll of carpet in the lobby of the Palace Theatre, which was undergoing renovations prior to the show's opening. Landing on the bare concrete floor, she shattered her knee-cap. Nevertheless, she was back at rehearsals in short order and even perse-vered—in a wheelchair—for a benefit performance on Long Island that was scheduled for the following weekend. In a March 21, 1991, column in the *New York Times* Susan Heller related how Comden joked about the situation: "Adolph will dance around me as usual," and how Green admired Comden's fortitude: "She's such a trouper and insisted we go on."

As previews progressed the writers felt that Will's concern with environ-mental issues needed to somehow be integrated into the show, and as a result the songwriters created "Look Around," which was put into the mu-sical just before opening. It was such a last-minute addition that the Playbills handed out on the show's May 1 opening night included an insert with the number added to the song list.

The reviews that ran on May 2 and after reflected critics' simultaneous respect for the show and sense of confusion about its style and format. In the *New York Times*, Frank Rich described the production as "the most dis-jointed musical of this or any other season," and on May 8, Edwin Wilson in the *Wall Street Journal* likened it to "a covered-dish supper where everyone brought desserts and no one thought to bring the main course." And still there were reviewers who championed it and even appeared to know Cossette's intent for the piece. One was Howard Kissel in the *Daily News*, who concluded his write-up with "'Will Rogers' is the homegrown musical Broadway has been awaiting a long, long time."

In most reviews Comden and Green's lyrics were praised. Clive Barnes in the *New York Post* labeled them "deft and winning"; Kissel noted that they were "simple and attractive"; and John Beaufort, who weighed in on the show on May 16 in the *Christian Science Monitor*, commented, "The Betty Comden–Adolph Green lyrics are also amusingly attuned to the now and the then."

Not only was the show Comden and Green's first brush with opening an original musical without the benefit of out-of-town tryouts, but it was also their first experience of having a show open just in the nick of time for Tony Award nominations (prizes that didn't even exist when their first two musicals hit Broadway). *The Will Rogers Follies* was the last entry in Broadway's 1990–1991 season, and that meant they only had to wait four days to learn that the production had earned 11 nominations, including one for Coleman, Comden, and Green's score and one for best musical. When the Tonys were presented in June, the show won both of these awards, as well as one for Carradine. In short order Columbia Records released the original cast recording, and just a year after the musical opened Comden and Green were able to pick up their first Grammy Award when the album won the prize for best musical show album.

Before the Grammy ceremony Comden and Green were feted as they received two other exceptional honors. Just before the June 1991 Tony ceremony they received the Johnny Mercer Award from the Songwriters Hall of Fame, the highest tribute that the organization pays writers already inducted into its ranks (Comden and Green were added in 1981). The Mercer Award recognizes a history of creating exceptional work. Then, in August 1991, the annual Kennedy Center Honors recipients were announced and Comden and Green were on the list, alongside country singer Roy Acuff, dancers Fayard and Harold Nicholas, actor Gregory Peck, and conductor Robert Shaw. Just before the ceremony in Washington, DC, in December, Green couldn't resist joking about it all: "We're getting all these awards while we can still get up and just walk to the podium."[9]

Kidding aside, Comden and Green, who were 77 and 74, respectively, at the Kennedy Center ceremony, were still professionally and personally active, even as they entered what could be described as a kind of semi-retirement. For the next 10 years, as the 20th century turned into the 21st, neither one shied away from an assignment to write or perform, but one thing eluded them: an entirely new musical for Broadway. They never stopped having their daily meetings, and Comden commented in 2000: "Adolph and I aren't content just being revived. We meet almost every day. I can't talk about what we're doing, but we'll get one done."[10]

Among the new scripts they worked on as the 1990s wound down was a stage version of *The Band Wagon*, which they started to revisit in 1999. This movie musical ultimately made its way to the stage in 2008 courtesy of playwright Douglas Carter Beane. Presented by the Old Globe Playhouse under the title *Dancing in the Dark*, the show later received a concert presentation as *The Band Wagon* as part of New York City Center's *Encores!* series in 2014. There were also press reports that Comden and Green were drafting a script based on Shakespeare's *A Midsummer Night's Dream* for a Disney animated feature.

Still, there were two new pieces from Comden and Green that did premiere in the 1990s. The first was a single song, "The Mamushka!," written for the 1991 movie *The Addams Family*. The number, with a melody by future Tony winner (for *Hairspray*) Marc Shaiman, was performed by Raul Julia and Christopher Lloyd, and the lyric includes the smile-inducing line "I swear by Mommy and Daddums/This detestable Fester's the echt Fester Addams!"

Also produced was an English-language book for Johann Strauss's *Die Fledermaus*, which bowed at the Metropolitan Opera in 1998. Comden and Green, who skewered populism at the staid company with "Catch Our Act at the Met" in the revue *Two on the Aisle*, might have seemed to be curious choices for the assignment, but they had loved opera since they were children and were frequent audience members at the august venue. Further, as Anthony Tommasini noted in a December 23, 1998, *New York Times* feature just before their work premiered, "Audiences now expect Strauss's wry operetta to be a gagfest," which he said had led to versions with "the inclusion of lame humor and dumb sight gags." Tommasini reported that the writers had described their task to him thus: "to spice up the dialogue without resorting to bawdy jokes and easy topical humor."

In their version of the libretto, the action no longer unfolds in 1874 but rather in 1899, a change instituted to give the work a millennial resonance. They also reframed the character of Dr. Falke as Dr. Freud and revamped a prominent feature of the operetta's third act, a monologue for a drunken jailer, which they transformed into scene for a chronically unemployed actor who performs a self-penned mini-play, "The Bell-Ringer of Notre Dame."

Reactions to their work included Allan Kozinn's "They have freshened the work nicely" in the December 26 edition of the *New York Times* and Charles Isherwood's observation in the January 11, 1999, edition of *Variety* that "Comden and Green's primary conception—a Freudian frosting on the traditional storyline—seems ably suited" to a production in which dialogue was delivered in English and songs were offered in German.

Ironically, while Comden and Green were striving to write another new musical, they found that they were—more often than not—tending to new presentations of their previously produced shows. In one instance (a 1992 starry concert presentation by Michael Tilson Thomas and the London Symphony Orchestra of *On the Town*) they developed continuity narration. Comden and Green performed this dialogue alongside such headliners as Thomas Hampson, David Garrison, Tyne Daly, and Frederica von Stade. Cleo Laine was also featured in the concert, offered at London's Barbican Centre, and she delivered the cut number "Ain't Got No Tears Left." The event prompted Michael Billington to contemplate how musicals had evolved in the 1980s in a July 9 column for the *Guardian*. After lamenting the rise of through-composed musicals, brought on after "the unholy triumph of *Jesus Christ Superstar*," Billington wrote, "In short, a musical is only as good as its book," and as an example he pointed to Comden and Green's for *On the Town*.

As if they were heeding Billington's concluding advice, "If you want a hit, get a book," Comden and Green began to revisit their script for *A Doll's Life* just over a year later. The impetus came from the York Theatre Company, which had produced a scaled-down version of *On the Twentieth Century* in 1985 and was planning a concert presentation of *A Doll's Life* for March 1994. Comden and Green used the opportunity to revise the book and score with composer Larry Grossman. Working with director Bob Brink, they condensed, cut, and added to the piece, paying particular attention to the show's ending. Critics were not invited to these presentations, but warm audience response, combined with the creative team's desire to continue working, prompted the York to slate a full production of *A Doll's Life* for its 1994–1995 season, which would be reviewed.

When the show, still further revised, officially bowed, Vincent Canby in a December 12, 1994, *New York Times* review offered guarded praise, saying, "It is a most melodic consideration of 'A Doll's House.'" As for the writing, Canby wrote: "Never have Comden and Green taken such risks, nor displayed such discipline and intelligence in meeting those risks." Four years later Comden and Green performed similar work on their 1945 musical, *Billion Dollar Baby*, when the York offered it in concert form, and while this revision did not result in a full production, it was preserved with an official cast recording featuring future Tony winner Kristin Chenoweth as the gold-digging Maribelle from Staten Island.

The York revisited two other Comden and Green shows during the late 1990s that were not as heavily revised. In 1997 the company presented *Fade Out–Fade In*, giving it its first return to the New York stage since 1965, and in 2000 the York offered *Hallelujah, Baby!* in a concert staging. Arthur Laurents returned to this piece four years later, heavily revising the book and reinstating several cut songs, including "When the Weather's Better." This new version also featured some lyric revisions by Green's daughter, Amanda, and played limited engagements at the George Street Playhouse in New Brunswick, New Jersey, and Arena Stage in Washington, DC. In an October 13 *Variety* review, Robert L. Daniels remarked, "The jaunty score remains a sunny souvenir of the '60s, when lyricists Betty Comden and Adolph Green designed crisply witty and fervently romantic lyrics for the infectious melodies of composer Jule Styne."

Comden and Green's shows were not limited to regional and off-Broadway revivals at the end of the millennium. *Peter Pan*, which had returned to Broadway in the late 1970s as a vehicle for Sandy Duncan, continued to be a popular work during this time, thanks to a production starring Cathy Rigby. The Olympic gymnast first crowed and soared for audiences in 1991 and was back in 1998, just as Comden and Green were celebrating their record-making 60th year together as writing partners.

At the same time, their first musical was back on Broadway in a new production helmed by Tony Award winner George C. Wolfe, then the artistic director of the Public Theater. Wolfe first staged *On the Town* at the Delacorte Theater in Central Park in 1997. For that production he worked closely with Comden and Green on revisions to the book, which included strengthening the character of Ivy, the Miss Turnstiles who inspires the three sailors to scour New York in search of her, and repositioning Gabey's "Lucky to Be Me." Also new for this al fresco incarnation of the tuner were dances by choreographer Eliot Feld, a Jerome Robbins protégé, whose work, primarily with the Feld Ballet, had been acclaimed by critics and audiences alike for years.

The Delacorte production, widely rumored as being a shoo-in for a Broadway transfer, received mixed notices, but Comden and Green's script and lyrics stood apart. Ben Brantley called the songs "abidingly clever" in his August 18, 1997, *New York Times* review. Speculation about what would become of the show after its limited run in Central Park was seemingly put to rest in November when the Public announced the musical would open at the St. James Theater the following April.

Financial issues (the nonprofit Public Theater eventually underwrote the entire $5 million enterprise) and a search for a new choreographer (briefly Christopher D'Amboise and later Keith Young, making his Broadway debut) stalled this timeline, but eventually *On the Town* opened at the Gershwin Theater on October 20, 1998, featuring a cast of performers relatively unfamiliar to Broadway audiences. Four of the principals were making their Broadway debuts, including Perry Laylon Ojeda and Tai

Jimenez, who played, respectively, Gabey and Ivy; Jesse Tyler Ferguson, who would go on to acclaim on television's *Modern Family*, as Chip; and downtown comedienne Lea DeLaria as Hildy the cabbie. And while critics generally admired the youthful energy that these performers, along with Robert Montano as Ozzie and Sarah Knowlton as Claire, brought to the show, they were unconvinced by Wolfe's production. In his November 23 *New York Times* review, Brantley complained about "an aura of exertion" that hung over it. Eventually, this new *On the Town* shuttered in early 1999, having played only 69 performances.

Unfortunately, a similar fate lay in store for the next Comden and Green musical that returned to Broadway, the 1956 hit *Bells Are Ringing*, which was revived in 2001. Directed by Tina Landau—who was known primarily for her work with experimental theater, garnered acclaim for her staging of the musical *Floyd Collins* off-Broadway, and was making her Broadway bow with *Bells*—it featured a book that Comden and Green had gently revised and starred Faith Prince in the role originated by Judy Holliday. Prince burst onto Broadway in a Tony-nominated turn in *Jerome Robbins' Broadway* and followed that with a Tony-winning performance as Adelaide in *Guys and Dolls* in 1992, and her combination of quirkiness and genuine warmth made her the ideal actress to step into the role of Ella Peterson. But while critics applauded her work, their response to Landau's staging was withering, and the result was a mere 68-performance run.

Happily, in between these two Broadway offerings, two of Comden and Green's other shows, *Do Re Mi* and *Wonderful Town*, returned to the stage in more highly praised outings as part of New York City Center's *Encores!* series. The musicals were presented in 1999 and 2000, respectively, as script-in-hand concerts with full orchestra and filled with top-name Broadway talent. Tony winners Nathan Lane and Randy Graff headlined *Do Re Mi*, playing the roles originated by Phil Silvers and Nancy Walker; and a two-time Tony winner, Donna Murphy, took on the role of Ruth in *Wonderful Town*. After this latter presentation, described as "jubilant" by Charles Isherwood in a May 15 *Variety* review, finished its limited five-performance run, speculation was rampant about a possible transfer to Broadway (the *Encores!* version of *Chicago* had done just this in 1996). This *Wonderful Town* did eventually arrive on Broadway in late 2003, but when it opened only Comden was on hand to celebrate its return to the Great White Way. Green had passed away in his Central Park West home, on October 23, 2002, at the age of 88.

Well before his death there had been reports of his failing health (physical and psychological), and yet, just a year before, he was on hand for rehearsals and previews of the *Bells* revival. Further, as late as March 1999 he and Comden, at the ages of 85 and 81, were still performing. In a March

18 *New York Times* review of their show, offered at Joe's Pub at the Public Theater on Lafayette Street, Stephen Holden wrote that they delivered with "winning verve and spirit" and that their lyrics contained "a wit and verbal energy that transcend headlines and celebrity name dropping to spill out a nonsensical kind of wisdom."

Green wasn't able to enjoy critics' reactions to *Wonderful Town* as it returned to Broadway. Charles Isherwood heralded it as "a gold-plated show" in a November 24, 2003, *Variety* review, and that same day Ben Brantley remarked in the *New York Times* that it featured lyrics that "percolate with the show-off spunk you associate with being brash, bright and eager to impress." During his last years, Green was able to savor the fact that in 1998 *Singin' in the Rain* was named to the American Film Institute's 100 best movies of all time and to enjoy a gala celebration thrown at Carnegie Hall in his and Comden's honor in 1999.

For her part, Comden persevered as a lone voice for the first time in her professional life. She attended *Wonderful Town* rehearsals and, as Wendy Wasserstein commented in a December 23 *Times* feature, "Even after a career of half a century in the theater, she still appears backstage at her shows nightly." For the piece, Comden told Wasserstein it was Green's "favorite" of their shows and also admitted, "It's been very difficult losing him. It's been a terrible blow. I'm trying to write a book about our collaboration now, because he isn't here to write a new show with me."

Two years later, when the English National Opera produced *On the Town*, Comden traveled to Britain to sit in on rehearsals and attend the opening. In one of her last interviews she spoke with Richard Morrison of London's *Times*. As she looked back on the show and her career, she told him, "The best thing for me is when people say 'You brought us such pleasure.'"[11] Comden passed away just 18 months later, on November 23, 2006.

Journalists' paeans to the work that she and Green wrote were abundant in the following day's obituaries, and, in the years that followed, tributes to their film writing continued to be plentiful as restored versions of various movies made their way to DVD.

However, while they had always been proud of their film work, theater was their first love, as a November 28, 2002, London *Times* obituary for Green noted: "If Hollywood was somewhat akin to a fickle mistress, the pair's enduring love affair was with Broadway." Appropriately, New York theatergoers got the chance to enjoy highly regarded revivals of two of their shows, *On the Town* and *On the Twentieth Century*, during the 2014–2015 Broadway season, which also coincided with the centenary of Green's birth.

But even as these shows played in theaters next door to one another on the Great White Way, no writer offered the kind of praise that two legendary critics had paid them while they were living. In his 1973 book *Astonish*

Me: Adventures in Contemporary Theater, John Lahr assessed their style, writing that they were "myth-makers, creating an image of their world so gaudy and mysterious that one is dazzled by the surface and unquestioning of what lies beneath."

Nine years later, when Comden and Green had the chance to finally offer their *A Party With* in London, Sheridan Morley unequivocally announced in a July 11 review in the *Spectator* that Comden and Green, who had been writing together for more than fifty years, were "the most adept American wordsmiths since Funk and Wagnalls."

A "READER'S DIGEST" FOR COMDEN AND GREEN

Nowhere was Comden and Green's linguistic deftness in more evidence than in their song-sketch "The Reader's Digest." In it they used just three lines to skewer classic works of literature, and they capped their witty reductions with a flourishing shout of "The End!" Each was such a succinct distillation of a book that it could induce hysterics among theatergoers. What might they have written about themselves? Perhaps this:

> Comden and Green wrote films and shows
> Many of which the whole world knows.
> They made us all forget our woes.
> The end!

NOTES

CHAPTER 1

1. Adam Green, "Innocents on Broadway," *Vanity Fair*, November 2014, http://www.vanityfair.com/culture/2014/11/on-the-town-broadway-making-of (accessed December 5, 2017).
2. Comden, *Off Stage*, 19.
3. Comden, *Off Stage*, 61.
4. Green, "Innocents on Broadway."
5. Newman, *Just in Time*, 84.
6. Comden, *Off Stage*, 64.
7. David Iams, "A Croquet Contest Costumed in White," *Philadelphia Inquirer*, June 29, 1986, 6-I.
8. Sheridan Morley, "The Lyricist Team at the Moment in Time," *Times* (London), June 5, 1980, 15.
9. Whitney Bolton, *Philadelphia Inquirer*, October 26, 1953, 17.
10. "What Is a Good Actor? Asks 'The Observer,'" *East Hampton Star*, August 11, 1938, 3.
11. "First Lady a Success," *East Hampton Star*, July 28, 1938, 2.
12. Green, "Innocents on Broadway."
13. Green, "Innocents on Broadway."
14. Carey, *Judy Holliday*, 23.

CHAPTER 2

1. Kasha and Hirschhorn, *Notes on Broadway*, 64.
2. Richard Manson, "Village Vanguard Sponsors 'Revue of Social Satire,'" *New York Post*, March 11, 1939, 10.
3. Theodore Straus, "News of Night Clubs," *New York Times*, June 18, 1939, section 9, 2.
4. Adam Green, "Innocents on Broadway," *Vanity Fair*, November 2014, http://www.vanityfair.com/culture/2014/11/on-the-town-broadway-making-of (accessed December 5, 2017).
5. Comden, *Off Stage*, 70.

CHAPTER 3

1. "What Hath Ureli Corelli Hill Wrought?," *New York Times*, November 29, 1992, H1.
2. "Young Talents Map Broadway Musical," *Variety*, June 7, 1944, 2.
3. Bernstein, *Making Music*, 87.
4. Richard Morrison, "An Accolade for One Helluva Show," *Times*, March 4, 2005, 12S.
5. Betty Comden and Adolph Green, "A Pair of 'Bookmakers' Tell All," *New York Times*, February 18, 1945, section 2, page 1.
6. Guernsey, *Broadway Song & Story*, 5.

7. Louis Sheaffer, "Ballet Theater Like Rotary and Kiwanis to Oliver Smith," *Brooklyn Eagle*, April 6, 1951, 12.
8. Sheaffer, "Ballet Theater Like Rotary and Kiwanis to Oliver Smith."
9. Abbott, *"Mister Abbott,"* 198.
10. K. C. Sherman, "Broadway Success Story," *Christian Science Monitor*, February 7, 1945, 5.
11. Betty Comden and Adolph Green, "Spotlight on Opening Nightmares," *New York Times Magazine*, May 7, 1961, 72.
12. Guernsey, *Broadway Song & Story*, 11.
13. Osato, *Distant Dances*, 234.
14. Sam Zolotow, "Anderson to Stage Max Gordon Show," *New York Times*, December 14, 1944, 30.
15. Tony Vallela, "Comden Is Back in 'Town,'" *Christian Science Monitor*, December 5, 2003, 18.
16. Osato, *Distant Dances*, 238.
17. Comden and Green, "Spotlight on Opening Nightmares."

CHAPTER 4

1. Betty Comden and Adolph Green, "Spotlight on Opening Nightmares," *New York Times Magazine*, May 7, 1961, 72.
2. James Thrasher, "Two 'Stage Struck Kids' Try New Musical Comedy Formula to Score Hit," *News-Herald* (Franklin, PA), March 23, 1945, 3.
3. Goodman, *Morton Gould*, 175.
4. Interview with Joan McCracken by Frank Chapman, *New York Journal-American*, July 20, 1946, 32.
5. Helen Ormsbee, "Authors of 'Billion Dollar Baby' Find It Hard to Write an Idea," *New York Herald Tribune*, May 19, 1946, D2.
6. Vail, *Somewhere: The Life of Jerome Robbins*, 124.
7. Goodman, *Morton Gould*, 176.
8. Fordin, *The Movies' Greatest Musicals*, 214.
9. Fordin, *The Movies' Greatest Musicals*, 214.
10. Thomas F. Brady, "Hollywood Awards," *New York Times*, March 23, 1947 section 2, page 5.
11. William Baer, "Singin' in the Rain: A Conversation with Betty Comden and Adolph Green," *Michigan Quarterly Review*, Winter 2002, 3.
12. Baer, "Singin' in the Rain," 3.
13. Simeone, *The Leonard Bernstein Letters*, 222.
14. A. H. Weiler, "Random Notes on the Film Scene," *New York Times*, June 8, 1947, section 2, page 2.

CHAPTER 5

1. Simeone, *The Leonard Bernstein Letters*, 222.
2. Simeone, *The Leonard Bernstein Letters*, 222.
3. Simeone, *The Leonard Bernstein Letters*, 222.
4. Lewis Funke, "News and Gossip Gathered on the Rialto," *New York Times*, March 30, 1947, section 2, page 1.
5. Mary Braggiotti, "Fussin', Writin' but No Feudin'," *New York Post Week-End Magazine*, December 13, 1947, 3.
6. Bert McCord, "News of the Theater," *New York Herald Tribune*, December 31, 1947, 7.
7. Sam Zolotow, "Logan Is Director of 'Miss Liberty,'" *New York Times*, November 8, 1948, 25.
8. Bloom, *Show and Tell*, 22.

9. Philip K. Scheuer, "Rogers-Astaire Reunion Brought about by Fates," *Los Angeles Times*, August 8, 1948, C1.
10. Astaire, *Steps in Time*, 294.
11. McGilligan, *Backstory 2*, 78.
12. Eyman, *Lion of Hollywood*, 402.

CHAPTER 6

1. Fordin, *The Movies' Greatest Musicals*, 257.
2. Hirschhorn, *Gene Kelly*, 180.
3. Silverman, *Dancing on the Ceiling*, 108.
4. Fordin, *The Movies' Greatest Musicals*, 258.
5. *Variety*, December 15, 1948, 4.
6. Sherman, *Dancing on the Ceiling*, 111.
7. Guernsey, *Broadway Song & Story*, 13.
8. Tom Donnelly, "When Two Think as One," *Washington Post*, May 17, 1973, B8.
9. Don Heckman, "Singin' Their Praises," *Los Angeles Times*, May 12, 1991, F1.
10. John Lyttle, "A Couple of Swells," *Independent* (London), July 1, 1992, 18.
11. Eells, *The Life That Late He Led*, 263.
12. Simeone, *The Bernstein Letters*, 275.
13. Simeone, *The Bernstein Letters*, 276.
14. Simeone, *The Bernstein Letters*, 281.

CHAPTER 7

1. Thomas F. Brady, "Plans for Hutton Dropped by Metro," *New York Times*, July 20, 1950, 21.
2. William Baer, "Singin' in the Rain: A Conversation with Betty Comden and Adolph Green," *Michigan Quarterly Review*, Winter 2002, 4.
3. Baer, "Singin' in the Rain," 4.
4. Baer, "Singin' in the Rain," 6.
5. Silverman, *Dancing on the Ceiling*, 149.
6. Betty Comden and Adolph Green, "How the Kids Made Movie Musical History," *Saturday Review*, April 22, 1972, 63.
7. Comden and Green, "How the Kids Made Movie Musical History," 60.
8. Bert McCord, "News of the Theater," *New York Herald Tribune*, March 5, 1951, 10.
9. Taylor, *Jule*, 153.
10. Taylor, *Jule*, 154.
11. Taylor, *Jule*, 155.
12. Brian Drutman, liner notes for *Two on the Aisle*, Decca Broadway (440 014 583–2), 2001.
13. Ballard, *How I Lost 10 Pounds in 53 Years*, 34.
14. Burrows, *Honest, Abe*, 223.

CHAPTER 8

1. Michael Kerman, "Comden and Green, Musical Magicians," *Washington Post*, February 1, 1979, B13.
2. Minnelli, *I Remember It Well*, 263.
3. Dietz, *Dancing in the Dark*, 295.
4. George Anderson, "The Music Never Ends for Comden and Green," *Pittsburgh Post-Gazette*, October 15, 1980, 21.
5. Minnelli, *I Remember It Well*, 270.

6. Griffin, *A Hundred or More Hidden Things*, 163.
7. "Holliday, Ives, Levenson, Loeb Deny Commy Taint in 2d McCarran Report," *Variety*, September 24, 1952, 40.
8. "Holliday, Ives, Levenson, Loeb," 40.
9. Russell, *Life Is a Banquet*, 154.
10. Betty Comden and Adolph Green, "My Sister Eileen Goes on the Town ... With Songs," *Theatre Arts*, August 1953, 20.
11. Bernstein, *Making Music*, 136.
12. Russell, *Life Is a Banquet*, 156.
13. Mark Barron, "Broadway," *Corsicana (TX) Daily Sun*, May 25, 1953, 6.
14. Engel, *This Bright Day*, 199.
15. Suskin, *The Sound of Broadway Music*, 579.
16. Engel, *This Bright Day*, 200.
17. Vaill, *Somewhere*, 214.
18. Engel, *This Bright Day*, 200.

CHAPTER 9

1. Bert McCord, "Producer of 'Wonderful Town' Cancels April 8 Performance," *New York Herald Tribune*, 18.
2. Leonard Lyons, "Lewis Looks through Glass Primly," *Philadelphia Inquirer*, September 13, 1956, 17.
3. Hedda Hopper, "Plan Another Movie to Star Fred Astaire, Cyd Charisse," *Los Angeles Times*, August 5, 1953, A2.
4. Simeone, *The Leonard Bernstein Letters*, 281.
5. Previn, *No Minor Chords*, 66.
6. Previn, *No Minor Chords*, 66.
7. Silverman, *Dancing on the Ceiling*, 212.
8. Hanson, *The Peter Pan Chronicles*, 199.
9. Hanson, *The Peter Pan Chronicles*, 200.
10. Hanson, *The Peter Pan Chronicles*, 202.
11. Hanson, *The Peter Pan Chronicles*, 204.
12. Hanson, *The Peter Pan Chronicles*, 203.
13. John Lyttle, "A Couple of Swells," *Independent* (London), July 1, 1992, 18.

CHAPTER 10

1. Joe Hyams, "Do You Feel You Want to Write a Musical? Then Look over a Mortuary," *Washington Post*, December 18, 1955, H8.
2. Silverman, *Dancing on the Ceiling*, 207.
3. Joan Hanauer, "Collaboration Comes Naturally," UPI wire in the *Herald* (Jasper, IN), April 7, 1978, 20.
4. Richard Gehman, "Bells Are Ringing for Syd Chaplin," *American Weekly* (supplement) for *Corpus Christi Caller-Times* (TX), September 15, 1957, 19.
5. Holtzman, *Judy Holliday*, 210.
6. Taylor, *Jule*, 10.
7. Taylor, *Jule*, 11.
8. Taylor, *Jule*, 11.
9. Taylor, *Jule*, 11.
10. Carey, *Judy Holliday*, 192.
11. Taylor, *Jule*, 14.

12. Vaill, *Somewhere*, 266.
13. Tom Prideaux, "They're Still Ringing Bells," *Life Magazine*, July 25, 1960, 47.
14. Prideaux, "They're Still Ringing Bells," 47.
15. Comden, *Off Stage*, 219.
16. "Iced Runway," *Washington Post*, December 26, 1956, B17.

CHAPTER 11

1. Secrest, *Stephen Sondheim*, 112.
2. Taylor, *Jule*, 192.
3. Jordan, *But Darling, I'm Your Auntie Mame!*, 107.
4. Jordan, *But Darling, I'm Your Auntie Mame!*, 108.
5. "Places of the Heart," *New York Times*, February 14, 1992, C18.
6. Newman, *Just in Time*, 68.
7. Barney Lefferts, "Two on the Town," *New York Times*, January 1, 1959, section 2, page 4.
8. Philip K. Scheuer, "Duo, Earning Filets, Just Frustrated Hams," *Los Angeles Times*, May 18, 1952, E1.
9. Scheuer, "Duo, Earning Filets."
10. Fordin, *The Movie's Greatest Musicals*, 434.

CHAPTER 12

1. Minnelli, *I Remember It Well*, 335.
2. Newman, *Just in Time*, 80.
3. Newman, *Just in Time*, 87.
4. Earl Wilson, "It Happened Last Night," *Newsday*, May 4, 1961, 6C.

CHAPTER 13

1. Love, *Subways Are for Sleeping*, 7.
2. Love, *Subways Are for Sleeping*, 8.
3. Stuart W. Little, "Comden and Green Teamed with Styne for 'Subways,'" *New York Herald Tribune*, 8.
4. Jack Gaver, "Screen Writers Watch Opening," *Republic* (Columbus, IN), July 12, 1960, 6.
5. Kissel, *The Abominable Showman*, 229.
6. Maurice Zolotow, "'Subways' in Transit," *New York Times*, December 17, 1961, section 2, page 5.
7. Zolotow, "'Subways' in Transit."
8. Walter Winchell, *Cincinnati Enquirer*, May 29, 1961, 5.
9. Bob Morris, "Window Shopping," *New York Times*, November 29, 1992, V8.

CHAPTER 14

1. Mike McGrady, "For the Record, Comden-Green Talk Softly," *Newsday*, October 5, 1964, 3C.
2. Sam Zolotow, "'48 'Madwoman' to Be a Musical," *New York Times*, June 11, 1963, 29.
3. "Carol Burnett, Hurt in Taxi, May Return to Role Tonight," *New York Times*, July 13, 1964, 24.
4. "Hamlet Regains Burton Tonight," *New York Times*, July 20, 1964, 18.
5. "Carol Burnett Into Hosp; 'Fade' Out of CBS-TV Also," *Variety*, October 14, 1964, 63.
6. Alan Patureau, "Carol Burnett Fires Back at Producer," *Newsday*, November 25, 1964, 2C.

7. Patureau, "Carol Burnett Fires Back at Producer."
8. Sam Zolotow, "'Bravo Giovanni' to End Saturday," *New York Times*, September 12, 1962, 32.
9. Sam Zolotow, "C.B.S. Backing 'The Skin of Our Teeth' Musical," *New York Times*, September 9, 1964, 17.
10. Vaill, *Somewhere*, 375.
11. Gottlieb, *Working with Bernstein*, 99.
12. Sam Zolotow, "'Skin of Our Teeth' Musical Dropped," *New York Times*, January 5, 1965, 24.
13. Leonard Bernstein, ". . . And What I Did," *New York Times*, October 24, 1965, section 2, page 19.
14. Vail, *Somewhere*, 376.

CHAPTER 15

1. Gay Pauley, "She's Nervously Combined Careers," *Washington Post*, June 19, 1964, C2.
2. Cynthia Lowry, "'TW3' Brings Out the Satirist in Her," *Washington Post*, January 11, 1965, B7.
3. Gay Talese, "The Intellectual Vote," *New York Times*, October 15, 1964, 31.
4. Eugene Sheppard, "This Is No Age for a 'Loner,'" *Kansas City Star*, October 19, 1965, 13.
5. Gloria Steinem, "The Party, Truman Capote Receives 500 'People I Like,'" *Vogue*, January 15, 1967, 134.
6. Michael Kernan, "Comden and Green, Musical Magicians," *Washington Post*, February 1, 1979, B13.
7. "Costly Music," *Variety*, May 22, 1968, 70.
8. Kernan, "Comden and Green, Musical Magicians."
9. Bryer and Davison, *The Art of the American Musical*, 133.
10. Gavin, *Stormy Weather*, 357.
11. Lena Horne and Richard Schickel, "Lena," *Chicago Tribune*, December 12, 1965, J34.
12. Sam Zolotow, "Broadway to See Absentees Again," *New York Times*, August 29, 1966, 23.
13. Bryer and Davison, *The Art of the American Musical*, 133.
14. Suskin, *Second Act Trouble*, 140.

CHAPTER 16

1. Gruen, *Close-Up*, 68.
2. Staggs, *All About "All About Eve,"* 284.
3. Bacall, *By Myself*, 392.
4. George Gent, "Comden and Green Talk All about the New Bacall Hit," *New York Times*, April 8, 1970, 36.
5. Bacall, *By Myself*, 400.
6. Strouse, *Put on a Happy Face*, 194.
7. Tom Donnelly, "When Two Think as One," *Washington Post*, May 17, 1973, B8.
8. "Chappell Rolls with Pop Sounds Plus Showtunes," *Variety*, June 28, 1972, 49.
9. George Gent, "Carol Channing to Do Lorelei Lee Again," *New York Times*, August 30, 1972, 45.
10. Gent, "Carol Channing to Do Lorelei Lee Again," 45.

CHAPTER 17

1. Howard Kissel, "A Party with Betty Comden and Adolph Green," *Women's Wear Daily*, February 11, 1977, 10.

2. Betty Comden and Adolph Green, "A New Head of Steam for the Old 'Twentieth Century,'" *New York Times*, February 19, 1978, section 2, page 6.
3. Viagas, *The Alchemy of Theatre*, 35.
4. Rex Reed, "Comden and Green Toss a Party for Themselves," *Independent Press-Telegram* (Long Beach, CA), February 12, 1977, L/S 2.
5. Prince, *Sense of Occasion*, 213.
6. Prince, *Sense of Occasion*, 214.
7. Prince, *Sense of Occasion*, 214.

CHAPTER 18

1. Comden, *Off Stage*, 212.
2. Betty Comden and Adolph Green, "Sink or Swim? Tipsy Goddesses Decide," *New York Times*, December 12, 1998, B7.
3. Ilson, *Harold Prince*, 317.
4. Susan Heller Anderson, "Earlier Broadway Date, Sept. 8, for 'A Doll's Life,'" *New York Times*, July 31, 1982, 9.
5. Marian Christy, "How Son, Celebrity Parents Interact," *Boston Globe*, May 17, 1980, 6.
6. Newman, *Just in Time*, 177.
7. Newman, *Just in Time*, 181.
8. Newman, *Just in Time*, 183.
9. Tharp, *Push Comes to Shove*, 297.
10. Sharon Churcher, "Still Kicking," *New York Magazine*, October 14, 1985, 44.
11. Churcher, "Still Kicking," 44.
12. Bryer and Davison, *The Art of the American Musical*, 57.

CHAPTER 19

1. Andrew L. Yarrow, "Regency Theater Is Closed Abruptly," *New York Times*, September 3, 1987, C18.
2. Donnie Radcliffe, "At the McLean Castle, Kennedy's Birthday Bash," *Washington Post*, February 23, 1988, D2.
3. Cossette, *Another Day in Showbiz*, 187.
4. Bell, *Broadway Stories*, 152.
5. Bell, *Broadway Stories*, 152.
6. Bell, *Broadway Stories*, 152.
7. Bell, *Broadway Stories*, 154.
8. Cy Coleman, "Adolph, Betty and a Piano in the Ladies Room," *New York Times*, November 3, 2002, A7.
9. Don Heckman, "Singin' Their Praises," *Los Angeles Times*, November 12, 1991, F1.
10. David Benedict, "What a Glorious Feeling," *Independent*, November 24, 2000, 11.
11. Richard Morrison, "An Accolade for One Helluva Show," *Times*, March 4, 2005, 12S.

SELECTED BIBLIOGRAPHY

BOOKS

Abbott, George. *"Mister Abbott."* New York: Random House, 1963.

Adams, Edie, and Robert Windeler. *Sing a Pretty Song: The "Offbeat" Life of Edie Adams.* New York: William Morrow, 1990.

Astaire, Fred. *Steps in Time: An Autobiography.* New York: Harper & Row, 1987.

Bacall, Lauren. *By Myself.* New York: Alfred A. Knopf, 1978.

Ballard, Kaye, with Jim Hesselman. *How I Lost 10 Pounds in 53 Years: A Memoir.* New York: Back Stage Books, 2006.

Bell, Marty. *Broadway Stories: A Backstage Journey through Musical Theatre.* New York: Limelight Editions, 1993.

Bernstein, Burton. *Family Matters, Sam, Jenny, and the Kids.* New York: Summit Books, 1982.

Bernstein, Shirley. *Making Music: Leonard Bernstein.* Chicago: Encyclopedia Britannica Press, 1963.

Blair, Betsy. *The Memory of All That.* New York: Alfred A. Knopf, 2003.

Bloom, Ken. *Show and Tell: The New Book of Broadway Anecdotes.* New York: Oxford University Press, 2016.

Brideson, Cynthia, and Sara Brideson. *He's Got Rhythm: The Life and Career of Gene Kelly.* Lexington: University Press of Kentucky, 2017.

Bryer, Jackson R., and Richard A. Davison (eds.). *The Art of the American Musical: Conversations with the Creators.* New Brunswick, NJ: Rutgers University Press, 2005.

Burrows, Abe. *Honest, Abe.* Boston: Atlantic Monthly Press Book, Little, Brown, 1980.

Burton, Humphrey. *Leonard Bernstein.* New York: Anchor Books, Doubleday, 1994.

Carey, Gary. *Judy Holliday: An Intimate Life Story.* New York: Seaview Books, 1982.

Carpozi, George Jr. *The Carol Burnett Story.* New York: Warner Paperback Library, 1975.

Chandler, Charlotte. *Not the Girl Next Door: Joan Crawford, a Personal Biography.* New York: Simon & Schuster, 2008.

Channing, Carol. *Just Lucky I Guess: A Memoir of Sorts.* New York: Simon & Schuster, 2002.

Chaplin, Saul. *The Golden Age of Movie Musicals and Me.* Norman: University of Oklahoma Press, 1994.

Comden, Betty. *Off Stage.* New York: Limelight Editions, 1996.

Conrad, Christine. *Jerome Robbins: That Broadway Man, That Ballet Man.* London: Booth-Clibborn Editions, 2000.

Cossette, Pierre. *Another Day in Showbiz: One Producer's Journey.* Toronto: ECW Press, 2002.

Davis, Ronald L. *Mary Martin: Broadway Legend.* Norman: University of Oklahoma Press, 2008.

Dietz, Howard. *Dancing in the Dark: An Autobiography.* New York: Quadrangle/New York Times Books, 1974.

Douglas, Kirk. *The Ragman's Son: An Autobiography*. New York: Simon & Schuster, 1998.

Eells, George. *The Life That Late He Led: A Biography of Cole Porter*. New York: G. P. Putnam's Sons, 1967.

Engel, Lehman. *This Bright Day: An Autobiography*. New York: Macmillan, 1974.

Eyman, Scott. *Lion of Hollywood: The Life and Legend of Louis B. Mayer*. New York: Simon & Schuster, 2005.

Filichia, Peter. *The Great Parade: Broadway's Never-to-Be-Forgotten 1963–1964 Season*. New York: St. Martin's Press, 2015.

Fordin, Hugh. *The Movies' Greatest Musicals, Produced in Hollywood USA by the Freed Unit*. New York: Frederick Ungar, 1984.

Friedwald, Will. *Sinatra! The Song Is You*. New York: Scribner, 1995.

Garrett, Betty, with Ron Rapoport. *Betty Garrett and Other Songs: A Life on Stage and Screen*. Lanham, MD: Madison Books, 1998.

Gavin, James. *Intimate Nights: The Golden Age of New York Cabaret*. New York: Grove Weidenfeld, 1991.

Gavin, James. *Stormy Weather: The Life of Lena Horne*. New York: Atria, 2010.

Goodman, Peter W. *Morton Gould: American Salute*. Portland, OR: Amadeus Press, 2000.

Gordon, Max. *Live at the Village Vanguard*. New York: St. Martin's Press, 1980.

Gottlieb, Jack. *Working with Bernstein*. New York: Amadeus Press, 2010.

Griffin, Mark. *A Hundred or More Hidden Things: The Life and Films of Vincente Minnelli*. Cambridge, MA: Da Capo Press, 2010.

Gruen, John. *Close-Up*. New York: Viking Press, 1968.

Gruen, John. *The Private World of Leonard Bernstein*. New York: Viking Press, 1968.

Guernsey, Otis L. Jr. (ed.). *Broadway Song & Story: Playwrights, Lyricists, Composers Discuss Their Hits*. New York: Dodd, Mead, 1985.

Hanson, Bruce K. *The Peter Pan Chronicles*. New York: Birch Lane Press, 1991.

Hess, Earl J., and Pratibha A. Dabholkar. *Singing in the Rain: The Making of an American Masterpiece*. Lawrence: University Press of Kansas, 2009.

Hirsch, Foster. *Harold Prince and the American Musical Theatre*. Cambridge: Cambridge University Press, 1989.

Hirschhorn, Clive. *Gene Kelly*. Chicago: Henry Regnery, 1974.

Hischak, Thomas S. *Word Crazy: Broadway Lyricists from Cohan to Sondheim*. New York: Praeger, 1991.

Holtzman, Will. *Judy Holliday*. New York, G. P. Putnam's Sons, 1982.

Ilson, Carol. *Harold Prince: A Director's Journey*. New York: Limelight Editions, 2000.

Janssen, Marian. *Not at All What One Is Used To: The Life and Times of Isabella Gardner*. Columbia: University of Missouri Press, 2010.

Jordan, Richard Tyler. *But Darling, I'm Your Auntie Mame! The Amazing History of the World's Favorite Madcap Aunt*. Santa Barbara, CA: Capra Press, 1998.

Jowitt, Deborah. *Jerome Robbins: His Life, His Theater, His Dance*. New York: Simon & Schuster, 2004.

Kasha, Al, and Joel Hirschhorn. *Notes on Broadway: Conversations with Great Songwriters*. Chicago: Contemporary Books, 1985.

Kashner, Sam, and Nancy Schoenenberger. *A Talent for Genius: The Life and Times of Oscar Levant*. New York: Villard Books, 1994.

Kissel, Howard. *David Merrick: The Abominable Showman*. New York: Applause Books, 1993.

Lahr, John. *Astonish Me: Adventures in Contemporary Theater*. New York: Viking Press, 1973.

Lahr, John. *Notes on a Cowardly Lion: The Biography of Bert Lahr*. New York: Alfred A. Knopf, 1969.

Laurents, Arthur. *Mainly on Directing: Gypsy, West Side Story, and Other Musicals*. New York: Alfred A. Knopf, 2009.

Laurents, Arthur. *Original Story: A Memoir of Broadway and Hollywood*. New York: Applause Theatre Books, 2000.

Lazar, Irving. *Swifty: My Life and Good Times*. New York: Simon & Schuster, 1995.

Leonard, William Torbert. *Broadway Bound: A Guide to Shows That Died Aborning*. Metuchen, NJ: Scarecrow Press, 1983.

Levinson, Peter J. *Puttin' on the Ritz: Fred Astaire and the Fine Art of Panache*. New York: St. Martin's Press, 2009.

Levy, Emanuel. *Vincente Minnelli: Hollywood's Dark Dreamer*. New York: St. Martin's Press, 2009.

Long, Robert Emmet. *Broadway, the Golden Years: Jerome Robbins and the Great Choreographer-Directors, 1940 to the Present*. New York: Continuum, 2001.

MacGilligan, Pat. *Backstory 2: Interviews with Screenwriters of the 1940s and 1950s*. Berkeley: University of California Press, 1991.

MacLaine, Shirley. *My Lucky Stars: A Hollywood Memoir*. New York: Bantam Books, 1995.

McBrien, William. *Cole Porter*. New York: Vintage Books, 1998.

McHugh, Dominic. *Loverly: The Life and Times of My Fair Lady*. New York: Oxford University Press, 2012.

Minnelli, Vincente, with Hector Arce. *I Remember It Well*. Garden City, NY: Doubleday, 1974.

Newman, Phyllis. *Just in Time—Notes from My Life*. New York: Simon & Schuster, 1988.

Novellino-Mearns, Rosemary. *Saving Radio City Music Hall: A Dancer's True Story*. Teaneck, NJ: TurningPointPress, 2015.

Oja, Carol J. *Bernstein Meets Broadway: Collaborative Art in a Time of War*. New York: Oxford University Press, 2014.

Osato, Sono. *Distant Dances*. New York: Alfred A. Knopf, 1980.

Peyser, Joan. *Bernstein: A Biography* (revised and updated). New York: Billboard Books, 1998.

Prince, Harold. *Sense of Occasion*. Milwaukee, WI: Applause Theatre & Cinema Books, 2017.

Previn, André. *No Minor Chords: My Days in Hollywood*. New York: Doubleday, 1991.

Reynolds, Debbie, and Dorian Hannaway. *Unsinkable: A Memoir*. New York: William Morrow, 2013.

Robinson, Alice M. *Betty Comden and Adolph Green: A Bio-Bibliography*. Westport, CT: Greenwood Press, 1994.

Rogers, Ginger. *Ginger: My Story*. New York: Dey Street Books, 2008.

Russell, Rosalind, with Chris Chase. *Life Is a Banquet*. New York: Ace Books, 1979.

Sagolla, Lisa Jo. *The Girl Who Fell Down: A Biography of Joan McCracken*. Boston: Northeastern University Press, 2003.

Schulman, Susan L. *Backstage Pass to Broadway: True Tales from a Theatre Press Agent*. New York: Heliotrope Books, 2013.

Secrest, Meryl. *Stephen Sondheim: A Life*. New York: Alfred A. Knopf, 1998.

Shapiro, Eddie. *Nothing Like a Dame*. New York: Oxford University Press, 2014.

Sheed, Wilfrid. *The House That George Built: With a Little Help from Irving, Cole, and a Crew of about Fifty*. New York: Random House Trade Paperbacks, 2008.

Silverman, Stephen M. *Dancing on the Ceiling: Stanley Donen and His Movies*. New York: Alfred A. Knopf, 1996.

Simeone, Nigel (ed.). *The Leonard Bernstein Letters*. New Haven, CT: Yale University Press, 2013.

Singer, Barry. *Ever After: The Last Years of Musical Theater and Beyond*. New York: Applause Theatre and Cinema Books, 2004.

Staggs, Sam. *All About "All About Eve."* New York: St. Martin's Press, 2000.

Strouse, Charles. *Put on a Happy Face: A Broadway Memoir*. New York: Union Square Press, 2008.

Suskin, Steven. *Second Act Trouble: Behind the Scenes at Broadway's Big Musical Bombs*. New York: Applause Theatre & Cinema Books, 2006.

Suskin, Steven. *The Sound of Broadway Music: A Book of Orchestrators and Orchestrations*. New York: Oxford University Press, 2009.

Taylor, Theodore. *Jule: The Story of Composer Jule Styne*. New York: Random House, 1979.

Tharp, Twyla. *Push Comes to Shove: An Autobiography*. New York: Bantam Books, 1992.

Vaill, Amanda. *Somewhere: The Life of Jerome Robbins*. New York: Broadway Books, 2006.

Viagas, Robert (ed.). *The Alchemy of Theatre, the Divine Science: Essays on Theatre and the Art of Collaboration*. New York: Playbill Books, 2006.

Whorf, Michael. *American Popular Song Lyricists: Oral Histories, 1920s–1960s*. Jefferson, NC: McFarland, 2012.

Wilson, Earl. *Sinatra: An Unauthorized Biography*. New York: Macmillan, 1976.

PUBLISHED SCRIPTS AND LIBRETTOS

Bissell, Richard, Abe Burrow, Marian Bissell, et al. *Say, Darling*. Boston: Atlantic Monthly Press Book, Little, Brown, 1958.

Comden, Betty, and Adolph Green. *The New York Musicals of Comden and Green*. New York: Applause Books, 1997.

Comden, Betty, and Adolph Green. *On the Twentieth Century*. New York: Samuel French, 1980.

Comden, Betty, and Adolph Green. *Singin' in the Rain*. New York: Viking Press, 1972.

Fields, Joseph, Jerome Chodorov, Betty Comden, and Adolph Green. *Wonderful Town*. New York: Random House, 1953.

Richards, Stanley (ed.). *Great Musicals of the American Theatre*. Vol. 2. Radnor, PA: Chilton, 1976.

SOURCE MATERIAL

Barrie, J. M. *Peter Pan*. New York: Random House Value Publishing, 1987.

Barrie, J. M. *The Plays of J. M. Barrie*. New York: Charles Scribner's Sons, 1929.

Bissell, Richard. *Say, Darling*. Boston: Atlantic Monthly Press Book, Little, Brown, 1957.

Dennis, Patrick. *Auntie Mame*. New York: Popular Library, 1955.

Fields, Joseph A., and Jerome Chodorov. *My Sister Eileen*. New York: Dramatists Play Service, 1968.

Kanin, Garson. *Do Re Mi*. New York: Boston: Atlantic Monthly Press Book, Little, Brown, 1955.

Love, Edmund G. *Subways Are for Sleeping*. New York: Signet Books, New American Library, 1957.

McKenney, Ruth. *My Sister Eileen*. New York: Berkley Highland Books, 1965.

Schwab, Laurence, B. G. DeSylva, and Lew Brown. *Good News, a Musical Comedy*. New York: Samuel French, 1932.

DIGITAL RESOURCES

Except where indicated by an asterisk, all are available as open-source websites. The others require access through subscriptions, usually through libraries.

Billboard—Google Books. Mountain View, CA: Google. https://books.google.com/books/serial/ISSN:00062510?rview=1

**Electronic Resources for Alumni*. Chicago: University of Chicago. http://guides.lib.uchicago.edu/alumni

**Entertainment Industry Magazine Archive*. Ann Arbor, MI: ProQuest. http://www.proquest.com/detail/eima.html

FamilySearch. Salt Lake City, UT: Intellectual Reserve, Inc. https://familysearch.org/

Fulton History. Fulton, NY: Old Fulton NY Post Cards. http://fultonhistory.com/

LIFE—Google Books. Mountain View, CA: Google. https://books.google.com/books/serial/ISSN:00243019?rview=1

NYS Historic Newspapers. Potsdam, NY: Northern NY Library Network. http://nyshistoric-newspapers.org/

ProQuest Historical Newspapers. Ann Arbor, MI: ProQuest. http://www.proquest.com/products-services/pq-hist-news.html

UNZ.org—Periodicals, Books, and Authors. Palo Alto: One Nation One California. http://www.unz.org/Pub/

Village Voice—Google News. Mountain View, CA: Google. https://news.google.com/newspapers?nid=KEtq3P1Vf8oC&dat=19770328&b_mode=2&hl=en

INDEX